616   Crook, William G. (William Grant), 1917–
.8589   Solving the puzzle of your hard-to-raise child /
05   William G. Crook and Laura J. Stevens ; illustrations by
Cro   Cynthia P. Crook. –– New York : Random House,
         c1987.
           xxix, 368 p. : ill.

         Includes index.
         Bibliography: p. 329 –358.
         03106187 LC:87009652 ISBN:039456054X :

         1. Food allergy in children – Psychological aspects. 2.
                                       (SEE NEXT CARD)

Solving the Puzzle of
Your
Hard-to-Raise
Child

Solving the Puzzle of
Your
Hard-to-Raise
Child

William G. Crook, M.D.,
and
Laura J. Stevens

Illustrations by Cynthia P. Crook

Random House   New York

Library of Congress Cataloging-in-Publication Data

Crook, William G. (William Grant), 1917-
Solving the puzzle of your hard-to-raise child.

Includes index.

1. Food allergy in children—Psychological aspects.
2. Behavioral disorders in children—Nutritional aspects.
3. Children—Nutrition.
I. Stevens, Laura J., 1945-. II. Title.
[DNLM: 1. Child Behavior Disorders—popular works.
2. Environmental Exposure—popular works.
3. Food Hypersensitivity—in infancy & childhood—
popular works. WD 310 C948s]
RJ386.5.C76   1987   616.85′8905   87-9652
ISBN 0-394-56054-X

Manufactured in the United States of America
23456789
First Edition

*This book is dedicated
to all hard-to-raise children . . .
especially those with hyperactivity
and related behavior and learning disorders.
It is also dedicated to their parents.*

A SPECIAL MESSAGE TO PARENTS

Laura Stevens and I have written this book to serve as a general guide and reference source for you and for those who are trying to help your child and your family. For obvious reasons, I cannot assume the medical or legal responsibility for having the contents of this book considered as a prescription for your child or for any child.

To help your hard-to-raise child you'll need assistance from a knowledgeable and interested physician or other licensed health professional. Accordingly, you and those who work with you and your child must take full responsibility for the uses made of this book.

William G. Crook, M.D.

THE COMPLEX CAUSES OF BEHAVIOR
AND LEARNING PROBLEMS

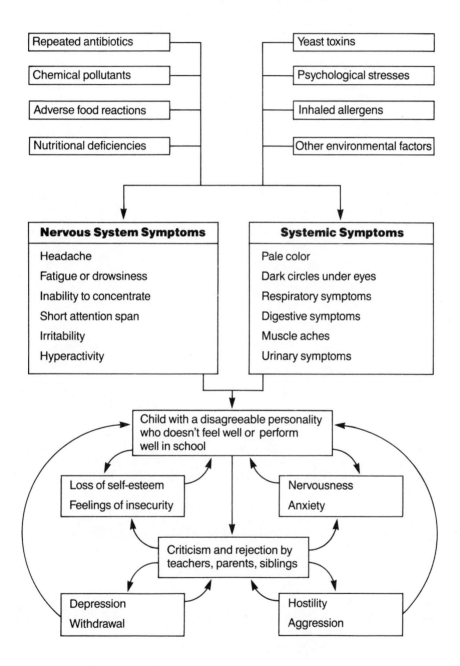

Preface

DR. CROOK'S STORY

I was born and reared in Jackson, Tennessee. I received my B.A. degree from the University of the South (Sewanee) and my medical degree from the University of Virginia. After receiving my internship and residency training at the Pennsylvania Hospital, Vanderbilt University Hospital, and the Sydenham and Johns Hopkins Hospitals in Baltimore, I returned to my hometown in 1949 to practice pediatrics.

In the middle 1950s, after reading reports in the medical literature by Drs. Albert Rowe,[1,2] Herbert Rinkel,[3] Theron Randolph,[4] Jerome Glaser[5,6] and Frederic Speer,[7] I learned (much to my surprise) that some of my patients felt better when they stopped eating their favorite foods. Such foods, especially milk, chocolate, corn, wheat and eggs, seemed to make these children pale, tired and nervous. Moreover, when their diet included these foods, many of them developed personality, behavior and learning problems.

So I began to search for more children in my practice with food-related problems, and I was amazed to find many of them. I reported my findings on twenty-three food-sensitive young-

sters at the allergy section of the American Academy of Pediatrics in 1958 and published a paper based on a study of fifty of these children in *Pediatrics* in 1961.[8]

During the sixties, my interest in the relationship of diet to poor behavior and to a whole host of other chronic health problems in children grew. I learned that food additives, air pollutants, odorous plastics and chemicals of all sorts caused adverse reactions in many of my patients. Yet, in spite of my observations and similar reports by John Gerrard, M.D., of the University of Saskatchewan,[9,10] the late William C. Deamer, M.D., and O. L. Frick, M.D., of the University of California,[11,12,13] and others,[14,15,16] most physicians[17,18] blamed headache, abdominal pain, muscle aches, bedwetting and nervous system symptoms in children on emotional causes.

During the seventies, my interest in the role of diet in contributing to systemic and nervous system disorders in children increased. And the general public also began to hear and read about a diet-behavior relationship. Much of the public awareness came from the work of the late Benjamin Feingold, M.D., who first reported his observations at a meeting of the American Medical Association in July 1973. Dr. Feingold observed that artificial colors and flavorings, and natural foods containing salicylates (an aspirin-like compound) caused hyperactivity in susceptible children. (See also Appendix A.)

About the same time, I began to see increasing numbers of difficult children in my general pediatric and allergy practice. Moreover, many of these children were brought in by parents who complained of the child's overactivity and irritability. Although my interest in children with hyperactivity may have attracted some of these youngsters and their parents to my office, I felt that the incidence of such problems was increasing. (See also Chapter 5.)

In evaluating the influence of diet on my patients, I used the controversial sublingual provocative test. In carrying out this test, small amounts of a food extract are dropped under the child's tongue and reactions are noted. Following such testing, elimination diets are prescribed for seven to ten days. If a child's behavior improves, the eliminated foods are returned to his diet, one food per day, and reactions are noted.

My interest in hard-to-raise children, including those with fatigue, headache, depression, hyperactivity, learning problems, bedwetting, constant colds, abdominal pain, muscle aches and other symptoms continued. And in 1973, I published a book describing my observations.[19] As my work with children with behavior and learning problems grew, I published a second book in 1975, entitled *Can Your Child Read? Is He Hyperactive?*[20] And in 1978, I published a third book, *Tracking Down Hidden Food Allergy,*[21] to provide parents with instructions for carrying out elimination diets.

Subsequently, I published data[22] from a five-year clinical study of 182 hyperactive children seen between 1973 and 1978. *Three out of four of the parents found that hyperactivity was related to one or more foods the child was eating.*

During the latter part of the seventies, I became aware of the role of other dietary factors in causing hyperactivity, irritability, headache, short attention span and other symptoms. These included deficiencies in vitamin B_6, magnesium, zinc and other nutrients. I also learned about toxicities of various sorts, including lead and cadmium, although I was able to obtain little objective proof of such toxicities in my own patients.

Then, in 1979, I became aware of the brilliant pioneer observations of C. Orian Truss, M.D. This Birmingham, Alabama, physician noted that many of his patients with chronic health disorders had a history of repeated or prolonged courses of antibiotic drugs. While such drugs are effective in helping a person conquer bacterial infections, they also tend to knock out friendly bacteria in the body. As a result, the common yeast *Candida albicans* multiplies in the gastrointestinal tract or vagina.

According to the Truss hypothesis, *Candida* toxins (produced by the overgrowth of yeasts) spread through the body. Truss found that by prescribing a safe antifungal medication, nystatin, and changing his patients' diets, their health would improve. Although most of these patients were adults, he noted that some children with irritability and other nervous system disorders responded favorably to an anti-*Candida* treatment program.[23]

In my own practice, I began to note marked improvement in the mental and nervous symptoms of hundreds of my adult patients and in some of my difficult pediatric patients when I prescribed a sugar-free, yeast-free diet. Among these patients were children with hyperactivity, allergies and recurrent infections. Moreover, the response of my patients to a yeast-control program was so gratifying and exciting that, in December 1983, I published a fourth book, *The Yeast Connection: A Medical Breakthrough.*[24]

In the course of my travels, I met Laura J. Stevens of West Lafayette, Indiana. Because Laura had successfully struggled to help her two hyperactive children, she wrote and published two books for other families who were experiencing problems with hyperactive children.[25,26]

Then, in the spring of 1983, Laura called me and said, "I've written another book, *The Complete Book of Allergy Control.*[27] I'd love for you to write the introduction." Laura mailed the manuscript to me and I read it from cover to cover. I was fascinated and delighted, and so I accepted her invitation. In my introductory remarks, I said, "This is the best and most complete book for the allergic person I've ever seen."

People like Laura and me who feel a burning desire to

write are forever working on new projects. I had sent my book on yeast-connected health disorders to the publisher about the same time Laura completed her book on allergies.

Soon thereafter, Laura and I met in person and began to talk more about our mutual interests. As you might guess our conversation soon turned to health problems in children and the many fascinating new developments in the field. These included yeast-connected health disorders, food allergies and a host of other dietary and environmental influences that were contributing causes of the growing "epidemic" of troublesome children, including those with hyperactivity and related behavior and learning problems.

I was fascinated by Laura's struggles in coping with and helping her own children. And her experiences, including her successes as well as her frustrations and failures, made me feel that, together, we could write a book on hard-to-raise children that would help a lot of people.

LAURA STEVENS'S STORY

I was born in Dayton, Ohio, and grew up in Cincinnati. I attended the University of Cincinnati, earning my B.A. degree in zoology and my M.A. degree in political science. As a graduate student I met and fell in love with George Stevens. We were married and moved to West Lafayette, Indiana, where George taught at Purdue University.

George and I didn't know much about raising children, but we felt confident parenting would come easily. But our two beautiful, healthy infants (born almost three years apart) became colicky, fussy babies and grew to be overactive, irritable toddlers. Yet at times they appeared cheerful and affectionate, played happily and seemed smart. We tried all the traditional approaches—psychological counseling, behavior modification and even medications such as Ritalin with no success. Several doctors predicted our boys would develop learning problems in school.

In desperation, we tried the Feingold diet and our children responded dramatically. We were so delighted with their responses that we shared our recipes and menu ideas with a local parents' support group. Then my mother said, "Why don't you write a book that will help other children?" So with the help and collaboration of my sister-in-law, Rosemary Stoner, a creative cook, George and I wrote *How to Feed Your Hyperactive Child.*

After a few months of adhering to the Feingold diet, much to George's and my distress, our children began to react to natural foods like milk, sugar, wheat, eggs and corn. I didn't understand these reactions because these foods contained no salicylates, artificial colorings, flavorings or other additives. Our pediatrician listened patiently to my story. He said:

> Laura, I don't understand why your children are continuing to experience problems with hyperactivity. But here's a possible source of further information and help. Pediatrician William G. Crook in a letter to the editor in one of my journals reports that adverse reactions to many different foods cause hyperactive behavior in many of his patients. Why don't you contact him?

So I wrote a six-page letter to Dr. Crook outlining my observations. Much to my delight, Dr. Crook called me and told me about hundreds of his patients who were "turned on" by common foods. He gave me many helpful suggestions and sent me two fascinating books he'd written, including *Tracking Down Hidden Food Allergy.*

Soon afterward we found an excellent doctor some miles from us who offered special allergy testing and treatment for hyperactive and learning-disabled children. During testing some of the test extracts caused my children to become irritable and overactive; other food extracts triggered aching legs, bloating, runny nose and headache. To my amazement, these symptoms closely resembled the symptoms my children showed when they ate foods that disagreed with them.

I was so excited by what I heard and observed I enlisted Rosemary's help in writing a new book that I felt would help even more children. It's title: *How to Improve Your Child's Behavior Through Diet.*

As I listened to the stories of our doctor's other allergy patients I realized that adults were also affected by what they ate. And I found through dietary experimentation that my fatigue, aching joints and depression were food related. As allergies run in families, I soon learned that other parents of hyperactive, difficult children were often bothered by both obvious and hidden allergies. And I said to myself, *"How ironic that the very parents who need the most patience and energy to deal with their children are often less able to cope because they're feeling crummy, too!"*

Foods were not the only villains that bothered us. Inhaled allergens including dusts, molds, pollens and animal danders made us sick, too. We also found that paints, gas fumes, formaldehyde, chlorine and other odorous chemicals caused symptoms including hyperactivity, irritability, headache and a feeling of being "spaced out."

Finally I learned the importance of a comprehensive nutritional program including the use of vitamin, mineral and fatty acid supplements.

To help other adults discover and cope with their allergies to foods, chemicals and inhaled allergens, I then wrote *The Complete Book of Allergy Control.*

Although we still have our ups and downs, our allergies are now well controlled. Both children are excellent students and are a joy to have around as long as we stick to our diets, allergy treatments and nutritional supplements.

Like Dr. Crook, I'm so excited that children like mine can be helped that I want to tell anyone who'll listen, "There's hope for your child, too." And that's why Dr. Crook and I teamed up to write this book.

Acknowledgments

First, I want to thank three pediatric mentors who played an important part in my life: the late Amos U. Christie, professor emeritus of pediatrics, at Vanderbilt University; James G. Hughes, professor emeritus of pediatrics, at the University of Tennessee; and Horace L. Hodes, professor emeritus of pediatrics, at Mount Sinai School of Medicine. Each of these men taught me, encouraged me and helped me in innumerable ways during my early years of pediatric training and throughout my many years of pediatric practice.

Special thanks are due also to John Gerrard, M.D., to Theron G. Randolph, M.D., and to the late William C. Deamer, M.D., Jerome Glaser, M.D., Albert Rowe, M.D., and Frederic Speer, M.D. These wonderful friends served as mentors who inspired me and helped me learn more about the challenging (and sometimes frustrating) field of allergy—especially food allergy.

Special thanks are also due to C. Orian Truss, M.D., who first made me aware of the role of the common yeast *Candida albicans* in causing nervous system disorders and other symptoms in both children and adults.

Laura and I are especially grateful to Sidney M. Baker, M.D., of the Gesell Institute of Human Development, New Haven, Connecticut, and to Leo Galland, M.D., of New York City. Drs. Baker and Galland have taught us many things about nutrition and about the importance of looking at the whole person. And the insights we've gained from them have helped us crystallize and organize many of the concepts presented in this book.

Special thanks are also due to the late Benjamin Feingold, M.D., who, beginning in 1973, worked untiringly to alert the medical community and the public to the importance of diet in causing hyperactivity in children. Thanks are also due to many of the members of the Feingold Association of the United States. I especially appreciate the friendship and help of Patricia Frederick, the longtime head of the Feingold Association of the greater Washington, D.C., area. "Trish" reviewed many parts of this manuscript and encouraged and helped me repeatedly during the past several years.

We also thank Gary Oberg, M.D., who spent many hours reviewing our complete manuscript and made many helpful suggestions and contributions. We also appreciate Sue Acheson, Dorothy Boyce, R.N., Elmer Cranton, M.D., Bernard Rimland, Ph.D., Mrs. Raymond Rubicam, Flo Stoner, Mary Campbell, Ph.D., and Aubrey Worrell, M.D., who made helpful suggestions and contributions.

Special thanks also go to those whom Laura interviewed and to those who completed our questionnaire: Stephen Davies, M.D., John Gerrard, M.D., Ellen Grant, M.D., John O'Brian, M.D., Donald Rudin, M.D., Morton Teich, M.D., Jonathan Wright, M.D., and Ray Wunderlich, M.D.

Special appreciation is due to John Wacker, head of the Scientific Studies Committee of the Association for Children with Learning Disabilities, Gerald Senf, Ph.D., former editor of the *Journal of Learning Disabilities,* Betty Lou Kratoville, editor, and John Arena, publisher, of *Academic Therapy.*

We're grateful to many other professionals and nonprofessionals who shared their knowledge and experience with us, including especially Jeff Bland, Ph.D., James Breneman, M.D., Robert Buckley, M.D., William Byrne, Ph.D., Brent Campbell, M.D., E. Cheraskin, M.D., D.M.D., Elmer Cranton, M.D., Hobart Feldman, M.D., the late Rudolf Flesch, Ph.D., Ira Fritz, Ph.D., Ken Gerdes, M.D., Ross Hume Hall, Ph.D., Harold Hedges, M.D., G. K. Hodenfield, Abram Hoffer, M.D., Ph.D., David Horrobin, Ph.D., George Kroker, M.D., Alan Levin, M.D., Allan Lieberman, M.D., John Maclennan, M.D., Marshall Mandell, M.D., Joseph McGovern, M.D., Audrey McMahon, Joseph Miller, M.D., David Morris, M.D., James O'Shea, M.D., Linus Pauling, Ph.D., William H. Philpott, M.D., Saul Pilar, M.D., Doris Rapp, M.D., William J. Rea, M.D., Bernard Rimland, Ph.D., Marshall S. Ringsdorf, D.M.D., Sherry Rogers,

M.D., Mrs. Raymond Rubicam, Phyllis Saifer, M.D., Douglas Sandberg, M.D., Alex Schauss, Ph.D., the late Charles Shedd, Ph.D., Del Stigler, M.D., Barbara Reed Stitt, Ida Lee Wacker, Robert Stroud, M.D., and Roger Williams, Ph.D.

Laura and I also appreciate the charming work of my daughter, Cynthia, whose pictures make this book easy to understand. We also thank Laura's husband, George Stevens, who patiently read and reread our manuscript and contributed many helpful suggestions.

We're also grateful to members of my staff: Ditzi Brittain, Georgia Deaton, Brenda Harris, Charlotte Jaquet, Sally Karlgaard, R.N., Brent Lay, Nancy Moss, Nell Sellers, Therese Shelby, Denny Spencer, Alice Spragins and Patrick Youngblood.

We're deeply indebted to hundreds of other people including friends, parents and patients, and to professionals whose work in the field of allergy, nutrition and learning disabilities stimulated us and taught us many of the things we've included in this book.

—William G. Crook, M.D.
—Laura J. Stevens

Contents

Section C: Allergy: The Great Masquerader

Section D: Helping Your Hard-to-Raise Child: What to Do First

Section E: Other Allergic and Adverse Reactions May Cause Health and Behavior Problems

Section F: Yeasts: Another Cause of Health and Behavior Problems

Section G: Nutritional, Metabolic and Biochemical Factors That May Affect Your Child

Section H: Other Nutritional Considerations

Section I: Meeting Your Child's Psychological and Educational Needs

Section J: Other Helpful Information

Section K: Checklist and Conclusion

Section A
INTRODUCTION

I
The Hard-to-Raise Child
Resembles a Jigsaw Puzzle

I F your child is bothered by

—Overactivity
—"Dr. Jekyll-Mr. Hyde" behavior and mood swings
—Irritability
—Aggressiveness and hostility
—Short attention span and inability to concentrate
—Learning problems
—Fatigue and listlessness
—Depression
—Headaches
—Recurrent ear infections
—Bedwetting
—Digestive symptoms
—Muscle and joint pains
—Respiratory symptoms

take him* to his physician for a careful checkup, including a history and physical examination, vision and hearing tests, complete blood count and urinalysis. Depending upon your child's symptoms and the findings on physical examination, your doctor may recommend other tests and studies.

To me, the hard-to-raise child with hyperactivity, irritability, learning problems, headaches, fatigue, depression, recurring allergies and other systemic and nervous system symptoms resembles a jigsaw puzzle with many pieces, a number of which are out of place. By contrast, the healthy, emotionally stable, nonallergic child resembles a completed puzzle.

To help your child overcome these problems, you and your physician will need to identify the out-of-place pieces, fit them in, and complete the puzzle.

In solving this puzzle, you'll need to learn about food allergies, food intolerances and other adverse reactions . . . how you recognize them and how you overcome them. And you'll

---

*We'll use only one gender, for convenience, and because the great majority of hard-to-raise children are boys we'll use "he," "him," or "his."

be delighted, even ecstatic, when after a five- to ten-day elimination diet, you find that your difficult Johnny "acts like a different child!"

Moreover, even if your child doesn't suffer from food allergies (or other adverse food reactions), you'll need to pay attention to what he eats and "clean up his diet." Most packaged, processed and refined foods lack essential nutrients including vitamins, minerals and essential fatty acids.

Such foods usually contain too much sugar, hardened (hydrogenated or partially hydrogenated) vegetable oil and refined carbohydrates (including white flour, corn syrup and sugars). When your child "fills up" on these foods, he doesn't leave room for vegetables, fruits, whole grains, nuts, seeds, eggs and other nutritious foods. So his brain (and other parts of his body), like a car filled with inferior fuel, sputters, jerks and seems to put out blue smoke.

You'll also need to know that chemicals of many types may affect your child's immune system and contribute to the development of many health problems, including hyperactivity. These chemicals include formaldehyde, odorous marking pencils (and other chemically treated school materials), floor waxes, bathroom chemicals, insecticides, deodorants, laundry detergents, perfume and tobacco.

You'll need to learn about the recently recognized connection between the common and usually benign yeast, *Can-*

dida albicans, and health problems in both children and adults. This yeast normally lives in the body (especially in the digestive tract) and causes few problems in the healthy individual with a properly functioning immune system. Yet, in the child who has received repeated rounds of antibiotic drugs, it may play a role in causing a variety of health problems. These include recurrent infections, fatigue, irritability, overactive behavior and other nervous system symptoms.

You'll also want to know more about vitamins and minerals, toxic metals and other biochemical factors that affect how your child feels and behaves.

As your child's obnoxious behavior leads to conflict with siblings, peers and teachers, you'll want to improve your skills in listening, talking and communicating. Moreover, your child will need help in handling the frustrations and rejections he's apt to experience at home, school and in the neighborhood.

Gary Oberg, M.D., of Crystal Lake, Illinois, a fellow of the American Academy of Pediatrics and the American College of Allergists, and a member of the Committee on Allergies in the School Setting, commented recently:

> I've seen hundreds of hard-to-raise children in my practice ... children with multiple health problems, including behavior and learning disorders, persistent allergies and symptoms involving just about any and every part of the body. To help these

children requires a cooperative team effort involving family members and professionals skilled especially in environmental medicine, nutrition, allergy, psychology and education.[1]

Right now, you're probably overwhelmed by the task facing you. You may be confused by the conflicting theories about the causes of your child's difficulties and the different methods of treatment recommended to you. You may also be frustrated if you've traveled down a long and often expensive road in search of help—especially if the treatment measures haven't been effective.

LAURA COMMENTS:

I know how you feel! I went through the same struggles. Changing our family's typical American diet, reducing our exposures to inhaled allergens and troublesome chemicals and understanding and correcting other nutritional and biochemical factors seemed monumental—even impossible—tasks.

Yet, take heart. You, your child and family will overcome these problems. Rome wasn't built in a day; neither will you solve all your child's problems overnight! Select diet changes, environmental control measures and nutritional supplements considering your available time, energy and finances.

Tommy: A Success Story

During the past twenty-five years, I've seen hundreds of difficult, hard-to-raise children. Here's a typical story about a hyperactive child (I'll call him Tommy), as told by his mother Linda:

> Tommy was a beautiful, healthy baby. Soon, however, he was screaming with colic, which continued for nine long months. At four months Tommy was hospitalized and again at eight months. Since no physical cause for his severe discomfort and crying could be found, the doctor insinuated that my husband and I were somehow causing Tommy's distress.
>
> Eventually, Tommy's colic subsided, but our problems continued. At times Tommy seemed happy, but it was a case of Dr. Jekyll and Mr. Hyde. At times he smiled, cooed and gurgled, but more often he fussed and screamed. He was especially sensitive to loud noises. He was always bouncing or rocking and quickly wore out two crib mattresses. Frequent temper tantrums plagued his toddler years. We read and reread various child psychology books, but they never seemed to describe Tommy's problems.
>
> Tommy also suffered from frequent ear infections. We seemed to pour "gallons" of antibiotics into him, yet his ear infections persisted or returned again. Finally, upon the recommendation of our pediatrician, ventilating tubes were placed in Tommy's ears.
>
> Although the tubes seemed to give Tommy temporary relief from his ear infections, his behavior problems continued. By the time Tommy reached the age of three and a half, we knew we needed expert help. Because his speech was hard to understand we consulted our university's speech and hearing clinic. They determined that his speech was developing normally but was too rapid to be easily understood. We also consulted several child psychologists.

Finally, we took Tommy to see a pediatric neurologist who said, "Your son shows the typical manifestations of severe hyperactivity. To help control his symptoms I'm prescribing Ritalin. He will probably be bothered by learning problems and require special education classes."

```
 Prescription
 Rx  Ritalin   10mg.

 Sig: Take 1 tablet before
 breakfast and lunch for
 hyperactivity.
              Fred J. Doe, MD
```

Then I read about Dr. Benjamin Feingold's diet for hyperactive children. I asked my doctor whether there was anything to this diet. He replied, "It's just a fad."

But the Ritalin turned Tommy into a zombie. In desperation, we tried the Feingold diet. Within five days Tommy improved greatly. He became calm, reasonable and seemed happy most of the time.

He could dress himself and sit at the table during meals without jumping up half a dozen times. He also played cooperatively with his friends in nursery school. Yet Tommy would relapse and his behavioral symptoms would return if he cheated on his diet and at times even when he didn't.

Tommy's now in kindergarten and doing okay. Yet at times he's anxious and restless. I'm worried about how he'll do in the first grade. I know he reacts to other foods besides those with additives. One day pure homemade chocolate pudding made him lie on the floor and cry for hours. Another time, adding soy powder to his bread made him extremely hyperactive.

The list of natural foods that "turn him on" has grown: eggs, chicken, milk, sugar, corn, wheat, rye and more. Exposures to gas fumes, tobacco smoke and paint also cause irritability and headaches. A friend suggested we visit you.

I saw Tommy and his mother Linda for the first time in January 1979. Although Tommy appeared calm, he looked pale and had dark circles under his eyes. His nose was runny and his nasal membranes appeared swollen. Eczema covered his thighs and lower legs, and the backs of his knees.

Because Linda had already tried an elimination diet for sugar, milk, eggs, corn, wheat, citrus and chocolate and believed Tommy to be sensitive to many of these foods, I scheduled special allergy tests. Hyperactive children often show deficiencies in various nutrients, so I prescribed a sugar and dye-free multiple vitamin and mineral tablet, extra vitamin C, and calcium and magnesium supplements.

In the meantime, my nurse talked to Linda about the importance of a rotated diet (see page 104) and told her how to reduce inhalant allergens and troublesome chemicals in the home. Testing Tommy with various food extracts suggested that he was sensitive to many foods. Sugar and corn extracts made him very hyperactive. Wheat made Tommy cry with leg cramps. Rye caused irritability and a runny nose. Linda remarked, "I'm amazed. These symptoms you're provoking with food extracts closely resemble those Tommy shows when he eats foods that disagree with him."

Tommy also reacted strongly to dust, mold and pollen extracts and to tests for petrochemicals, tobacco and formaldehyde.

I outlined and prescribed a comprehensive program for Tommy, including a special diet and allergy extracts. A month later, Tommy's mother reported, *"Tommy is like a different child.* He acts calmer and happier. His legs have stopped aching and his nose doesn't run anymore."

Tommy continued to improve. In June 1979, his mother wrote:

> Tommy successfully completed kindergarten. His teacher is delighted with his progress and he's a joy to have around the house as long as we stick to his diet, and give him his allergy extracts for foods and inhalants, and nutritional supplements.

A year later his mother reported:

> Tommy has had an excellent year in first grade. I can't believe this is the same child who was supposed to be learning disabled!
> Sugar is still the number one troublemaker for Tommy. We had hoped he could have occasional birthday treats at school. But he became so hyperactive then extremely depressed after eating one sugar cookie that *he* decided it wasn't worth feeling so awful. He's usually—but not always—content to eat special treats I send for him.

Tommy continued to make excellent progress. When occasional sugary treats exacerbated his symptoms, I suspected that Tommy was sensitive to yeast and prescribed nystatin (see Section F), a safe antiyeast prescription medication. I also recommended oil of primrose capsules and linseed oil (both of these supplements provide essential fatty acids (EFA's). (See chapters 34 and 35.)

Recently Tommy's mother reported:

> Tommy is doing great on the nystatin and oils. His food allergies and chemical sensitivities are much best better. His eczema has cleared completely.
>
> Tommy is in fifth grade now and is an excellent, well-behaved student. He loves baseball, tennis, video games, and rock music. We're thrilled with his progress. His future looks bright.

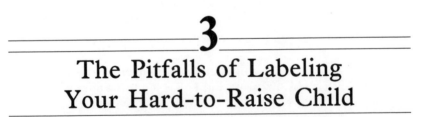

3
The Pitfalls of Labeling
Your Hard-to-Raise Child

During my early years of pediatric practice, I read a fascinating book by Johns Hopkins psychiatrist Leo Kanner, entitled *In Defense of Mothers*. The author discussed the child who wouldn't eat or sleep. He also talked about the child whose behavior didn't always measure up to the parents' expectations. It was an easy-to-read book and full of practical advice and comments. And one chapter was entitled, "Labeling Labels."

In this chapter Dr. Kanner pointed out that physicians and other professionals often label children. They're apt to come up with a diagnosis such as brain dysfunction, hyperactive or dyslexia. Moreover, in my experience, parents and teachers

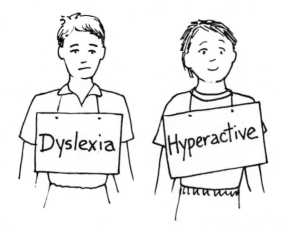

who are frustrated and driven up the wall by a difficult, hard-to-raise child may at times say, "Johnny is lazy, dull and un-coordinated. He could do better if he only wanted to."

Although children may exhibit these behaviors occasionally—or frequently—I feel that labeling them doesn't help for many reasons. First, it doesn't solve the problem. Then relatives, teachers and neighbors will start using the same label. As a result, the child will believe what people say about him. His self-esteem will suffer and his obnoxious and difficult behavior may continue.

Some fifteen to twenty years later, I read an article written for physicians by Emanuel Cheraskin, M.D., D.M.D., of the University of Alabama. In this article, entitled "The Name of the Game is the Name," Dr. Cheraskin discussed traditional medical education and training. He said physicians are taught to diagnose, classify and label diseases. And as a general rule they feel if they can put a diagnostic label on each patient they see, they've done their duty. Then they can prescribe drugs, surgery or psychotherapy. Cheraskin emphasized, "There's a better way."

In his numerous publications, he pointed out that many health problems in both children and adults that affect different parts of the body are usually related. And by making changes in their life-styles and more especially in their diets, symptoms such as headache, fatigue, joint pain, depression and hyperactivity may vanish.

C. Orian Truss, M.D., expressed a similar approach in his recent book, *The Missing Diagnosis.* He said:

> I would like to call attention . . . to the pitfall inherent in dividing human illness into "diseases." The organs and systems of the body are so integrated (that) . . . if one organ malfunctions, it is likely there will be repercussions in most other systems.[1]

Eight years ago, I met Sidney M. Baker, M.D., a member of the clinical faculty of Yale University and director of the Gesell Institute of Human Development of New Haven, Connecticut. Dr. Baker, like Drs. Cheraskin and Truss, emphasized the relationships among the different parts of the body. In working with hard-to-raise children, Dr. Baker emphasized the importance of looking at the whole child as a person rather than putting a label (or a diagnosis) on him. Although Dr. Baker acknowledged that labels such as "dyslexia" or "hyperactivity" may help people communicate, such labels also cause problems and lead to confusion.

In a recent article on dyslexia Dr. Baker commented:

> As soon as we start talking about treating dyslexia (or acne, or depression, or hyperactivity, or arthritis, or allergies or any other disease or condition), it becomes essential to recognize the difference between treating a child and treating a disease. . . .
>
> Two children may have the same problem—difficulty with reading—for very different reasons. Similarly, two children with very similar kinds of biochemical or psychological imbalance may show this imbalance in entirely different ways.
>
> This means that labels such as dyslexia are helpful only to tell us the ways in which a given child is like others, but not as a guide for treatment. Treatment is intended for the *child,* who is unique, and not for the *problem.*[2]

In a series of other articles[3] and lectures,[4] Dr. Baker urged physicians and other professionals to look for the causes of a problem rather than to hang a label on a person and prescribe a drug to counteract his symptoms. In approaching the irritable, overactive child, he emphasizes the importance of "biochemical imbalance." And he feels that this imbalance is often related to "consumption of altered adulterated, sweetened, fatty and refined foods."[5]

In discussing the way he approaches the study of a child with health problems of various types, including behavioral problems, he commented:

> Since the days of Hippocrates in ancient Greece, some people, including Hippocrates, have held to the notion that balance, or harmony, is the basis for health and that poor health—of whatever kind—comes from being out of balance. We are still a long way from knowing all the substances that must be brought into balance to help . . . any . . . person achieve his or her best state of health. But enough is known to take very practical and effective steps.
>
> These steps follow two connected paths. One helps to answer the question that asks if Michael could be *lacking* something. The other question is, "Is there something Michael could be *getting too much of* that contributes to his problem?" Together, these two questions form the basis for detective work aimed at uncovering imbalance in people of all ages with all sorts of problems.[6]

The teachings of Dr. Baker along with those of Drs. Cheraskin and Truss have influenced my thinking and the way I go about studying and managing my hard-to-raise patients. Labels such as *migraine, hyperactivity, dyslexia* or the *attention deficit disorder* help parents, physicians and other professionnals communicate. Yet I try to find out *why* a child is irritable, overactive and hard-to-raise rather than put a label on him and treat him with drugs.

FOR GOOD PHYSICAL, MENTAL AND EMOTIONAL HEALTH

Things your child may be lacking

1. Amino acids (proteins)

2. Complex carbohydrates

3. Essential fatty acids

4. Dietary fiber

5. Other nutrients such as iron, calcium, magnesium, and dozens of micronutrients, including vitamins A, B_1, B_2 B_3, B_6, B_{12}, C, D, E, and the trace minerals (zinc, chromium, selenium, and many others)

6. Light, air, water

7. Love, praise, touch and other psychological nutrients

8. Exercise

Things your child must avoid (or limit his exposure to)

1. Metallic poisons:
   Lead, cadmium, mercury, and aluminum;

2. Air, food, water and soil pollutants:
   Petrochemicals, insecticides, weed killers, formaldehyde, disinfectants, perfumes and tobacco

3. Nutritionally poor foods:
   Refined sugar
   White flour
   Saturated fats
   Hydrogenated vegetable oils

4. Allergens:
   Foods
   Molds
   Dusts
   Pollens
   Animal danders

5. Harmful microorganisms (germs) including bacteria, fungi, viruses, and parasites

Adapted from the work of Sidney Baker, M.D., and associates of the Gesell Institute of Human Development, New Haven, Connecticut.

4

Defining Terms
You'll Run Into

Labeling a difficult child with a diagnosis, such as "hyperactivity" or "dyslexia" or "attention deficit disorder" and treating him with a drug may help him "settle down," concentrate and get along with people. Yet, it doesn't really solve his problem unless the causes can be identified and appropriately treated.

Nevertheless, as you work to help your child, you'll bump into all sorts of labels and diagnoses. Although I don't like these labels, I feel I should define and explain some of them.

HYPERACTIVITY, HYPERKINESIS, MINIMAL BRAIN DYSFUNCTION AND ATTENTION DEFICIT DISORDER

First, I'd like to focus on three terms that have confused many of my patients: *hyperactivity, hyperkinesis* and *hyperkinetic*. These terms mean exactly the same thing. *Hyper* means over or excessive and *kinetic* means movement. So the hyperactive or hyperkinetic child can be said to be one who is always on

the go, who experiences trouble sitting still and settling down and paying attention.

Here are two other terms you may have run into: *minimal brain dysfunction* and *minimal brain damage.*

During the 1950s and early '60s, a number of papers describing difficult, hard-to-raise children appeared in the medical literature. All sorts of terms were used to describe these children, including *perceptual handicap, learning disability, developmental imbalance, minimal brain damage* and many others.

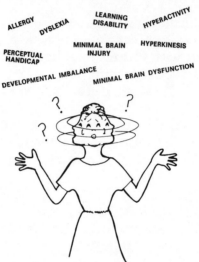

Because these terms confused everyone (including both professionals and parents), a conference of experts was held in 1966 to talk about these difficult children. Neurologists, psychiatrists and other professionals at the conference coined a new term, "minimal brain dysfunction," to describe children who were blessed with average or above-average intelligence, yet were bothered by learning or behavioral disturbances. This term was commonly used during the ensuing fifteen years.

Even before I met Dr. Baker and began using his sound and simple approach, I disliked the term *minimal brain dysfunction.* Here's why: Parents, on receiving such a diagnosis, would often say to themselves, "Since Johnny has something wrong with his brain, I guess there's isn't much I can do about it."

A lot of other people, including physicians, psychologists and educators also disliked the term *minimal brain dysfunc-*

tion. Several years ago, the American Psychiatric Association came up with a new label for the attentional problems of hard-to-raise children: "attention deficit disorder" or "ADD." The child given such a label is said to show the following manifestations:

    A. Inattention. At least three of the following:
        1. often fails to finish tasks
        2. often doesn't seem to listen
        3. easily distracted
        4. has difficulty concentrating on schoolwork or other tasks requiring sustained attention
        5. has difficulty sticking to a play activity
    B. Impulsivity. At least three of the following:
        1. often acts before thinking
        2. shifts excessively from one activity to another
        3. has difficulty organizing work (this not being due to cognitive impairment)
        4. needs a lot of supervision
        5. frequently calls out in class
        6. has difficulty awaiting turn in games or group situations.
    C. Hyperactivity (not always present). At least two of the following:
        1. runs about or climbs on things excessively
        2. has difficulty sitting still or fidgets excessively
        3. has difficulty staying seated
        4. moves about excessively during sleep
        5. is always "on the go" or acts if "driven by a motor"[1]

Some children who are labeled as having an attention deficit disorder are overactive. Others are less active but experience problems concentrating and paying attention and acting impulsively.

LEARNING DISABILITIES

While I'm sorting out terms and trying to help make things less confusing for you, I'll review, define and explain several educational terms you'll run into.

A child with a *learning disability* (LD) or *specific learning disability* (SLD) is a child who isn't learning his readin', 'ritin' and 'rithmetic. And when he struggles unsuccessfully to master these fundamentals, he experiences trouble with all his subjects.

These terms are often used to describe or label the child who:

1. Enjoys good physical health, including normal vision and hearing
2. Has normal or above intelligence
3. Is well motivated
4. Consumes an apparently good diet
5. Lives in an average or better social, cultural and economic environment
6. Receives proper emotional support

yet who, nevertheless, experiences problems in one or more of the following areas:

1. Listening
2. Thinking
3. Talking
4. Reading
5. Writing
6. Spelling
7. Arithmetic
8. Remembering

Putting it another way, you might say the child who is said to have a specific learning disability (SLD) possesses good health and an "okay" brain. And he *isn't* bothered by: cerebral palsy, mental retardation, bad eyesight, impaired hearing, an emotional disturbance or an environmental disadvantage.

Just as is the case with all children (including those who make A's in almost every subject), the child with a specific learning disability is unique. Different. So some children with SLD experience trouble only in writing. Others write beautifully but struggle and hesitate when they're confronted with simple math problems.

Other children with learning problems may experience trouble only in reading and are often said to be troubled with primary or "true dyslexia" and they're labeled "dyslexic." So the label *dyslexia* (*dys* = difficult; *lexia* = reading) is used to describe the child who experiences difficulty in reading. This type of reading problem has also been called "word blindness."

Boys suffer from it more than girls (in a ratio of six to one).

The child with a reading disability may often experience difficulty in writing and reproducing symbols. He may also have trouble telling his right hand from his left. He may confuse words that sound alike . . . such as shoe and chew. So his parents and teachers may complain, "Johnny doesn't listen . . . he must be hard of hearing," or "Johnny doesn't pay attention." Yet, hearing tests rarely show a problem.

One language specialist commented:

> Many children with hyperactivity and learning problems hear well but they don't understand what they've heard or don't remember it. So sometimes when they don't follow orders, it isn't because they're misbehaving; it's because they didn't understand what was wanted of them.

These children usually enjoy normal vision, yet their eyes seem to play tricks on them. They may confuse a "b" with a "d" and a "p" with a "q." They may reverse numbers like 24 and 42. They may show upside-down confusion and write "M" for "W."

RELATIONSHIP OF HYPERACTIVITY AND LEARNING DISABILITIES TO ALLERGIES

Hyperactivity, learning disabilities and allergies are commonly seen in the same child. Yet, I've known hyperactive youngsters who made A's in all their subjects—except behavior and deportment. And I've seen other hyperactive youngsters who had none of the usual symptoms of allergies (nasal congestion, skin rashes, cough, fatigue or dark circles under their eyes).

Similarly, I've seen hundreds—even thousands—of allergic children who are calm, well-behaved youngsters. Moreover, most of these youngsters performed well in school—on a par with their peers.

Nevertheless, most of my hyperactive patients have been troubled by allergies and learning disabilities. And such disabilities have often developed in children with normal intelligence because their allergies and hyperactivity interfered with their performance.

THE RELATIONSHIP OF HYPERACTIVITY AND LEARNING DISABILITY TO ALLERGY

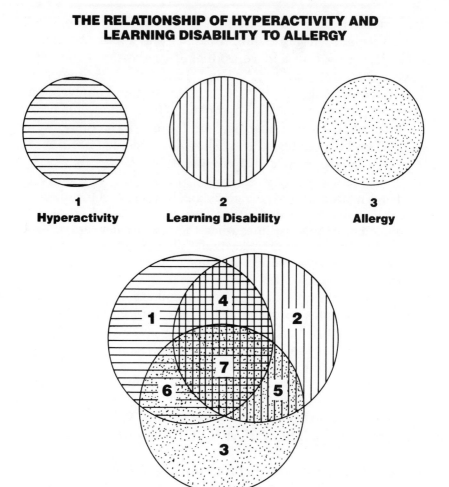

1. A hyperactive child with no allergy or learning disorder.
2. A learning disabled child (with no hyperactivity or allergy).
3. An allergic child (with no learning disability or hyperactivity).
4. A hyperactive learning disabled child.
5. An allergic learning disabled child (without hyperactivity).
6. An allergic hyperactive child (without learning disability).
7. An allergic hyperactive child with a learning disorder.

Section B

WHY MORE CHILDREN TODAY ARE BOTHERED BY ALLERGIES AND BY BEHAVIOR AND LEARNING PROBLEMS

5

Is the Incidence of
Hard-to-Raise Children Increasing?

Difficult, contrary, irritable and hyperactive children have been described in the medical and lay literature for decades . . . even for centuries. So have allergic children. However, as I reviewed my professional journals, it seemed to me that physicians, psychologists and other professionals have been talking about these troublesome children more often during the last two or three decades.

Is increased attention being paid to hyperactivity because a greater percentage of children today are developing behavioral disorders? Or are there other reasons today why so many physicians, teachers and parents are concerned about them?

It depends on whom you ask. Several years ago, a friend sent me a book entitled *The Myth of the Hyperactive Child.* In this book, the authors said that hyperactivity and learning disability are current "fads" being promoted by special interest groups, including teachers, physicians, overconcerned parents and drug companies.[1]

I possess no data to "prove" there are more difficult children today than there were twenty-five, fifty, a hundred or a thousand years ago. Yet, I was amazed to see this book. While I agreed with the authors that too many children today are given behavior modifying drugs, I disagreed strongly that "hyperactivity is a myth and its management shouldn't concern us."

As a pediatrician I've always been interested in the growth and development of my patients—including those with behavior and learning problems. Yet during my early years of practice (even though I was the only full-time pediatrician in my community) I rarely saw a child with hyperactivity. By contrast during the past decade (as has been the experience of many of my pediatric peers), irritable, hard-to-manage, hyperactive children (and their parents) are literally banging on my office door seeking help. So I'm convinced that more of today's children are troubled with these problems.

It also seems to me that learning disorders and allergies are increasing. Moreover, both of these disorders have been present in over 75 percent of the hyperactive children I've worked with in the past ten years.

David E. Rogers, M.D., president of the Robert Wood Johnson Foundation of Princeton, New Jersey, in his keynote address at the fiftieth anniversary meeting of the American Academy of Pediatrics in 1980, commented that the pediatrician in practice is now primarily concerned with problems relating to school health, with allergies, with problems requiring parent and child counseling, and with the supervision of child growth and development.

Why are there more of these hard-to-raise children today? Life has changed dramatically in this century and especially during the past forty years—due to antibiotics, fabricated foods, television, windowless schools, soil, water and air pollution, and so on. And I feel that these changes (and others) are adversely affecting the health of many children in the Western world.

6

The Nutritional Disaster
of the Twentieth Century

hen I was a small boy in the 1920s, my parents lived at the edge of town on what you might call a "mini-farm" (all of three acres!). We had four cows, a hundred chickens, forty oak trees and lots of vegetables and flowers. In the corner of our back lot were compost piles containing food scraps, decaying leaves and cow manure. From time to time, material from these piles was scattered over the vegetable garden as well as on the flower beds and around shrubs and trees.

We grew so many vegetables that I earned pocket money by selling them to our neighbors. And my mother sold thousands of sweet peas and asters to the local florists. Neighbors and friends would often say, "Millian Crook has a 'green thumb'! Her flowers and vegetables grow better than anyone else's."

I had almost forgotten about my mother's "green thumb," until about fifteen years ago. Then, at a meeting in Miami, I heard several fascinating presentations on nutrition. Each speaker said that much of the food Americans are eating today is refined and processed. And it's loaded with fat, sugar, artificial flavorings, colorings, preservatives and other additives.

Moreover, these nutritionists commented that even good foods (such as fruits and vegetables) may be laced with pesticides and other chemicals. And such foods may lack vital nutrients because they're grown on poor soil, soil that has been depleted of many of its vital minerals including chromium, zinc, copper, manganese, cobalt, selenium and other essential trace minerals.

I was fascinated by these remarks. What these nutritionists said made sense. I saw for the first time that my mother's green thumb was related to the soil enrichment program she systematically carried out. Those ever-present compost piles returned to the soil important nutrients that might otherwise have been lost.

During my years of medical training, like most pediatricians I learned that children needed sufficient protein if they were to grow and thrive, and carbohydrates and fats for energy. I also knew that if a baby didn't get enough iron or vitamins D and C, he'd become anemic or develop rickets or scurvy. I also learned about the fluid and mineral needs of children with diarrhea, especially their requirements for sodium, potassium and chloride. Yet I can recall few lectures in medical school devoted to other aspects of nutrition. So like most physicians I knew little about the subject.

In the August 1975 issue of *Southern Medicine* (published by the Southern Medical Association and reprinted from *Hospital Tribune*, June 16, 1975), this statement appeared:

> Medicine confronts a disturbing dilemma. Linus Pauling, Roger J. Williams, Albert Szent-Györgi and other leaders have pointed to the failure of the "medical establishment" to undertake proper training of young doctors in the field of nutrition.
>
> There has been an *educational blackout* in a key area of medicine . . . nutrition. A significant portion of the improvement of our general health . . . is attributable to improved nutrition. Yet little is taught . . . (on this important subject).

And when Emanuel Cheraskin in his Miami presentation commented, "The average physician knows as much about nutrition as his secretary . . . unless his secretary belongs to Weight Watchers. . . . Then he only knows half as much," I said to myself, "He's talking about me!"

For a long time, I had been interested in what children ate and how it affected the way they felt. Yet my interest had been limited to food allergy. So with the impetus of the Miami meeting, I began to read everything I could get my hands on that dealt with nutrition. The more I read, the more fascinated I became. Today I'm just as interested in nutrition as I am in

food allergy. Moreover, I've found that the two fields overlap to a remarkable degree.

In their books *Diet and Disease* and *Psychodietetics,* Emanuel Cheraskin, and his associate W. M. Ringsdorf, Jr., D.M.D., also from the University of Alabama, said that dietary surveys during the past two decades have revealed that progressive worsening of the average American's nutrient intake is largely because of an increased consumption of refined carbohydrate foods—white flour and sugar in precooked bakery products, ready-to-eat cereals, soft drinks, punches and beverage products. These and other snack foods supply little more than energy and are slowly but surely depriving the American of essential nutrients.[1,2]

Roger Williams, Ph.D., of the University of Texas, discoverer of pantothenic acid and folic acid, and former president of the American Chemical Society, likewise observed that excessive sugar consumption provides only "naked calories." Poorly nourished children eat more sugar than those who are well nourished. "Greater sugar consumption spells poorer nutrition because sugar provides calories that have been stripped of all minerals, amino acids, and vitamins," stressed Dr. Williams.[3]

Ross Hume Hall, Ph.D., professor and past chairman of the Department of Biochemistry at McMaster University in Hamilton, Ontario, commented:

> The all-American diet has largely become the all-fabricated diet—consisting of foods that have literally been taken apart and put together in new form. They are "engineered" from ingredients that may or may not include chemical additives, vitamins and minerals. . . .
>
> At least 75 percent of the food consumed in North America

has been factory-processed in one way or another. Some 1800 chemicals have been added to the cans, bottles, boxes and packages for sale on our supermarket shelves. . . .

What you buy at the grocery store or eat in a restaurant is becoming less nourishing and increasingly hazardous to your health. [4]

Several years ago, I read the comments of a food industry spokesperson who said it is useless to try to persuade the American people to eat foods that are nutritionally good for them. Instead, foods will have to be "nutrified"—enriched with health-promoting chemicals. Frankfurters should be fortified with extra protein and candy bars with vitamins and minerals.

But are enriched foods really better than other foods? In my opinion the answer is no. Moreover, such foods are actually inferior to whole, unrefined foods.

According to the late Henry Schroeder, M.D. (professor at the medical schools of Washington University and, later, Dartmouth), when whole wheat is refined and converted to white flour, 60 to 90 percent of its thirty-seven micronutrients are removed.[5] Only four nutrients are returned to the flour in the "enriching" process: B_1, B_2, B_3 and iron.

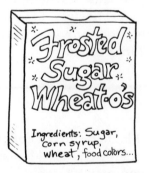

So when food processors "enrich" bread, white flour and cereals, the resulting foods are still inferior to those containing whole grains. And they're especially bad when combined with sugar and food colors and other additives found in most of the highly advertised breakfast cereals. Many of these cereals contain over 40 percent sugar and one contains 68 percent. *This means that a fourteen ounce box of such a cereal contains up to sixty-four teaspoons of sugar.*

POPULAR BREAKFAST CEREALS

CEREAL	PERCENT SUCROSE (SUGAR)
Shredded Wheat	0.0%
Cheerios	2.2
Puffed Rice	2.4
Grape-Nut Flakes	3.3
Post Toasties	4.1
Special K	4.4
Grape-Nuts	6.6
Corn Flakes	7.8
Total	8.1
Rice Krispies	10.0
Life	14.5
Team	15.9
Sugar Frosted Flakes	29.0
Frosted Mini-Wheats	33.6
Sugar Pops	37.8
Cocoa Puffs	43.0
Cap'n Crunch	43.3
Kaboom	43.8
Frosted Flakes	44.0
Fruit Loops	47.4
Apple Jacks	55.0
Sugar Smacks	61.3
Super Orange Crisp	68.0

Source: *Journal of Dentistry for Children,* reprinted by permission.

Each year I become more convinced that man isn't smart enough to manufacture foods that compare with those provided by nature. This holds true whether we're talking about feeding infants, children or adults.

Take the matter of infant feeding. Over a hundred years ago, Oliver Wendell Holmes said, "Human breast milk is ideally suited for the human infant. And it's better than any substitute. Moreover, a team of the wisest professors can't design a milk that equals breast milk."

Since I finished medical school, I've seen several situations when artificial formulas (which supposedly were "complete and equivalent to human breast milk") were proved to be devastatingly inadequate. For example, during the late 1940s, I saw a number of formula-fed infants with severe anemia. Their supposedly "complete" formulas were subsequently found to be lacking in folic acid, an essential ingredient in preventing an unusual type of anemia.

A few years later, many babies around the country were found to be hyperactive and irritable. The cause: a popular infant formula lacking sufficient vitamin B_6.

As Shakespeare said some three hundred years ago, "You can't make a silk purse out of a sow's ear." Today, in the mid-1980s, you can't add a few vitamins and minerals to nutritionally deficient manufactured foods consisting of sugar, white flour and hydrogenated fat,* and end up with food that provides adequate nutrition.

I'm also concerned about the philosophy of many government officials, food processors and supposedly knowledgeable nutritional "authorities." Such individuals seem to feel that you can fortify a soft drink or orange breakfast drink with vitamin C and make it as good as pure orange juice. They also seem to feel they can take doughnuts and most breakfast cereals and "fortify" them with a few vitamins and end up with a truly nutritious food.

THE ROLE OF TELEVISION

Television brainwashes your children and encourages them to eat junk food. Numerous research studies have shown that the average American child spends more hours in front of the TV set than at school and sees and hears countless thousands of commercials for sugary food every year.

Judith J. Wurtman, Ph.D., a mother and a biologist at the Massachusetts Institute of Technology, declared:

*Each month, the *Nutrition Action Health Letter* focuses on one of these incredibly poor foods under the heading "Food Porn." For more information, write to: CSPI, 1501 16th St., N.W., Washington, D.C. 20036.

Television advertising is probably the most persistent force undermining good eating habits. [Messages that promote well-balanced meals and nutritious foods] tend to be overwhelmed by the huge number of ads for junk foods that appear during prime TV time for children.[6]

Peggy Charren, president of Action for Children's Television (46 Austin St., Newtonville, MA 02160), in a number of her comments had this to say:

The television ads come fast and furious, coaxing children to try "Mars bars," "M&M's" and sweetened cereals as between-meal snacks. . . . Adults whom the children respect, father figures, famous athletes, competent older children . . . are hourly heard encouraging children to eat candy bars, soft drinks and make friends by sharing snacks. The familiar cartoon characters, the friendly announcer, the superstars all entice children to try the latest gooey, munchy, crunchy sweet snacks.

Food advertising directed to children sets up a conflict between the parent and child and between the child and authority figures . . . including doctors, dentists and teachers, as well as parents.[7]

Joan Gussow, nutrition educator, testifying before a U.S. Senate subcommittee about commercials shown on children's television, reported, "What our survey has told us is that nutrition messages are numerous on children's television, that few of them even hint at proper eating habits, and that altogether they encourage poor eating habits."[8]

As I look back on my thirty-eight years of general pediatric and allergy practice, I've seen a tremendous rise in the incidence of allergies, hyperactivity and related health disorders. When I ask myself why, one answer seems clear: *The "explosion" of sweetened, colored, additive-laden, fabricated, nutritionally deficient foods plays a major role in causing these health problems. And the continuing daily seduction of our children by television makes them hard to resist.*

7

Our Polluted Planet and Chemical Sensitivity

If you've been reading your newspapers and magazines, or looking at television, you know something about toxic chemicals. You've heard not only about Love Canal, where thousands of barrels of poisonous chemicals were buried, but also about chemical dump sites in or near your own community. You've also heard or read about agent orange, PCB's and acid rain. And I'm sure you've heard about formaldehyde, indoor air pollution, DDT in human breast milk and chemicals in our food.

I don't want to sound like a prophet of doom, but I'm

concerned about the growing pollution of our planet. This chemical pollution plays a role in causing hyperactivity and other health problems in adults and children.

CHEMICALS IN OUR OCEANS, RIVERS, SOIL AND DRINKING WATER

Before the Clean Water Act was enacted in 1972, oceans, rivers and other bodies of water were commonly used as dumping grounds for some of the most toxic substances imaginable, including arsenic, cadmium, mercury, lead, polychlorinated biphenyls (PCB's) and toxic pesticides.

Francesca Lyman, a former editor of *Environmental Action,* commented:

> Baltimore wants to deepen its ship channel to be able to handle deep draft ships that carry more bulk cargo. To do this it must dredge some 120 million cubic yards of silty mud, contaminated with heavy metals, pesticides and other industrial wastes dumped there for a century. . . .
>
> It's better not to move these toxic substances because moving them can further spread the contamination and disrupt the chemical, physical and biological integrity of the aquatic ecosystem.[1]

Lyman pointed out that cadmium and lead were among the substances found in silty mud and that such silt was sometimes spread over cultivated areas where vegetables and fruit crops could absorb them.

CHEMICALS IN OUR FOOD

Over thirty thousand chemicals are being used in today's modern, industrialized society. Thousands of them can be found in our foods. Some get in there unintentionally; for example, insecticides and weed killers. Others are added on purpose.

To illustrate how far out of hand things are, the government does not even know how many additives are being used or by whom, or for what; official estimates range from three thousand to ten thousand. Between 1958 and 1974, government approval was granted to over three thousand additives and nearly one thousand were put on the GRAS ("Generally Recognized as Safe") list. Governmental acceptance gives no assurance, however, that future evidence will not show that an "approved" substance actually harms us. Many additives once thought to be safe are now banned.

In their book *An Alternative Approach to Allergies,* Theron G. Randolph, M.D., and Ralph Moss, Ph.D., tell of a patient who developed "searing attacks of head pain" after eating apples. Dr. Randolph said, "I naturally diagnosed him as allergic to apples."[2]

Subsequently, the patient gathered apples from trees in an abandoned orchard which hadn't been sprayed in years. And, surprisingly, he was able to eat them with complete abandon. He developed no headache or other adverse reactions.

Following up on this clinical observation, Randolph noted that many patients who reacted to fruit (and other foods) weren't reacting to the food, but to the chemical pollutants in or on the food.

In discussing chemicals in our food, Randolph and Moss point out that foods can be contaminated with many different chemicals, including chlorinated hydrocarbons in meats, which enter the animals' bodies by way of sprayed feed. Also, fruits which have been sprayed, fumigated or preserved are often contaminated with sulfur and other chemicals.

As long ago as the late 1940s, Stephen D. Lockey, Sr., M.D., of Pennsylvania, warned that artificial colors in drugs caused adverse reactions in both adults and children.[3]

More recently, the late Benjamin Feingold, M.D., publicized the effect of food colors and other additives in contributing to hyperactivity in children.[4]

Even our water has been "chemicalized." Chlorine added to our drinking water stops the spread of gastrointestinal and other infections, and fluoride lessens the incidence of tooth decay. Yet these widely used chemicals cause adverse reactions in susceptible individuals. Moreover, all sorts of other chemicals, including industrial wastes, insecticides and weed killers that find their way into our water supply cause toxic and allergic reactions in susceptible individuals.

According to an article in the October 1984 issue of *Environmental Action,* entitled "Poisoning the Well," "a shocking one-fifth of U.S. ground water is poisoned." In the discussion the author of the article commented:

> After four years of procrastination, the Environmental Protection Agency (EPA) finally released a "Ground Water Protection Strategy" in late August [1984], declaring what everyone has known for some time—contamination of underground drinking water sources "may be a widespread problem."
>
> EPA strategy is actually a non-strategy: It places primary responsibility for protecting underground water supplies on the states; it suggests weak protection *guidelines*—but not mandatory requirements—for the states to follow; and it provides far too little money . . . to aid the state protection programs.[5]

Francis S. Sterrett, Ph.D., a professor of chemistry at Hofstra University, commented:

> Several hundred different organic chemical substances have been found in a variety of drinking waters. For this reason, I and many other people on Long Island and in other parts of the country filter their drinking water through an activated carbon water filter.*[6]

CHEMICALS IN OUR HOMES

Theron G. Randolph, M.D.,† a Chicago internist and allergist, warned:

> While it is true that outdoor . . . air pollution is a significant source of exposure, a far greater threat is posed by the presence

---

*Information on water filters can be found in the book *Water Fit to Drink,* by Carol Keough, and in the February 1983 issue of *Consumer Reports.*

†Randolph, a fellow of the American Academy of Allergy and the American College of Allergists, over thirty years ago noted that some of his patients reacted adversely to chemicals. In 1961 he published a book called *Human Ecology and Susceptibility to the Chemical Environment.* He also founded the Society for Clinical Ecology. This group of physicians was interested in people who were made ill by things in the environment. The organization has since been renamed the American Academy of Environmental Medicine.

of indoor . . . air pollution. . . . Many household products give
off noxious fumes. Indoor air pollution is particularly dangerous
because exposure to it is so constant.[7]

William Rea, M.D., of Dallas, past president of the American Academy of Environmental Medicine, has for over a decade been studying patients with chronic health disorders
related to chemical overload. And he stresses the importance
of chemical overload in contributing to many chronic illnesses.[8]

Do chemicals play a part in causing behavior and other
health disorders? In my opinion, the answer is *yes*. Hyperactivity occurs more often in allergic children, and the more
chemicals a child is exposed to, the worse his allergies become.

Here's a list of symptoms I've seen caused by (or ag-
gravated by) chemical exposures:

Coughing, wheezing
Nasal congestion
Burning eyes
Headache
Burning, tingling and flushing of the skin
Muscle aches
Irritability
Drowsiness
Mental confusion
Incoordination
Hyperactivity

But in spite of growing evidence that our "chemical load"
is increasing every year and that chemicals may play a role in
causing many health problems, you may have heard other
voices saying, "Chemicals are a normal part of our life today.
To maintain a high standard of living in our modern industrialized society, we must use chemicals. Although a rare person
may be bothered by such chemicals, the average person
doesn't need to worry about them."

People who make such remarks resemble ostriches with
their heads in the sand. Although I agree that chemicals may
promote "better living" in a variety of ways, they may harm

more than they help—especially when they're used indiscriminately.*

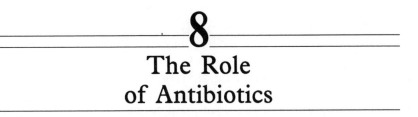

8
The Role
of Antibiotics

My grandfather, a country doctor, began practicing medicine in western Tennessee over a hundred years ago. My father followed in his footsteps and joined him in practice around 1900. They were both "people doctors" who tried to help their patients with the limited resources available to them at the time. No X rays; no polio vaccine; no corticosteroids; no birth-control pills; no endoscopic examinations; no

---

*A report on *NBC Nightly News*, April 5, 1987, told of a tremendous increase in the use of insecticides and weed killers during the past decade. Moreover, when these toxic chemicals are sprayed on crops, they're inhaled by unprotected people. In addition, they're contaminating the drinking water in many communities. Some of these chemicals are so toxic they've been banned for use in the United States. Yet, they're being sold to food producers in Mexico and other countries. Increased quantities of tomatoes and other fruits and vegetables which are sold in American supermarkets are imported from these countries.

CAT* scans; no cataract or open heart surgery and no hip replacements. *And no antibiotics.*

In medicine, just as in transportation, communication and every other area of our lives, changes have been amazing, fantastic and breathtaking. And because of these advances in medicine, many lives have been saved and much suffering relieved.

At the age of four my oldest daughter developed severe peritonitis following a ruptured appendix. Antibiotics helped save her life.

Antibiotics save the lives of thousands of children and adults each year. Moreover, they could save your child's life. *Yet these drugs are a two-edged sword.* When your child takes antibiotics, especially if he takes them repeatedly, friendly germs in his body (including *Lactobacillus acidophilus*) are "wiped out." Yet, another kind of germ, *Candida albicans,* a usually benign yeast organism, isn't affected by antibiotics.

Accordingly, when your child takes antibiotics, especially ampicillin, amoxicillin, Keflex, Septra, Bactrim or Ceclor, yeasts multiply and have large families. Symptoms of a yeast overgrowth include bloating, diarrhea, skin and diaper rashes and vaginal discharge.

Even more important, clinical observations and laboratory studies show that yeasts can put out toxins that enter the circulation and play a part in causing many health problems. These include disorders affecting the immune system[1,2] and the nervous system. Common symptoms include irritability, memory loss, depression, headache and a feeling of being "spaced out."[3,4]

Obviously, if your child develops a "strep throat," bacterial pneumonia or meningitis, he'll need an antibiotic to help his immune system fight off the attacking bacteria. However, if your child "catches" a cold or flu, antibiotics won't help, as these infections are caused by viruses. And antibiotic drugs, especially when they're taken repeatedly, promote yeast overgrowth.

In my experience, yeast toxins play an important role in

*Computerized axial tomography is a specialized radiological technique that provides the examining physician with much more information than the ordinary X ray.

causing nervous system symptoms and persistent infections in children. Accordingly when your child takes antibiotic medication (especially a broad-spectrum drug), he should also take an antifungal agent, such as acidophilus, garlic, caprylic acid or nystatin (see Section F).

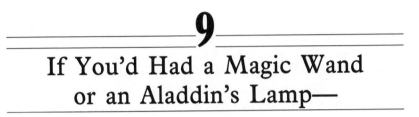

9

If You'd Had a Magic Wand or an Aladdin's Lamp—

Your child, whether he is hard to raise or not, is one of a kind. And your family is also unique. Different genes and different family medical history. Different food choices and different economic resources. Different exposure to pollutants and different loads of allergy troublemakers. Different medical and educational resources that are available to you.

Accordingly, your child deserves to be treated as an individual. His special requirements should be considered in planning a treatment program. Yet, in spite of their differences, all children—including those with problems—share certain basic needs that must be met if they are to enjoy good physical, mental and emotional health and a reasonable chance for a useful, productive and happy life.

Admittedly, no child and no family enjoys an ideal situation. Nevertheless, the closer a child can approach such an ideal, the fewer problems he'll experience. And the better he'll cope with the challenges he'll meet and overcome the obstacles he must face.

So let's talk about the child of parents who had been given a magic wand or an Aladdin's lamp, plus infinite wisdom, un-

limited financial sources, a crystal ball and 20/20 foresight—
even before he was conceived!

1. *Genetic factors.* This child would be free of genetically
transmitted diseases, including those that might handicap him
in early life. His parents would consume a good diet prior to
conception so that both egg and sperm cells would be healthy.

2. *Maternal nutrition.* During pregnancy, the child's
mother would eat nutritious foods (derived from many, many
different sources). Such foods would provide the essential nutrients that an unborn baby needs for optimum intrauterine
growth. She would avoid tobacco, caffeine, alcohol, and toxic
drugs and chemicals that can pass through her placenta to her
infant.

By consuming good foods and avoiding toxic substances
she'd reduce the risks of toxemia and other complications of
pregnancy and lessen her chances of delivering a low birth-
weight infant.[1] She'd also increase her chances of delivering a
healthy infant.

3. *Labor and delivery.* "Birthing a baby" shouldn't be
looked on as an illness. Parents who plan an infant and receive
proper preparation during pregnancy improve their chances
of producing a healthy baby. When a father (or any caring
person) participates in and furnishes emotional support to a
mother during labor and delivery, the labor is shorter and
easier for the mother and child. Moreover, complications
occur less frequently and the subsequent physical and emotional welfare of the child and his family are improved.

4. *Breast-feeding.* The ideal child would be fed *only human milk* during the first six to nine months of life, so as to lessen his chances of developing allergies and infections. Breast milk contains large amounts of immunoglobulin A, which acts as a kind of "antiseptic paint" on the intestinal membranes, keeping harmful invaders (including allergens and disease-causing microorganisms) from getting in. It also contains zinc and many essential nutrients uniquely designed to promote the physical and mental health of the infant.

5. *Infant stimulation.* He would be held, patted, petted, nurtured and cared for by loving parents who would look at, smile at and talk to him. (Many recent scientific studies have shown that early infant stimulation plays an important role in the physical, emotional and intellectual development of the child in later life.)

6. *Home environment.* His home would be as free as humanly possible of pollutants. These include tobacco smoke and odorous chemicals of all kinds, including petrochemicals, toxic insecticides and formaldehyde. Such substances may not only irritate the respiratory membranes, but also cause adverse or toxic reactions in other parts of the body, including the nervous system.

7. *Child guidance.* During the second six months of life, he'd receive not only affectionate care but also guidance and limits. Such limits would be based on a sound knowledge of child development. Accordingly, he'd be stimulated to grow and learn according to his capacities. And he'd rarely be frowned at and never punished.

Desirable behavior would be reinforced and rewarded with a smile or a love pat and undesirable behavior ignored unless it could cause injury or property damage, or interfere with the rights of others.

8. *Nutritional factors.* Although he'd be breast-fed for nine months to a year (or longer), he'd need foods other than breast milk during the second half of his first year of life. Such foods would be appropriately selected. As he grew, he'd continue to eat nutritious food.

9. *Family factors.* He'd be reared by a loving and supportive family. He'd receive liberal amounts of "unconditional love," plus praise and acceptance. His parents would also pro-

vide him with wise counsel and guidance and would set appropriate and consistent limits for him.

10. *Kindergarten and school.* He'd start kindergarten and school when he was physically, mentally and emotionally "ready" and not at some predetermined time based solely on his chronological age. Louise Bates Ames, Ph.D., of the Gesell Institute, in her book *Is Your Child in the Wrong Grade in School?* commented, "The drop-out problem starts right down there in kindergarten and first grade with children whose parents start them in school before they're ready. They fail early, come to hate school and drop out as soon as the opportunity presents itself."[2]

I agree with Dr. Ames and I've seen countless children during my years in pediatric practice whose behavior and learning problems were caused mainly by, or were related to, overplacement in school.

Few parents can fulfill all of these requirements for rearing an "ideal child." Moreover, you can't turn the clock back and change things that happened years ago—or even yesterday. But don't feel guilty. Today is the first day of the rest of your child's life. Your child is resilient. He wants to conquer his problems and enjoy good physical and mental health. With your help and that of those who work with you, he can overcome many problems.

To cope with your hard-to-raise child (with the guidance and cooperation of your physician and other professionals), you must first identify the main causes of his difficulties. When you do, you can more effectively help him overcome them.

Section C

ALLERGY:
THE
GREAT
MASQUERADER

10

Types of Allergy
and the Allergy Controversy

THE ALLERGY "ICEBERG"

Allergy has been recognized for thousands of years. But it wasn't until 1906 that the Austrian pediatrician von Pirquet coined the term *allergy*. He put together two Greek words, *allos*, meaning "other," and *ergon*, meaning "action." To von Pirquet, allergy meant "altered reactivity."

As translated today, most physicians feel that allergy means hypersensitivity to a substance that does not bother other people.

However, if you consult different physicians, you may find that they do not always concur on how allergy should be defined, diagnosed or treated. Although most pediatricians and allergists agree that allergies occur commonly in children, you'll discover different opinions about food allergies.

Allergy can be compared to an iceberg. Asthma, hay fever and eczema resemble the part above the surface of the ocean. Such disorders are easy to recognize. Yet allergy also causes less obvious (or "submerged") manifestations. And their allergic cause is often overlooked by parents and physicians. These hard-to-recognize allergies are usually caused by common foods your child eats every day. I call them *hidden food allergies*.

When I entered practice in 1949, I hadn't heard or read about this kind of allergy. Although I knew that foods could make a susceptible person break out in a rash, I didn't realize that they could cause headache, fatigue and other symptoms.

Then, in the middle 1950s, I read reports by physicians who described food-induced systemic and nervous system symptoms.[1,2,3,4] When offending foods were avoided, these symptoms would disappear.

So I began to look for food-sensitive patients in my own practice. Using elimination diets, I was able to help hundreds of people each year by changing their diets. Moreover, I found that food-induced reactions played a major role in causing behavior and learning problems in many of my patients.

Yet in spite of my observations (and those of a handful of other physicians), most of my colleagues paid little attention to hidden food allergies. Moreover, most allergists and immunologists agreed with Charles D. May, M.D., professor of pediatrics, emeritus, of the University of Colorado, who said:

> Controversy over food allergy confuses the public. Our troubles begin when we leap from a suspicion that eating a food causes symptoms to the assumption that these symptoms are due to allergy.
>
> Until we prove scientifically by immunologic tests that food is responsible for hyperactivity, nervousness and other manifestations of the tension-fatigue syndrome, we ought to stop talking about it.
>
> Rather than calling food allergy "the great masquerader," we should call it the current crutch for neurotic patients.[5]

Dr. May expressed these sentiments in a commentary on food allergy in the February 1975 issue of *Pediatric Clinics of North America.* However, in the same issue, in an article entitled "Food Allergy—The Great Masquerader," I said:

> Food allergy is the most common cause of chronic unwellness seen in pediatric office practice. Yet, if the "scientific" immunologist (or any other physician) closes his eyes and never puts his patients on an elimination diet and never looks for this sort of allergy, he'll surely never find it.[6]

There are two types of food allergy:

1. Obvious food allergy
2. Hidden or unsuspected food allergy

OBVIOUS FOOD ALLERGY

As the name implies, you know when your child is bothered by this sort of allergy. Such an allergy is usually caused by uncommonly eaten foods, such as fish, strawberries, cashew nuts or lobster. However, it may be caused by any food, including eggs, peanuts or chocolate. An obvious food allergy will usually make your child break out in a rash. Or it may make him swell, sneeze, wheeze or develop a headache or digestive symptoms.

Let's suppose that your child itches and breaks out in hives when he eats a candy bar. Moreover, his nose stops up. In studying his problem, your physician uses allergy prick or scratch tests.

If an itching welt appears on your child's skin at the site of the peanut test, your doctor will usually say, "This test shows he's allergic to peanuts."

No one argues about this sort of allergy. Here's why: It's easy to diagnose. Moreover, scientists understand what happens in this sort of allergy. They know that it occurs because of a reaction that takes place in the immune system. This system resembles our army, navy, marines and air force and is composed of specialists with many different capabilities.

Among the components of your child's team of defenders are protein fractions of his blood called *immunoglobulins.* These substances are made by blood cells (lymphocytes) in the bone marrow. Canadian pediatric allergist and immunologist John Gerrard has suggested we might call these cells

"soldier cells," whose duty it is to fight invading enemies. The shock troops, the cells called up in an emergency when an enemy is seen for the first time, make IgM (immunoglobulin M). They hold the enemy in check while the reserves are brought up and the army as a whole is mobilized. The ammunition of the reserves is called immunoglobulin G or IgG.[7]

A third class of "soldiers" that dwell in the linings of the nose, bronchial tubes and stomach, bowel and bladder are called "secretory IgA's" (immunoglobulin A). They lie in wait (like the booby traps and antitank mines laid by soldiers in the field) for unwary germs and other invaders that try to enter the body.

Around 1967, two Japanese scientists (the Ishizakas) studying immunoglobulins found that the body makes still another immunoglobulin, which they named *immunoglobulin E* or *IgE.*[8] IgE, like the other immunoglobulins, helps protect the body from harmful invaders. In addition it becomes attached to special groups of cells called *mast cells* and *basophils.* These cells contain a powerful chemical called *histamine.* For reasons we don't clearly understand, in some persons IgE is formed against harmless substances including inhalants and foods.

For example, the ragweed- and lobster-sensitive person develops elevated blood levels of IgE—especially to ragweed and lobster. This sensitivity can be measured by several laboratory tests including the RAST test.

Moreover, individuals with this type of allergy also show positive allergy skin tests. Here's why: When IgE on the surface of mast cells combines with ragweed, lobster (or other extract the person is allergic to) a reaction takes place. As a part of this reaction mast cells break open releasing histamine. This substance causes blood vessels to leak fluid, producing an itching welt or wheal.

Because allergies of this sort can be readily identified, little controversy surrounds IgE-mediated allergies. But with hidden food allergies, it's a different story.

HIDDEN OR UNSUSPECTED FOOD ALLERGY

Hidden food allergy is usually caused by foods your child eats every day, including milk, cane sugar, corn, wheat, legumes, chocolate, citrus and eggs. However, other commonly eaten foods such as potatoes, beef, yeast, apples, lettuce and oats may also cause hidden allergies. When your child develops an allergy to these foods, he tends to develop it gradually . . . so gradually that the relationship of his symptoms to the foods is rarely recognized.

Unfortunately, the mechanisms responsible for these reactions haven't yet been explained.* These food-induced reactions are not mediated through immunoglobulin E. Accordingly, the allergy scratch test is usually negative, as are the RAST test and other sophisticated immunologic tests that measure only IgE.

In discussing adverse food reactions, the late Frederic Speer, M.D., of the University of Kansas, commented, "While immunological mechanisms are undoubtedly important in explaining allergic diseases, they don't tell the whole story."[9]

The late William C. Deamer, M.D., of the University of California, commented:

> It would certainly clear up some of the confusion among both doctors and patients if we had a laboratory test to identify hidden or delayed-onset food allergy. But we don't. Yet we needn't sit back and wait for such a laboratory test. Instead, we can identify and successfully treat patients with food-related problems using simple elimination diets followed by challenge to determine which foods are the trouble makers.[10]

Happily, more allergists and immunologists are becoming interested in food-related health problems. For example, over five hundred physicians attended a seminar sponsored by the Committee on Adverse Reactions to Foods at the March 1983 meeting of the prestigious American Academy of Allergy.

In April 1984, and again in January 1986, at national meetings of the American College of Allergists, William T. Kniker, M.D., professor of pediatrics and microbiology at the University of Texas, San Antonio, urged allergists attending these conventions to look for hidden food allergies in their patients. Dr. Kniker's remarks were published in the *Annals of Allergy*. Here are excerpts:

> The estimated group of 40 million citizens with classical allergies is probably the most underserved of all diseases in the U.S.

*However, new research may well reveal the underlying mechanism, immunologic or otherwise, which should help to throw light on this perplexing problem.

. . . In addition, there are countless other millions of individuals who have unrecognized adverse reactions to the various antigens, foods, chemicals and environmental or occupational triggers. . . .

The acquired disease . . . may involve a puzzling array of organ systems causing the patients to visit a number of different kinds of specialists who are unsuccessful in recognizing that an adverse or allergic reaction is going on.[11]

In over thirty-five years of pediatric office practice, I've found that thousands of my patients showed adverse or allergic reactions to foods they were eating every day. Moreover, *food reactions were the most common cause of persistent and recurring symptoms in my patients.*

Based on my experiences and those of many of my peers, I feel there are millions of other people who suffer from similar food-induced reactions. And recognizing and helping these food-sensitive people is more important than arguing over whether or not their symptoms are caused by a "true allergy."[12]

II
Allergy Can Make Your Child Hyperactive, Tired or Nervous

THE ALLERGIC TENSION-FATIGUE SYNDROME

When children show symptoms of hyperactivity and irritability, alternating with fatigue, listlessness and drowsiness, plus complaints in other parts of the body, many physicians refer to the symptom complex as the *allergic* *tension-fatigue syndrome.** Symptoms characteristic of this disorder include:

TENSION
Motor tension (hyperactivity):
    Overactivity, restlessness
    Clumsiness
    Poor manual behavior
    Inability to relax
Sensory tension:
    Irritability
    Oversensitivity
    Insomnia
    Oversensitivity to light, pain, noise

FATIGUE
Motor fatigue:
    Tiredness
    Achiness
Sensory fatigue:
    Sluggishness
    Mental dullness or "brain fatigue"

OTHER MENTAL AND NERVOUS SYSTEM
SYMPTOMS
Headache
Mental depression
Feeling of unreality
Bizarre and irrational behavior
Paranoid ideas
Inability to concentrate
Nervous tics, abnormal skin burning or prickling

ASSOCIATED SYSTEMIC SYMPTOMS
Almost invariably present:
    Pale appearance
    Dark circles under eyes
    Stuffy nose

*Credit for coining this term goes to the late Dr. Frederic Speer.

Common, but not present in all patients:
Puffiness around eyes
Increased salivation
Increased sweating
Abdominal pain, limb pain (especially in the legs)
Headaches
Bedwetting, daytime bladder-control problems

Reprinted (but slightly modified) from W. G. Crook in F. Speer, *The Allergic Child* (New York: Hoeber, 1963), p. 333. Used with permission.

Observant parents and doctors have known for many years that allergies can make a child irritable and hyperactive and can interfere with his behavior in many ways.*

Yet when I entered practice in 1949 I didn't know that what a child ate could affect his behavior. Then in 1956 an alert mother convinced me—against my will—that when her twelve-year-old son, Mack, drank cow's milk he became irritable and nervous. Soon afterward I came across an article by Dr. Speer, describing children with food-related symptoms, including those involving the nervous system.[8] I was fascinated by this article and was amazed to learn that many other physicians (cited by Speer) had described similar allergy-related nervous and other systemic symptoms.

So I began to look for food reactions in my own patients.

---

*In 1916, pediatrician B. R. Hoobler described disturbances of the nervous system in allergic infants and young children. He commented on their "restlessness, fretfulness and sleeplessness" and their tendency to irritability.[1]

Subsequently, in 1922, W. R. Shannon, M.D., described seven patients with generalized symptoms due to allergy. He especially emphasized the involvement of the nervous system with symptoms of irritability and peevishness.[2]

Then, in 1927, I. S. Kahn, M.D., described a group of children who developed tension, fatigue and pallor in the pollen season.[3] And in 1930, Albert Rowe, Sr., M.D., reported that food allergy could cause hyperactivity, drowsiness, irritability, fatigue, weakness, slowness and behavior problems.[4]

In 1947, Randolph published the first of a series of observations on children with fatigue, irritability and other nervous system reactions caused by allergies. He described for the first time the facial pallor and puffiness and the dark shadows under the eyes often seen in children with allergy.[5]

Moreover, during the 1940s and 1950s many other physicians, including especially the late Frederick Speer, reported similar findings.[6,7]

Much to my surprise, I found numerous youngsters whose behavior improved when I changed their diets. Moreover, I saw so many children with diet-related systemic and nervous system symptoms that I published my observations on fifty such youngsters in 1961.[9]

My interest in food-related disorders continued and in January 1973, I began to collect data on the relationship of food sensitivity to hyperactivity. At the end of five years, I had studied and treated 182 hyperactive youngsters using elimination diets. *Three out of four of the parents found that their child's hyperactivity was diet related.*[10]

FOODS CAUSING HYPERACTIVITY
A FIVE-YEAR STUDY OF 182 CHILDREN

OFFENDING FOODS	CHILDREN AFFECTED (NUMBERS OF)
Sugar	77
Dyes, additives and flavors*	48
Milk	38
Corn	30
Chocolate	28
Eggs	20
Wheat	15
Potatoes	13
Soy	12
Citrus	11
Pork	10

Many other foods were reported as causing trouble, including beef, apples, chicken, grapes, peanuts, tomatoes, oats, rice and lettuce.

*Especially food dyes

In 1978 pediatric allergist Doris Rapp studied twenty-four hyperactive children using elimination diets and double-blind sublingual tests for foods and artificial colors.[11] Here's what she found:

FOODS CAUSING HYPERACTIVITY IN DR. RAPP'S STUDY* OF TWENTY-FOUR CHILDREN

OFFENDING FOODS	CHILDREN AFFECTED
Food dyes	52%
Sugar	33
Milk	29
Corn	24
Cocoa	19
Wheat	14
Eggs	10

*Since 1978, Dr. Rapp has studied hundreds of children with food-related hyperactivity. She has published her observations and presented them both to physicians and to the public. Moreover, she made films to further support her studies. One of the most impressive of these was presented on the *Today* show in December 1982.

A three-year-old youngster who was known to be sensitive to bananas was sitting quietly in his mother's lap. He then ate a banana. Within a few minutes, he became irritable, hyperactive, aggressive, hostile and unmanageable.

Sublingual extracts using double-blind techniques were then adminstered to the child. The examiner, child and parent did not know which extract was "the real thing" and which one was a blank. Extracts containing the placebo (blank) had no effect on the child's behavior. By contrast, banana extract (which had previously been found to be the "neutralizing dose") was followed by a return of the child's behavior to normal.

Dr. Rapp has also published her extensive experiences in dealing with hyperactive children in a book entitled *Allergies and the Hyperactive Child* and in a more recent book, *The Impossible Child*.[12,13]

In yet another report James O'Shea, M.D., and Seymour Porter, Ph.D., studied fifteen hyperactive children using sublingual testing and treatment.[14] Here's what they found:

SUBSTANCES CAUSING HYPERACTIVITY IN DR. O'SHEA'S STUDY OF FIFTEEN CHILDREN

OFFENDING SUBSTANCES	CHILDREN AFFECTED
Foods	
Milk	73%
Peanuts	47
Tomatoes	47
Apples	40
Cane Sugar	40
Corn	40
Grapes	40
Oranges	40
Chocolate	33
Wheat	27
Eggs	20
Dyes	
Red	87
Yellow	80
Blue	80
Inhalants	
Tree	33
Dust	27
Mold	13

Even more recently, in the March 9, 1985, issue of *Lancet,* J. Egger, M.D., and associates published a carefully designed and executed study of seventy-six overactive children.[15] Sixty-two children improved on elimination diets.

Then twenty-eight of the children who improved completed a scientific trial in which foods suspected of causing symptoms were reintroduced by disguising them mixed with other "safe" foods. Symptoms returned or worsened much more often when patients were fed foods thought to cause symptoms than when given other foods.

If your child is tired, depressed, irritable or hyperactive, chances are he's troubled by allergy—especially allergy to foods he eats every day. Because the allergic nature of these complaints often goes unrecognized, I've frequently used the term "the great masquerader" in discussing this type of food allergy.

FOODS CAUSING HYPERACTIVITY IN DR. EGGER'S AND ASSOCIATES' STUDY

OFFENDING FOODS	NUMBER OF CHILDREN TESTED	PERCENT REACTED
Colors and preservatives	34	79%
Soy	15	73
Milk	55	64
Chocolate	34	59
Wheat	53	49
Oranges	49	45
Eggs	50	39
Sugar	55	16

Many other foods were noted to cause hyperactivity, including grapes, peanuts, corn, fish, melons and tomatoes.

"HYPER" OR TENSION SYMPTOMS

The mother of one of my patients commented:

If my child eats chocolate every day, by the end of the fourth day he acts so hateful you can't stay in the house with him. He can't sit still in the daytime and he rolls and bumps around in his bed at night. He won't mind and, worst of all, no matter what I do, I can't please him. When I eliminate chocolate from his diet his behavior improves so much, I can't believe he's the same child!

Such is the typical description of the "hyper" group of symptoms many of these children manifest. These hyper symptoms fall into two main groups: those involving motor tension and those involving sensory tension.

Typical of the motor symptoms of some of these children is their restlessness and constant state of activity. They fidget, twist, turn, grimace, jump and jerk. They're clumsy and awkward. As a result, they drop things, make noise, damage family possessions and bring on even more trouble for themselves.

The sensory tension symptoms are equally striking in

many of these children. Of these symptoms, irritability and inability to be pleased are perhaps most common. These personality traits, when exhibited repeatedly, gain for the child the reputation of being spoiled. Parents often wonder where their methods of child care have been faulty and may seek medical assistance for these reasons alone. They may feel they're to blame for what seems to be a primary emotional disturbance of the child.

Other sensory symptoms include insomnia, hypersensitivity to light, pain and noise. The insomnia may be blamed on anything from worms to television. The hypersensitivity to light and related eye symptoms sometimes cause the parent to consult an ophthalmologist.

As a result of these "hyper" symptoms, these unfortunate youngsters are unpleasant little people to have around. They're apt to be reprimanded and punished by parents and teachers and rejected or ignored by their siblings and contemporaries. Thus are planted the seeds of more trouble. As a secondary response to the allergic mental and nervous syndrome, the child is often puzzled and secretely ashamed of his inability to cope successfully with his contemporaries. As a result, he may become irritable, hostile, unusually aggressive, mean, disobedient and stubborn.

FATIGUE SYMPTOMS

Although your difficult child may be "swinging from the ceiling" from the time he gets up in the morning until you and other family members collapse into bed in the evening, many of these children at times appear tired and listless. And in my general pediatric and allergic practice, I've found that the tired, listless child (who shows no other chronic disease) nearly always is troubled by allergies. Furthermore, fatigue, rather than tension, is often the major complaint of parents seeking medical help for children with this syndrome.

Allergic fatigue, like allergic tension, has both motor and sensory components. The children with motor fatigue (or

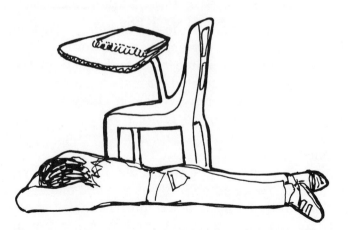

movement fatigue) seem to feel tired and weak. They may interrupt their play to rest. Others who are more severely affected are too tired to sit at their desks at school and may ask the teacher for permission to lie down on the floor and rest. Allergic children with motor fatigue often sit on the sidelines while their more energetic contemporaries play games.

Equally dramatic is the drowsiness, sluggishness and stupor of the child with sensory fatigue. Parents have a difficult time rousing him, and when the child wakes up, he may appear spaced out and not "with it." Schoolchildren with this malady will often be found sleeping at their desks even though they slept ten hours or more during the preceding night.

Naturally, before concluding that your tired child suffers from allergy, take him to your doctor for a careful checkup. Make sure he isn't anemic or suffering from some other chronic disease, including rheumatic fever, thyroid deficiency or a malignancy. But if your doctor says, "I can find no physical cause for your child's symptoms," don't conclude that your child's fatigue and apparent laziness are caused by an emotional disorder.

Moreover, put your child on an elimination diet before you subject him to a lot of expensive, invasive and painful tests.*

---

*Such tests include gastrointestinal X rays, EEG's, CAT scans and endoscopic examinations.

HEADACHES

If your hard-to-raise child complains frequently of headaches, you've probably thought about eye strain. So you may have consulted an eye specialist, only to find that his vision is normal. Then you may have taken him for a checkup to see if he is troubled by high blood pressure, kidney trouble or infected sinuses. When a careful examination shows no abnormal findings either you or your doctor may have concluded, "Johnny is complaining of headaches to get attention." Or, "Johnny is suffering from an emotional problem."

If Johnny's headaches continued to bother him, you may have consulted a neurologist or a neurosurgeon for skull X rays, brain wave tests, CAT scans and other studies. But rarely are headaches in children caused by a brain tumor or similar serious disease. Instead they're usually caused by hidden or unsuspected food allergies.

Remarkably, the role of foods in causing migraine and other headaches has been recognized by many observers since the early 1900s.[16,17,18] In my own practice I've been able to help dozens of youngsters with troublesome headaches by using elimination diets. (Many of these children had been subjected to a variety of tests including brain wave tests and CAT scans before I saw them.) In spite of these reports in the medical literature documenting the food-headache connection, it has been and continues to be overlooked by most physicians.

However, recent scientific studies in England by Munro, Egger and associates seem to be attracting the attention of more physicians. A study carried out at the Great Ormond Street Hospital in London found that in eighty-seven out of ninety-two children with chronic recurrent headache, one or more foods was the culprit.[19]

Here's how allergies may cause headaches: During the allergic reaction, spasm and other changes take place in blood vessels. Fluid leaks out. Tissues within the skull swell, causing headache and other systemic and nervous symptoms.

OTHER MENTAL AND NERVOUS SYSTEM SYMPTOMS

Any part of the nervous system can be affected by allergies. During my years of practice I've seen many almost unbelievable "reactions." Here are a few examples: Charlie, an eighteen-month-old youngster, showed unusual aggressiveness. He'd attack any child who came near him, hitting, biting and slapping. As a result, he was expelled from nursery school. When sugar, food coloring, milk and corn were removed from his diet, his aggressive behavior vanished.

At the age of seven, Virginia began to tell her parents about what she called, "funny feelings." She'd say, "Sometimes I feel as though I'm outside of my body," or, "People aren't real." Elimination diets, challenges with suspected foods and further dietary experimentation showed that these bizarre nervous symptoms were triggered when Virginia ate wheat or chocolate.

Tammy, a seven-year-old, would sit in the corner of her room as though she were in a trance. She'd compulsively count things (like the number of window panes in the windows or the circles in the design of the wallpaper in her room). When her mother would try to talk to her, Tammy would ignore her. She'd act as if she were in another world. Her mother commented, "If I interrupted her, she'd go into hysterics."

Tammy also complained of headaches and showed what her mother called "unbelievably dark circles under her eyes." Tammy (a youngster I saw in the 1950s) developed her bizarre symptoms within a few weeks after the family bought their first TV set. Tammy started looking at the ads and began drinking a quart of chocolate milk a day. When chocolate was eliminated from her diet and the quantity of milk reduced, her symptoms disappeared.

I've heard that Confucius said that a journey of a thousand miles begins with one step. Identifying hidden food troublemakers and removing them from your child's diet may not make all your child's physical and behavioral symptoms vanish, but it could be that important first step.

12
Allergy Can Make Your Child Sick

Allergy can make your child "sick all over." Here's why: adverse and allergic reactions affect tiny blood vessels (capillaries), circular muscles and mucous-secreting glands found throughout the body. Here are a few of the more common manifestations.

FALSE ANEMIA

Children with anemia ("low blood") look pale and sallow. So do chronically sick children with rheumatic fever, kidney disease or malnutrition, even when they aren't anemic.

Allergy also makes children look pale even though their blood tests show no abnormality. Here's the probable cause of allergic pallor: excess clear fluid leaks from capillaries, giving the face a puffy, pale and pasty appearance.

So if your child looks pale, with dark shadows under his eyes (even though he has taken iron tonics to "build his blood"), an undetected food allergy may be causing his pallor. When such an allergy is brought under control, your child's color will usually improve.

RECURRENT ABDOMINAL PAIN

Many different things can make a child complain of stomachache. For example, he may become tense because he doesn't read as well as his classmates. Or he may be afraid of his teacher who has been criticizing him and making him stay after school. Or he may feel nervous because he isn't pleasing his parents and siblings and isn't getting enough "psychological vitamins."

Such a child could also be infested with roundworms or his symptoms could be caused by a hidden kidney disorder. He might even be bothered by a chronic infection of his appendix (although most doctors feel this type of appendicitis rarely occurs).

But all over the country, children are being taken to doctors because of recurring stomachaches. Many of these children are given comprehensive head-to-toe examinations with blood studies, urine tests and X rays. When the reports are "negative" or "normal," parents and doctors usually conclude the child is suffering from "an emotional problem."[1,2,3]

Although emotional stress can cause your child to say, "Mama, I'm tired and my stomach hurts," allergy can cause similar symptoms. You should especially suspect a hidden food allergy if your child with recurrent abdominal pain looks pale (with dark circles under his eyes), is tired and nervous, and also complains of headache and aching in his legs or other muscles.

Allergic abdominal pain is apparently caused by tightening of the smooth (circular) muscle which surrounds every part of the digestive tract. However, other mechanisms may also be involved, including increased mucous gland secretion and leakage of fluid from small capillaries. As a result, the child with digestive-tract allergies may complain of nausea, constipation, diarrhea, excessive gas and pain in any part of the abdomen.

So before blaming your child's recurrent stomachache on an emotional cause, rule out a hidden allergy. Usually, such an allergy is caused by milk or some other food your child eats every day.

LEG ACHE AND
OTHER MUSCULOSKELETAL COMPLAINTS

Many children complain of pains in their muscles and joints . . . especially their legs. Doctors and parents, for generations, have tended to blame such symptoms on "growing pains," even though there's no evidence that suggests growing can cause pain.

Obviously, many disorders can cause aching or swelling in the muscles and joints, including orthopedic abnormalities, rheumatoid arthritis, rheumatic fever, inadequate exercise or too much exercise without proper preconditioning. However, a common and often overlooked cause of musculoskeletal discomfort is allergy.

Here are possible mechanisms that may be involved: The blood vessels that supply oxygen and other nutrients to the muscle and joint tissues are surrounded by the same circular muscles that surround the bronchial tubes, intestine and bladder. When these muscles go into spasm, pain may occur. Or pain and swelling may develop when capillaries leak fluid into the tissues.

Over fifty years ago, the late Albert H. Rowe, Sr., M.D., of

Oakland, California, first described swelling and aching muscles, bones and joints caused by allergy.[4] Since that time, many other physicians have noted that allergy, especially food allergy, often causes leg ache and discomfort in other parts of the musculoskeletal system.

Joseph Bullock, M.D., William Deamer, M.D., O. L. Frick, M.D., and associates of the University of California (San Francisco) said:

> We've seen patients who have been diagnosed as rheumatic because of leg aches and fever. One patient had a muscle biopsy because of leg ache and fatigability. . . . (His) symptoms disappeared following elimination of chocolate and milk from the diet.[5]

BEDWETTING AND OTHER URINARY DISTURBANCES

Parents and doctors do not usually think of allergy when a child wets the bed, shows albumin in the urine or suffers from repeated urinary tract infections. But allergy can be a factor in causing diseases and disorders in any part of the urinary tract.

James Breneman, M.D., of Galesburg, Michigan, and John Gerrard, M.D., have documented the relationship of allergy to bedwetting in children.[6,7] Apparently, when some children eat foods they're sensitive to, smooth muscle in the urinary bladder contracts, making the bladder smaller. As a result it can hold less urine. So the child urinates more often during the day and wets the bed at night.

Allergy may also play a much more important role than commonly recognized in causing other disturbances of the urinary tract. For example, Ann Harrison, M.D., of Scottsville, New York, and John Gerrard, M.D., have suggested that allergy may be related to recurrent urinary tract infections in children.[8,9] And Japanese allergist Tatsuo Matsumura has documented the relationship of food allergy to albuminuria.[10]

Allergy can also cause other types of genitourinary symptoms, including vaginal discharge and urinary frequency. The causes of symptoms of this type include foods, food dyes and contact sensitivity to bubble baths, soaps and other irritants.

FREQUENT COLDS AND RESPIRATORY INFECTIONS

 In offices, clinics and emergency rooms every day (especially during the winter months), frustrated mothers are going to equally frustrated doctors and complaining, "Johnny has one infection right after another. I can't keep him well. No matter what I do, he's forever catching a cold. And even when he doesn't have a cold, he sniffs, snorts and coughs."

Clues suggesting an allergic respiratory disorder include:

1. Frequent sneezing and nasal itching
2. Night cough that continues for days and weeks at a time
3. Cough on exertion
4. Recurrent attacks of bronchitis or pneumonia
5. *Other family members do not seem to "catch the cold"*

Respiratory allergies are commonly caused by house dust, house dust mites, animal danders, molds, pollens and other inhalants. Yet, foods a child eats every day can also play an important role in causing nasal congestion, recurrent ear or bronchial problems. Although any food can provoke respiratory symptoms, I've found that cow's milk leads the list of offenders.

MIDDLE EAR DISEASE

Although ear disorders (including recurrent infections and fluid in the middle ear) occur in children who aren't allergic, such problems are seen with far greater frequency in allergic children. Here's why: Allergy congests the membranes of the respiratory tract and swollen membranes are less able to resist bacterial and viral invaders. Moreover, as a part of the allergic reaction, membranes swell, blocking the eustachian tube, which connects the throat to the middle ear.

Youngsters with respiratory allergies often experience repeated bouts of ear infection or obstruction. They're especially apt to develop "glue ear" (the name was coined to describe the thick, sticky fluid that forms in the middle ear). In some of these children, the adenoids may be removed and plastic tubes may be inserted through the ear drum to ventilate the middle ear. In others, tubes alone are used.

In a study of 512 children with allergy and ear trouble, John P. McGovern, M.D., and associates found that, following careful allergic study and management, 97 percent of these patients showed a marked lessening in the frequency of ear infections.[11]

Recent clinical observations by C. Orian Truss, M.D., plus my own experiences, suggest that recurrent ear problems in children may be related to the common yeast, *Candida albicans.* Here's a possible explanation:

THE VICIOUS CYCLE

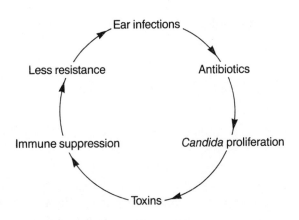

Candida proliferation occurs following repeated or prolonged administration of antibiotic drugs. *Candida* produces toxins that cause immune suppression, lessening the child's resistance and resulting in further infections.

In his book *The Missing Diagnosis,* Dr. Truss tells of a sixteen-month-old boy who had been given repeated courses of antibiotics for ear infections. At ten months tubes were put in both ears. His ear infections continued to recur.

The child was then put on the antifungal medication, nystatin. His respiratory and ear infections subsided. When the nystatin was discontinued his symptoms returned. Nystatin was again prescribed and continued for four months and the child remained well through the entire ensuing winter.

In commenting on this child Dr. Truss noted:

Perhaps the single most fascinating and potentially important aspect of this case was the abrupt cessation of the ear infections. This suggests that *Candida albicans* was actually causing this problem, and makes one wonder about the possible relationship of this yeast to what seems almost a national epidemic of otitis and "tubes in the ears."[12]

In 1982 I began prescribing nystatin and a sugar-free, yeast-free diet for a few children with recurrent ear problems. Although my series of patients is small I have been gratified— even excited—by their response.

CONSTIPATION AND SOILING

Although persistent constipation with soiling is often blamed on "improper bowel training" or an "emotional problem," it is often related to a hidden food allergy. Milk and chocolate are especially common offenders.

Allergy seems to cause spasms of the circular muscles of the bowel, interfering with normal elimination. Once the elimination mechanism is disturbed, waste material accumulates in the lower colon and rectum. This causes a stretching and loss of muscular tone, making it more difficult for the child to expel the stool in a normal manner. So he tends to "hold it" and soil himself. As a result, he may be ridiculed and rejected by his schoolmates. This in turn causes anxiety and tension that further interferes with his ability to control his bowel function.

During my years of practice, I have successfully treated many of these unhappy youngsters using a comprehensive treatment program that includes sympathetic treatment of the child, a diet eliminating milk and other foods the child is sensitive to, plus a systematic plan of bowel reeducation.

Every part of your child's body is connected to every other part. So if your child develops measles or chicken pox he'll usually break out in a rash from the top of his head to the soles of his feet. If he has the flu, he'll usually ache all over. Some diseases affect certain parts of the body more than other parts (for example, the mumps virus usually affects the salivary glands, yet it can also involve the testicles, brain, pancreas and other organs and tissues). Similarly, allergy commonly affects the respiratory tract (hay fever and asthma) and the skin (itching, hives and eczema). Yet involvement of other organs occurs commonly, even though such allergies still go unrecognized by physicians and the public.

<h1 style="text-align:center">13</h1>

Is *Your* Child Allergic?

If your child is troubled by a persistent stuffy nose, asthma or eczema, you know he's allergic. Yet, you may have been surprised to learn that allergies commonly affect the nervous system. And the symptoms that result can be caused by foods, chemicals and inhaled particles.

To help you evaluate the role of allergies, complete the following questionnaire. *The more "yes" answers, the greater the chances that allergies are contributing to your child's problems.*

FAMILY MEDICAL HISTORY

Allergies run in families. If an allergic individual shakes his family tree, all sorts of allergic ancestors will usually fall out!

LAURA COMMENTS:

Our family is loaded with allergies. Like my mother, I've been bothered by allergies all my life. My brother was troubled by asthma and hay fever as a child and developed allergy-related headaches and colitis as an adult. My husband's nose stuffs up from dust and molds and several foods cause indigestion, bloating and aching legs. His sister suffered from childhood asthma.

So, since I'd been bothered by food allergies, when my children were toddlers I wouldn't have been surprised if their noses had dripped when they ate trouble-making foods. But I never knew that behavior problems could be allergy-related.

Answer the following questions regarding:

Your Child's Medical History

FAMILY

1. Do (did) any blood relatives (parents, siblings, grandparents, aunts or uncles) suffer from
   *a. Seasonal hay fever, allergic rhinitis, asthma, eczema or hives?   Yes   No
   *b. Food allergies?   Yes   No
   c. Addictive disorders such as compulsive eating, alcoholism or drug abuse?   Yes   No
   d. Diabetes or hypoglycemia?   Yes   No
2. Do (did) any blood relatives suffer from
   a. Arthritis?   Yes   No
   b. Headaches?   Yes   No
   c. Digestive disorders?   Yes   No
   d. Autoimmune diseases (for example, rheumatoid arthritis, multiple sclerosis, lupus, Crohn's disease, etc.)?   Yes   No
   e. Nervous or mental disorders?   Yes   No
   f. Hyperactivity or learning disabilities in childhood?   Yes   No

YOUR CHILD'S MEDICAL HISTORY

Infancy:

3. Did you (or your child's biological mother) experience significant physical or emotional problems during pregnancy? **Yes** No

Was the birth difficult? Were there complications? **Yes** No

4. Did your child experience problems
   *a. while you were breastfeeding him? (If yes, he may have been sensitive to foods you were eating.) Yes **No**
   b. tolerating his formula? Yes **No**
   c. gaining weight? Yes **No**
   d. with colic, spitting up, bloating, diarrhea, stomachaches or vomiting? **Yes** No
   *e. with respiratory ailments (stuffy nose, noisy breathing, frequent ear infections or colds)? **Yes** No
   f. with eczema or other skin rashes? **Yes** No
*5. Was your child a "difficult" baby? **Yes** **No**

Did his irritability, sleeplessness and overactivity continue during most or all of his first year of life? Yes **No**

6. Did your child receive three or more "rounds" of broad-spectrum antibiotics during his first year of life? **Yes** No

Childhood:

*7. Has your child been bothered by hay fever, chronic runny nose, asthma, eczema or hives? **Yes** No

8. Has your child experienced frequent
   a. Ear infections, sore throats, swollen glands, colds, bronchitis, or croup? **Yes** No
   b. Stomachaches, constipation, diarrhea, or bloating? **Yes** No
   *c. Headaches? Yes **No**

9. Has your child shown other puzzling or unexplained symptoms, such as
   *a. Recurrent leg or other muscle aches? Yes **No**
   *b. Fatigue or exhaustion even though he gets plenty of sleep? **Yes** No
   *c. Dark circles or puffiness around the eyes? **Yes** No

*d. A pale, washed-out complexion even though examinations and tests for anemia and other chronic disorders are normal? Yes No

*e. Itchy nose, constant clearing of throat? Yes No

*10. Does your child's behavior worsen during some seasons of the year? Yes No

11. Has your child wet the bed frequently after age three? Yes No

*12. Does your child act like a "Dr. Jekyll-Mr. Hyde"? (Does he behave for a few minutes or an hour or so, then without apparent cause act as though he's possessed by a demon?) Yes No

Does he do well in school one day and poorly another? Yes No

13. Is your child a picky eater? Yes No

Do certain foods make him sick? Yes No

Does he act worse after eating? Yes No

Does his behavior deteriorate if he doesn't eat on time? Yes No

Does his behavior improve if he skips meals? Yes No

14. Does he experience frequent mouth ulcers or canker sores? Yes No

Does his tongue show a rash that looks like a map (we call this rash a "geographic tongue")? Yes No

Is bad breath a problem? Yes No

15. Does your child crave certain foods? Yes No

Does he binge on favorite foods? Yes No

Is he a "sugarholic"? Yes No

Has he ever stolen food or candy? Yes No

*16. Does his behavior or health worsen around holidays (especially Halloween, Christmas, Easter and Valentine's Day) when he consumes more sugary, artificially colored and flavored treats? Yes No

In using this questionnaire look especially at the fifteen starred questions. If you answered "yes" to seven or more of these questions, allergies probably play a significant role in causing your child's problems.

If you answered "yes" to questions 1a, 5, 7 and 10, your child is probably allergic to things he breathes. If you answered "yes" to questions 4, 5, 8c, 9a, 9b, 9c, 9d, 12 and 16, he's probably allergic to foods.

Section D

HELPING YOUR HARD-TO-RAISE CHILD: WHAT TO DO FIRST

14
Getting Started

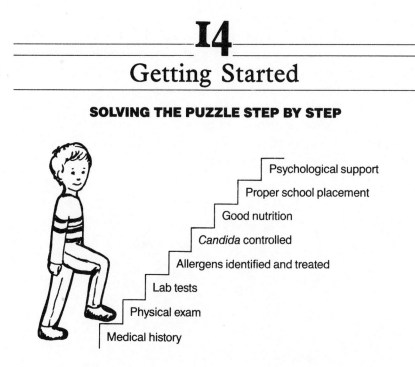

Psychological support
Proper school placement
Good nutrition
Candida controlled
Allergens identified and treated
Lab tests
Physical exam
Medical history

YOUR CHILD'S HISTORY IS IMPORTANT

Your child's history is important. A good history gives a doctor more information than a physical examination, laboratory studies, allergy tests and X rays.

In a recent issue of *Hospital Practice,* Gene H. Stollerman, M.D., professor of medicine at Boston University, said that as medicine gets more complicated and new tests become available, doctors should place increasing emphasis on the medical history. Moreover, the history can help physicians even more as they learn better questions to ask. And he said, "Clinical experience is the gold standard on which patient care should be based."[1]

This is not to say that I never use diagnostic studies. Yet, in working to help a hard-to-raise child I always start by taking a comprehensive medical history. I've found that history questionnaires filled out by the child's parents tell me a lot of things that I need to know in evaluating a child's problem.

I'm especially interested in his mother's pregnancy history, his birth history, his developmental milestones, allergies, illnesses and diet. I also like to know about his family. (How do his parents get along? Is there much sibling rivalry? Are there interfering in-laws? Alcohol or drug problems? Economic problems? And so on.) I also want to know about medications, diet, tutoring, behavior modification and other treatment measures that have been tried. I always ask parents to send me a report from nursery school, kindergarten or schoolteachers.

I realize that filling out a questionnaire isn't easy and it takes time. Moreover, even though every question is completed, I like to spend unhurried and uninterrupted time with the child and his parents together and then separately. By so doing, I have a better chance of determining which pieces of the child's puzzle are out of place and what needs to be done to put them back into place.

So before taking your hard-to-raise child to a physician or other health professional, prepare as much information as possible. I especially like a longhand narrative report written like a letter. Your physician may provide you with forms or you may want to copy and fill out my history questionnaire at the end of this chapter. Also get copies of any tests, school records or other documents that will provide your physician with pertinent information.

PHYSICAL EXAMINATION

I try to make a child feel comfortable before my staff and I begin carrying out strange and even frightening procedures. I get acquainted with him just as I would with a new neighbor or a doctor who has just moved to town.

I then take a careful look at Johnny—an "all over" look. I want to see if he looks happy or unhappy, depressed or elated, calm or jittery, clumsy or well coordinated. Usually I ask him to walk down the hall outside my office. I also ask him to write his name and to read a paragraph or two out of a book.

The child's overall appearance often provides important information. Because I've found that most difficult children are troubled with allergies, I look for these characteristic signs of allergy:

—A pale color (in the absence of anemia)
—Allergic "shiners" (dark shadows or wrinkles under the eyes)
—A congested nose with a crease across it.*
—Allergic gape (the child tends to keep his mouth open because his nose is stopped up)
—Chapped lips or patches of rash on the face and other parts of the body
—Spots on the tongue, called "geographic tongue" or "wandering rash" because the spots look like a map and tend to move around

I then give him a thorough going-over. However, except in the occasional troubled child who suffers from asthma, the remainder of the physical examination is often remarkably normal.

Is a neurological examination important? Some physicians (including many who specialize in pediatric neurology) feel

---

*The child with nasal congestion tends to sniff and snort or show one or more characteristic mannerisms. These include nose or face twitching, pushing the tip of his nose up with the palm of his hand, and throat clearing.

that much valuable information can be obtained by carrying out performance tests. These include balance tests, coordination tests, eye movement tests, finger and thumb tests, alternating-movement-of-the-hands tests, right to left tests, and others.

Although I do limited neurological testing on my own patients as a part of my overall work-up, I rely more on the child's birth history, past medical history, dietary history, family history and response to an elimination diet.

Moreover, even if a child shows nervous system abnormalities on initial testing, including brain wave abnormalities and so-called "soft signs," I don't usually become too concerned. Numerous studies over the years have shown that brain wave abnormalities and a wide variety of other neurological manifestations—even convulsions—can be caused by adverse or allergic reactions to foods and food additives.[2,3,4,5] When offending substances are removed from the child's diet, his neurological symptoms often disappear.

Because I've found that adverse reactions to common foods play an important role in causing symptoms in almost all difficult children, after the history, physical exam and a few simple tests have been completed, I prescribe an elimination diet.

Comprehensive Health Record*

Name_____ Birthday_____ Date_____
List your child's main problems: When did each problem begin?
1._____   _____
2._____   _____
3._____   _____
Other problems or symptoms that concern you:_____

_____

A. Family History: Have your child's parents, grandparents, siblings or other relatives been troubled with food allergies, learning disabilities, hyperactivity, hay fever, asthma, hypoglycemia, alcoholism or mental illness?†

*To obtain a copy of this Comprehensive Health Record, send a stamped self-addressed envelope and $2.00 to: Professional Books, Box 3494 Jackson, TN 38302
†Circle terms that apply.

Comments:

B. Pregnancy, Labor and Delivery: Normal, abnormal, repeated vomiting, high blood pressure, toxemia, alcohol, smoking, exposure to toxic chemicals, difficult delivery, breech, caesarian?*
   Weight gain during pregnancy_____ Duration of labor_____

   Comments:

C. Your Child's Past History:

1. Birth and First Week of Life:
   Normal_____ Abnormal_____
   Birthweight_____
   If adopted, age at adoption_____

   Comments:

2. One Week to Three Months:
   Persistent colic and/or digestive problems, nasal congestion, rattling, wheezing, troublesome rashes.*
   Feeding: Breast only_____ Breast plus bottle_____ Bottle only_____ Formula changes_____ Solid foods_____

   Comments:

3. Three to Twelve Months:
   Excessive crying and irritability, overactive, good baby, slept well, happy, normal development, nasal congestion, rattling, wheezing, troublesome skin

*Circle terms that apply.

rashes, digestive problems, formula changes, allergies, frequent ear infections, hospitalization?*

Comments:

4. One to Four Years:
Happy, unhappy, frequent colds, many ear infections, tubes in ears, allergies, calm, overactive, sleep problems, destructive, hard to toilet train, accident prone, speech problem?*

Developmental History:_____
When did he/she sit alone?_____
When did he/she crawl or creep?_____
When did he/she walk with support?_____
When did he/she walk alone across the room?_____
When did he/she say ten words anyone could understand?_____
When did he/she say two hundred words anyone could understand?_____

Diet History:

Good eater_____ Poor eater_____
Favorite foods: milk_____ orange juice_____
apple juice_____ sugar-coated cereals_____
Kool-Aid_____ colas_____ tea_____
vegetables_____ fruits_____ chocolate milk_____
cookies_____ hamburgers_____ chicken_____
fish_____ other meats_____ bread_____
crackers_____ other foods_____

Age on weaning_____ Average milk intake_____ ozs.

Comments:

Family and Social History:

Was the home reasonably stable?_____ Did parents cooperate to a reasonable degree?_____ Divorce or separation?_____ Change

*Circle terms that apply.

of residence?_____ Interfering in-laws?_____ Severe health problems of parents?_____ Alcoholism?_____ Economic problems?_____ Were you pleased with the sitter or day-care arrangements?_____

Comments:

5. Four to Seven Years:

Frequent or constant colds? Ear infections? Antibiotics more than three or four times a year? Adenoidectomy? Tonsillectomy? Ear tubes? Accident prone? Stitches more than once? Convulsions? Bedwetting? Soiling? Food allergies? Inhalant allergies? Hay fever? Asthma? Hives? Headache? Abdominal pain? Muscle aches? Irritability? Overactive? Uncooperative? Bizarre behavior? Skin problems? Digestive problems? Frequent masturbation?* Other_____

Kindergarten and School Progress:

Problems in: Paying attention?_____ Staying in seat?_____ Getting along with other children?_____ Reading?_____ Writing?_____ Other_____

Comments:

Family and Social History:

Stable home?_____ Cooperative parents?_____ Separation?_____ Divorce?_____ Change of residence?_____ Interfering in-laws?_____ Health problems of parents?_____ Alcoholism?_____ Economic problems?_____

Comments:

*Circle terms that apply.

Diet: Did he or she . . .
    Eat to suit you?   Yes ( ) No ( )
    Like fruits and vegetables?   Yes ( ) No ( )
    Crave sweets?   No ( ) Yes ( )
    Eat many sugar-coated cereals?   No ( ) Yes ( )
    Favorite   beverages: milk_____   chocolate   milk_____
       water_____   apple juice_____   orange juice_____
       Kool-Aid_____   Tang_____   Hawaiian Punch_____
       tea_____ coffee_____   colas_____ other_____

Comments:

D. Systems Review (Symptoms your child has now):

1. *General:*
Recent weight gain or loss, energetic, tired, fever, run down, pale, eats well, coaxed or forced to eat, overeats, trouble going to sleep, restless sleep, wakes in night, nightmares*

2. *Eyes:*
Tearing, burning, itching, discharge, circles under eyes, cross-eyes, doesn't see well*

3. *Ears, Nose, Mouth and Throat:*
Ears: Stop up, hurt, drain, have bad odor, hears poorly*
Nose: Runs, stuffs up, sniffs, sneezes, picks nose, thick discharge, postnasal drip*
Mouth: Sore gums, canker sores, bad teeth, grinds teeth*
Throat: Sore, clears throat, swollen glands, bad breath, mouth breather*

4. *Heart and Lungs:*
Chest hurts, heart races, heart pounds, faints, short of breath, hoarse, coughs, rattling sounds, wheezes when breathing in or out, spits*

5. *Stomach and Intestines:*
Nausea, vomiting, loose stools, constipation, soils clothing, pain in abdomen, passes excessive gas, blood in stools, mucus in stools, worms in stools*

*Circle terms that apply.

6. *Kidney, Bladder and Sex Organs:*
   In Infants: Diaper rash, strong or ammonia odor to urine, strains to pass urine, urinates too often*
   In Older Children: Complains of burning when urinating, wets bed, can't hold urine in daytime, has discharge from vagina, has discharge from penis or foreskin, plays with sex organs or masturbates*

7. *Nerves, Muscles, Bones, Joints and Skin:*
   Headache, dizziness, nervous habits, convulsions, twitching, muscle or joint pains or aching, limp, growing pains, change in walking, change in handwriting, clumsiness, bruises, itching, dry skin, oily skin, rashes, pimples*

8. *Behavior and Personality:*
   Calm, high-strung, overactive, lazy, happy, unhappy, pleasure for you, cross, irritable, stubborn, special fears, outgoing, confident, secure, insecure, shy, "loner," minds well, disobeys frequently, cooperative, self-centered, leader, follower, jealous, speech problem, likes school, dislikes school, favors one parent over the other*

   Children are often difficult to live with. What does your child do that irritates you most?

E. Present Nutritional Habits of Child and Family:

   How would you rate your family's diet, including especially the consumption of fresh fruits, vegetables, whole grains, vegetable oils, seeds and nuts, and avoidance of soft drinks, refined, sweetened, processed foods?*

Superior	Excellent	Good
Fair	Poor	Lousy

   Your child's usual diet:

   Average amount of whole milk per day (including chocolate milk)_____
   Average ounces of sugar-containing beverages (such as Coke, 7-Up, Kool-Aid, lemonade, Tang, tea with sugar)_____
   Average ounces of artificially sweetened soft drinks_____
   Average number of ounces of tea or coffee with saccharin_____
   Average number of ounces of pure fruit juice_____
   Does your child eat hot cereals (oats, Wheatena, etc.)?   Yes ( ) No ( )
   What dry cereals does he/she usually eat?_____

*Circle terms that apply.

How many eggs does he/she eat a week?_____
What brand of peanut butter do you use?_____
Does he/she like (and eat) such vegetables as baked potatoes, baked yams, black-eyed peas, string beans, squash, lettuce, tomatoes, lima beans?*
Other_____
Does he/she like (and eat) bananas, oranges, apples, grapes, melons?*
Does he/she tend to eat the same foods every day?   No ( ) Yes ( )
What are his/her favorite meal-time foods?_____
What are his/her favorite snacks?_____

Comments:

Vitamins, minerals, and other nutritional supplements:

List the vitamin, mineral or other supplements your child takes_____
_____

Comments:

F. Miscellaneous Information About Your Child and Your Family:

1. Have you tried an elimination diet?   Yes ( ) No ( )
   Was the diet carried out systematically?   Yes ( ) No ( )
   How long were foods eliminated?_____
   Did the diet make a difference?   No ( ) Yes ( )
   Was your child's behavior worse on the first one to three days on the diet?   No ( ) Yes ( )
   If he/she improved, how long did it take him/her to improve?_____
   Was the improvement obvious?   No ( ) Yes ( )
   What foods caused obvious reactions?_____
   _____
   What foods caused less obvious reactions?_____
   _____
   What foods caused no reactions even though they were given in quantity?_____
   _____

*Circle terms that apply.

2. Has your child been given Ritalin, Cylert, Tofranil or Mellaril? (circle drugs which were tried)   No ( ) Yes ( )
How long did he/she take the medication?_____
What was his/her response . . . (circle)
   Excellent?   Good?   Fair?   Poor?
Were there side effects?   No ( ) Yes ( )

Comments:

3. Would you term the degree of cooperation that exists among the different adults who play a role in guiding this child's life . . . (circle)
   Superior?   Excellent?   Good?   Fair?   Poor?   Lousy?

Comments:

4. Is his/her school situation, including the interest and cooperation of his/her teachers . . . (circle)
   Superior?   Excellent?   Good?   Fair?   Poor?   Lousy?

Comments:

5. What are your child's (and your family's) greatest strengths, resources, assets or accomplishments at this time?

6. What are your child's (and your family's) greatest problems, difficulties and frustrations at this time?

7. Are the psychological and emotional support and help this child receives from his parents, grandparents, siblings, peer group and teachers . . . (circle)
   Superior?   Excellent?   Good?   Fair?   Poor?   Lousy?

(Some resources and individuals are undoubtedly better [or worse] than others. Briefly comment on the sources or resources which are most helpful to your child.)

8. Helping a hard-to-raise child can drain a family physically, psychologically and financially. How would you rate your family's ability and resources when it comes to meeting the physical, emotional, educational, nutritional and financial costs of providing for his/her needs?

9. During the past year, describe this child's
   a. Physical health, including allergies and respiratory infections. Have things been better or worse (bronchitis, head colds, ear infections, strep throats, etc.)?

   b. New allergies (seasonal hay fever or asthma)

   c. Other health problems (surgical operations, accidents, etc.)

   d. School progress (or lack of it) in
   Reading_____
   Writing_____
   Math_____
   Special tutoring_____
   Acceptance by peers_____

   Comments:

   e. Emotional status and behavior (circle):
   Happy   Unhappy   Accepted (or rejected) by siblings

   f. Acceptance (or rejection) by other family members. Frequent punishment

   Comments:

10. What does this child do best? What talents or interests does he/she possess?

11. What frustrates or discourages him/her?

12. Chemical and other environmental substances may contribute to your child's physical, emotional and behavioral problems.
    Is your home new or old?_____
    When was it built?_____
    How long have you lived there?_____
    Does it or did it smell strongly of chemical odors (paint, glues, foam rubber, plastics, etc.)?_____
    Have changes in your residence made any difference in your child's physical or behavioral symptoms (for better or worse)?_____
    Do you use odorous chemicals in your home (Lysol, Pine-Sol, Bounce, perfumes, colognes, bubble baths, glues, etc.)?_____
    Do you cook with gas?_____
    What sort of heating system do you have?_____
    What insecticides are used?_____ How often?_____
    How about chemicals in your yard or outside environment? (Check)
       Insecticides? ( )
       Aerial spraying of weed killers? ( )
       Other agricultural chemicals? ( )
    Are the pipes in your home made from copper?   No ( ) Yes ( )
    Do you use aluminum cookware?   No ( ) Yes ( )
    Are the vegetables or fruits you eat contaminated with insecticides or environmental chemicals (your answer will usually be "yes")?   No ( ) Yes ( )
    Do you live on or near a heavily traveled road?   No ( ) Yes ( )

    Comments:

G. Narrative Report of Your Child's Problem:

School Inventory

Date_____

Appointment date_____

_____is scheduled to be seen for an evaluation. Because a large part of the day is spent in school, a description of his/her behavior and your impressions of this child will be extremely useful as we work with him/her. We have received the parents' permission to contact you; we hope you'll be able to answer these questions for us prior to the above appointment.

Date of Birth:_____ Grade:_____

Attendance Record:_____

We'd like information about his/her academic skills and progress.

Subjects	Grades (last report)	Subjects	Grades (last report)
_____	_____	_____	_____
_____	_____	_____	_____
_____	_____	_____	_____
_____	_____	_____	_____
_____	_____	_____	_____

His/her strongest academic areas are_____

His/her weakest academic areas are_____

Is this child in danger of failing this year?_____

He/she is in a slow_____, average_____, accelerated_____,
    group in his/her class.

He/she is in a slow_____, average_____, accelerated_____,
    class in his/her school.

What standardized academic or psychological tests has this child taken?

Name of test	Date	Grade in school	Results
_____	_____	_____	_____
_____	_____	_____	_____
_____	_____	_____	_____

Please check all words that are appropriate for this child:

Generous_____ Aggressive_____ Shy_____ Restless_____

Sensitive_____ Friendly_____ Irritable_____ Whining_____

Affectionate_____ Cruel_____ Withdrawn_____ Nice_____

Resentful_____ Nervous_____ Happy_____ Jealous_____

What special strength does this child have that can be used in helping him/her?

_____

_____

_____

Does he/she have any physical problems (including headaches, poor coordination, etc.), and how do these affect school activities?

_____

_____

_____

Handedness?_____ Glasses?_____ Vision?_____ Hearing?_____
If this child experiences difficulty in school, how long has this existed?
_____

How does he/she relate to you and to the other teachers?

_____

_____

_____

_____

What about his/her relationship with the other children?

_____

_____

_____

He/she has few_____, some_____, many_____ friends. These friends can be described as_____
How often are there teacher-parent conferences in your school?_____
How many conferences have you had this year with these parents?_____

How willing or able were the parents to carry out any suggestions?

_____

_____

_____

_____

As a professional person who has worked with this child, your opinion is highly valuable to us. Please use the space below to give us your opinion and comments in regard to this child.

_____

_____

_____

_____

_____

_____

_____

_____

_____

_____

_____

_____

_____

Please check the following list so that we may have a better understanding of the special education facilities available in your area.

	Available in your building Elem. Sec.	Available in your district Elem. Sec.	Being planned for next year Elem. Sec.	Available to your pupils elsewhere Elem. Sec.
Classes for remedial reading	_____	_____	_____	_____
Classes for speech and hearing therapy	_____	_____	_____	_____
Classes for emotionally disturbed	_____	_____	_____	_____
Homebound teaching services	_____	_____	_____	_____
(other)	_____	_____	_____	_____

We appreciate your filling in this form. With the parents' permission, we'll send you additional information from our medical records that we feel can help you in your work with this child.

Please mail this report directly to Dr._____

_____
(address)

Reported by_____(Teacher)

15

Behavior
Inventory

This inventory will help you evaluate and follow the progress of your hard-to-raise child. By periodically comparing the child's scores recorded at intervals, you and those working with him can get a clearer picture of his progress and his response to various treatment measures.

Score each item checked in the first column, 0; in the second column, 1; in the third column, 2; in the fourth column, 3. There are thirty-five items to be evaluated, so the highest score your child could receive would be 105 and the lowest score he could receive would be zero.

Younger children and allergic children will normally have higher scores than older children and nonallergic children.

Obviously, the lower your child's score, the better. Yet, no child . . . even a healthy, easy-to-manage child . . . is expected to achieve a score of zero.

BEHAVIOR INVENTORY

	Rarely or never	Occasion- ally	Often	Usually or constantly
Overactive				
Doesn't finish projects				
Fidgets				
Can't sit still at meals				
Doesn't stay with games				
Wears out toys, furniture				
Talks too much				
Talks too loud				
Doesn't follow directions				
Clumsy				
Fights with other children				
Unpredictable				
Interrupts				
Teases				
Doesn't respond to discipline				
Gets into things				
Speech problems				
Temper tantrums				
Doesn't listen to whole story				
Defiant				
Hard to get to bed				
Irritable				
Hard to please				
Cries				
Reckless				
Unpopular with peers				
Impatient				
Lies				
Accident-prone				
Wets in daytime				
Wets bed at night				
Destructive				
Can't read well				
Can't write well				
Performs poorly in other schoolwork				

16

Elimination
Diets

THE FIRST ELIMINATION DIET?

Several years ago a young physician in training, from the University of Tennessee Family Practice Program, walked into my office with a Bible in his hand. And he told me that elimination diets had been described in the first chapter of Daniel.

Daniel and three of his friends were being trained to serve in Nebuchadnezzar's royal court and were offered the same food and wine as other members of the court. But Daniel and his friends didn't want to partake of the royal fare.

So Daniel went to the guard, whom Ashpenaz had placed in charge of him and his three friends. "Test us for ten days. Give us vegetables to eat and water to drink. Then compare us with the young men who are eating the food of the royal court and base your decision on how we look."

He agreed to let them try it for ten days. When the time

was up, they looked healthier and stronger than all those who had been eating the royal food. So from then on the guard let them continue to eat vegetables instead of what the king provided.

At the end of the three years set by the king, they became members of the king's court. No matter what questions the king asked or what problems he raised, these four knew ten times more than any fortune teller or magician in his whole kingdom.[1]

TRY AN ELIMINATION DIET*

I usually ask parents to try an elimination diet before they bring their child in for his first visit. Here's why:

During the past fifteen years, *over three fourths of the hundreds of hyperactive, hard-to-manage children I've seen improved when they stopped eating foods they were sensitive to.* Moreover, many families solved a major part of their child's problem *before* they came to my office.

Take the case of nine-year-old Eddie Brown (not his real name), the son of a calm, caring Methodist minister and his equally calm and caring wife. In telling me about Eddie, Mrs. Brown said:

> We often wondered where Eddie came from. Most days he acted irritable, peevish, fussy, hostile and aggressive. He wouldn't sit still in class and he was forever getting into fights with his classmates. He'd often come home and say, "Nobody likes me."
>
> Four days after we put him on your Elimination Diet A, he was "like a different child." Then when we added the foods back, we found that sugar and milk made him hyperactive. *We could scarcely believe our eyes.* Milk also stuffed his nose up and caused him to develop a headache, dark circles under his eyes and nighttime leg cramps.
>
> In the three months since we eliminated milk and sugar from Eddie's diet, his entire personality has changed. His

*The diets in this chapter are adapted and condensed from *Tracking Down Hidden Food Allergy,* by William G. Crook, M.D. (Professional Books, Box 3494, Jackson, TN 38302, 1978).

grades on his daily work have gone from fifties and sixties to nineties or better. The change in his behavior is almost *miraculous*!

Naturally, I've seen other patients who showed little or no improvement on the initial trial diet. Yet, most parents who tried it found at least a part of the answer to their child's problems. They did this by carefully eliminating sugar, food colors and additives, milk, corn, wheat, eggs, yeast, chocolate and other frequently consumed foods from their child's diet for five to ten days, occasionally longer. Then when his hyperactivity (and other symptoms) improved, eliminated foods were eaten again (one food per day) and reactions noted.

Over the years I've experimented and I now use two different elimination diets. I call the easier diet *Diet A* and the more difficult one *Diet B* (or the *"cave man"* diet). I nearly always begin with Diet A. With a little study and planning (and the cooperation of other family members), you'll find this diet easy to follow.

ELIMINATION DIET A

1. Since your child is apt to be sensitive to his favorite foods, you may need to modify Diet A depending on what your child usually eats. For example, if he is an "apple juice freak" and drinks a pint of apple juice every day, eliminate apples. If he craves potatoes and eats them every day, eliminate potatoes. Any food can cause trouble. The goal of Diet A is to provide you and your child with a diet that won't drive you and your family crazy, yet which will uncover one or more common offenders.

2. While on this diet your child may eat (or drink):

Any meat except hot dogs, sausage, bacon or luncheon meats

Any vegetable except corn and legumes (peanuts, peas and beans)

Any fresh fruit except citrus (oranges, grapefruit, lemons, limes and tangerines)

Hot oat or rice cereals from a health food store or Quaker
rolled oats or plain rice
Rice cakes (such as Arden, Chico-San or Lundberg)
Safflower and sunflower oils
Any nuts except peanuts; purchase nuts in the shell or get
unprocessed nuts from a health food store
Water—this should be his only beverage; if possible use
spring water, filtered water or bottled water such as
Mountain Valley

3. *Your child must avoid:*

Milk, cheese, ice cream and all other dairy products
Sugar and sugar-containing foods, including soft drinks,
candies, ice cream and most processed and packaged
foods; also low-calorie soft drinks sweetened with Nutra-
sweet
Wheat in all forms, including dry cereals, breads, cakes,
crackers and cookies
Eggs and products containing eggs
Corn (found in candies, syrups, carbonated beverages,
chewing gum, pastries, peanut butter, puddings, sher-
bets and many other packaged foods)
Food colors* and dyes and artificial flavors (found in hun-
dreds of commercial foods and beverages)
Chocolate and cola
Oranges, lemons, grapefruit and other citrus fruits
All fruit juices, because they contain yeasts
Legumes (peanuts, peanut oil, soybeans, soybean oil, peas
and all beans)
Mushrooms and yeast-containing foods
Honey and maple syrup

4. Before starting the diet:
a. Prepare menus and purchase the foods you'll need.
Avoid all processed, canned and packaged foods on the grocery store shelves. (Almost all of them contain sugar, milk,

*Food colors to be avoided are those artificial colors derived from petrochemicals, and
not the colors from tomato, beet powder, turmeric, saffron and other natural foods.

corn, food coloring and other "hidden" ingredients.) Instead, go to a farmers' market or the produce and meat section of your supermarket or neighborhood food store.

b. Buy a notebook and record each and every food your child eats. *Keep a symptom diary. Start your diary three days before your child begins the diet.* Note especially his behavior and at what times during the day he becomes overactive, inattentive, "spaced out," uncoordinated or irritable. Also note whether he acts tired, nervous or depressed, or whether he complains of headaches, stuffiness, burning of the eyes, sneezing, coughing, abdominal pain, itching, backache, leg ache, or frequent urination.

c. Get the cooperation of your spouse, grandparents, siblings, neighbors, teachers and other school or nursery personnel. (Get down on your knees if necessary!)

5. *Eliminate food suspects for five to ten days (occasionally longer) or until your child's symptoms show a significant improvement lasting forty-eight hours.* During the first two or three days of the diet, he may feel more irritable, tired and cross. He may also develop a headache or leg cramps. Such "withdrawal" symptoms resemble those experienced by a smoker who gives up cigarettes. He develops such symptoms because he is apt to be "hooked" or "addicted" to foods causing his hyperactivity, or his other symptoms.

6. After you're certain your child looks and acts better and his improved behavior continues for forty-eight hours, begin adding back the eliminated foods. *Add back only one food each day.* When you return a food to your child's diet, add it in pure form. For example, use whole wheat from the health food store rather than bread, since bread contains milk and yeast. Or you may use Shredded Wheat.* Use corn on the cob, popcorn or grits rather than mixed forms of corn; milk rather than ice cream; soft- or hard-boiled eggs rather than eggs cooked in butter; and so on.

If eating a food makes his symptoms return, don't give him any more of it. And wait until his symptoms subside (at least twenty-four hours) before adding another food. If the reaction

---

*Shredded Wheat contains the additive BHT, which could cause a reaction. So I prefer an additive-free wheat product.

persists—especially if your child tends to be constipated—give him a dose of unflavored milk of magnesia to speed the removal of the offending food from his digestive tract.

7. Menu suggestions for Elimination Diet A:

Breakfast

Potato cakes, french fries cooked in safflower or sunflower oil, plain oatmeal, rice cakes, hamburger patties, pork chops (no bacon or sausage), whole fruits of all kinds except citrus

Lunch

Tuna, baked chicken, almonds, cashews, pecans, hamburger patties, pork chops, fruits (except citrus), rice cakes

Dinner

Baked or broiled chicken, fish, beef, pork, lamb; any vegetables except corn and legumes; lettuce and tomato salad; for dessert, ambrosia made with pineapple, banana and unsweetened coconut

Snacks

Fruits except citrus, rice crackers, nuts (in shells or unprocessed) except peanuts

ELIMINATION DIET B

On this diet, the "cave man" diet, in addition to the foods eliminated on Diet A, avoid pork, beef, chicken, white potatoes, tomatoes, rice, oats and *any other food your child eats more often than once a week.* For example, if your child

eats bananas every day, eliminate them. If he snacks on pecans, avoid them.

Carrying out this diet takes careful planning. Here are suggestions:

Stock up on foods your child doesn't usually eat. Examples: asparagus, avocados, carrots, cherries, mangos, pears, pineapple, pomegranates, strawberries, sweet potatoes, lamb, fresh fish, shrimp or other seafoods.

From your health food store get unrefined sunflower, safflower or walnut vegetable oils,* additive-free nuts and cashew-nut butter. Wild game, including deer, rabbit, squirrel and quail are great foods if you you can obtain them. (A source of organic foods and exotic meats is Czimer Foods, Inc., Route #7, Box 285, Lockport, IL 60441.)

Carry out Diet B just as you did Diet A, with this exception: When you return foods to the diet, add one food back each meal.

LAURA COMMENTS:

At first, just thinking about trying an elimination diet may make *you* feel tired and depressed. I know because I've used these diets and have helped many friends through the frustrations.

Careful organization and planning ahead will keep you from arriving at the dinner hour with nothing safe to serve.

You're probably thinking to yourself, "Eddie likes orange juice, 'frosted junkies' and chocolate milk for breakfast; hot dogs and corn chips for lunch; and a cola after school. He isn't going to like this diet. And I may run into trouble getting him to cooperate and not cheat."

Most children like games and prizes. Say to your child, "I'm going to buy extra special foods for you to eat for the next two weeks. And we're going to play the 'the diet game.' You can win prizes.

"Here's how we play the game. Eat foods like a hamburger patty and french fries for breakfast; bananas, cashew

---

*Such oils haven't been treated with high heat. Brand names include Arrowhead, Golden Harvest and Hain.

butter and rice crackers for lunch; pineapple, raisins and pecans for a snack.

"If you eat only the foods on your diet, you'll earn six stars a day to paste on your chart that we'll keep on the refrigerator door. Each night at bedtime, you'll win a little prize! And when you've finished the diet—if you don't cheat—you'll win a *big* prize!"

If possible, put your whole family on the diet. Your child will be more apt to cooperate if he doesn't see the rest of his family eating his favorite foods. You won't have to prepare two separate meals. You may discover why you're irritable and your husband complains of headache and fatigue!

17

Helping Your Food-Sensitive Child

Fortunately, when your child avoids a food he's allergic to for three to six weeks (or longer), the allergy to that food may gradually subside or slowly disappear. Dr. William Deamer often compared this phenomenon to logs burning in a fireplace. When left alone, such a blaze will gradually die down.

For example, many a child who is bothered with stuffy nose, stopped-up ears, headache, fatigue, stomachache and leg ache when drinking three or four glasses of milk a day, may safely drink a few ounces of milk or eat an occasional ice cream cone or a cheese and cracker sandwich . . . after he has eliminated all dairy products for two to three months.

However, if you say to yourself, "Johnny ate that ice cream

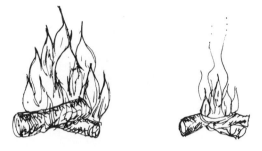

cone and it didn't bother him, so maybe he isn't allergic to milk," you may feel it's all right for him to drink milk regularly. His symptoms will gradually return. Before you know it, he'll be experiencing the same health problems he had before you eliminated milk. Putting it another way, *if your child is allergic to a food, he'll probably remain allergic to that food all of his life, if he eats the food as much and as often as he ate it when you first discovered his allergy.*

Accordingly, when you feel your child is developing a cold or other infection, tighten up on his diet and avoid any and every food that has given him trouble in the past. Be careful especially during the winter months. Cold weather seems to lessen a person's tolerance to foods.

THE ALLERGIC LOAD

A child can develop allergic reactions to many different substances . . . pollens, dusts, molds, animal danders, tobacco smoke and chemical fumes. (See Section E.) When these various troublemakers "pile up," they overcome his resistance and cause him to develop symptoms. For example, the child who is sensitive to ragweed, milk, corn, tobacco smoke and cat dander may be able to tolerate a little of any of these substances without developing symptoms. Yet, if he watches TV in a room where people have been smoking, while he drinks milk, eats popcorn and pets the cat, he's apt to become hard to handle and to develop nasal congestion, headache, irritability and fatigue.

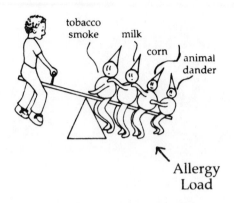

tobacco
smoke   milk
        corn animal
              dander

Allergy
Load

A ROTATED DIET*

An important aid in helping allergic individuals remain well is the rotated diet. In following this diet, do not repeat the same foods every day, even foods your child isn't allergic to. A four-day rotation preserves tolerance and minimizes allergic reac-

Rotated Diets

Day	1	2	3	4	5
Meats	Beef	Chicken	Shrimp	Pork	Trout
Fruits	Orange	Banana	Pineapple	Grape	Apple
Vegetables	White potato	Sweet potato	Carrot	Squash	Peas, beans or other legumes
Grains	Wheat	Oats	Rice	Barley	Corn

*You can obtain more information about food allergies (including menus and recipes for grain-free products) from the following sources: *The Allergy Self-Help Cookbook* by Marjorie Hurt Jones (Emmaus, Pa.: Rodale Press, 1984) and *Mastering Food Allergies* (a monthly newsletter) by Marjorie Hurt Jones, MAST Enterprises, Inc., 1500 Wilmot Road, Deerfield, IL 60015.

tions. However, if your child has shown a clear and definite sensitivity to a particular food, avoid it for several months. When he appears to have regained tolerance to it, offer it only occasionally, in small amounts, perhaps once every few weeks.

Rotating foods such as apples, oranges, bananas and grapes, or potatoes, carrots, broccoli and yams usually poses no problem, because such foods are easy to identify and are rarely mixed in other foods. On the other hand, rotating grains isn't easy, as wheat-free breads are hard to find (and don't usually taste as good!) So if your child is sensitive to wheat, you may need to bake bread from corn, rice, oats or other special flours—including arrowroot, amaranth, and quinoa.*

Many (and perhaps most) difficult, allergic children who improve on a comprehensive program of management may not need a rotated diet. Furthermore, such a diet can put a lot of stress on you, your child and your whole family. Nevertheless, if your allergic, hard-to-handle child continues to experience problems, careful rotation of his diet may help.

TREATMENT WITH FOOD-ALLERGY VACCINES

In June 1963, Drs. Herbert Rinkel, James Willoughby, Carleton Lee and Dor Brown described a new method of testing and treating patients with food sensitivity.[1] In carrying out this test, a minute amount of food extract is injected between the superficial layers of the skin, producing a small bump or welt called a *wheal*. The appearance of the patient, including symptoms that may be present, is carefully noted and recorded just before the administration of the test injection.

The patient is then carefully observed for ten minutes. If the small welt increases in size and remains hard and raised, or if the patient shows symptoms, the test is said to be "posi-

*For more information on and help with rotation diets, see N. Golos and F. Golbitz, *If This Is Tuesday It Must Be Chicken* (Dallas: Human Ecology Research Foundation of the Southwest, 1981); also S. Rockwell, *The Rotation Game* (Seattle: Rockwell, 1984) and *Allergy Recipes* (Seattle: Nutrition Survival Press, 1984); also V. Nichols, *The Cookbook and Guide to Eating—Diversified Diet for Allergies* (Xenia, OH: Nichols, 1977).

tive." And such a positive test usually indicates the patient is apt to be sensitive to the food being tested.

If this provocative test shows a positive reaction, additional weaker doses of extract of the same food are then administered in a similar manner. If a second test is also positive, additional test doses are administered at ten-minute intervals until a negative test wheal is obtained and symptoms that were provoked by the previous dose subside or disappear. That amount of food extract is the neutralizing or optimal dose and is used (by injection or drops placed under the tongue) in treating the patient with food sensitivity.

Moreover, clinical reports by many professionals,[2,3,4,5] and double-blind studies,[6,7,8,9,10,11] show the efficacy of this method of testing and treating the food-sensitive patient. Such food extracts may enable a person to consume foods that had previously bothered him. Symptoms that have been helped by this method of therapy include headache, rhinitis, gastrointestinal and urinary problems, hyperactivity and other nervous system symptoms.

In spite of these studies and the clinical experiences of hundreds of American physicians who use these methods of testing, they are considered to be "controversial and unproven."[12]

Nevertheless, in my own practice I have found that provocative testing followed by neutralization treatment has helped many children with multiple food sensitivities.

However, such testing and therapy is time consuming and expensive if many foods are tested. Moreover, only a few doctors have been specially trained in performing these tests. So if you identify and put into place many other pieces of your child's puzzle, food-extract therapy probably won't be needed.

Section E

OTHER ALLERGIC AND
ADVERSE REACTIONS
MAY CAUSE HEALTH
AND BEHAVIOR
PROBLEMS

18

Is *Your* Child Allergic to Airborne Particles He Breathes?

If your hard-to-raise child is troubled by persistent or recurrent respiratory problems, including allergic rhinitis, sinusitis, recurrent ear problems (infections, fluid in ears or hearing loss), bronchitis or asthma, he's apt to show a sensitivity to pollens, molds, house dust or animal danders. These airborne particles he breathes may also make him tired, irritable and hyperactive. And in some children who aren't bothered by respiratory symptoms, inhalant allergies may cause other physical and behavior problems.

LAURA COMMENTS:

Even though my first son's nose often streamed and his eyes watered, I was surprised when testing for mold, dust and pollens provoked behavior changes. However, I was amazed when these tests made my other son hostile and irritable, because he'd never been bothered by respiratory allergies. Yet I soon learned that controlling both children's dust and mold exposures and treating them with allergy extracts filled important gaps in their puzzles.

HOUSE DUST

You can see tiny particles of this ever-present substance floating or dancing in the air. You'll especially notice them when the morning sun shines through your window. You will, of course, see quantities of this dust when you empty your vacuum cleaner. (This fine gray powdery substance is formed when mattresses, carpeting, curtains, papers, books and other household items deteriorate.) Dust settles and accumulates in areas that aren't frequently cleaned and floats constantly in the air even in the best-kept homes. House dust also contains a microscopic, spider-like mite . . . a tiny bug that lives and feeds on human skin and nests in bedding and mattresses.

MOLDS

Like house dust, inhaled molds may also contribute to difficult behavior and other miseries. Molds belong to a group of plants called *fungi,* which lack true roots, stems, leaves, flowers or green pigment and which reproduce by spores. (You're probably familiar with the furry mold that grows on old bread, leftover food or on damp bathroom grout.) Thousands of different molds are found in the soil, air and water; they flourish in damp, dark areas, both inside and outside.

Weather affects the number of mold spores you breathe. Rainfall, high humidity and wind promote the growth and spread of spores, making the mold-sensitive person miserable. Although mold spores always surround us, molds, like other outdoor plants, tend to die when winter comes and snow and ice cover the ground.

Foods containing mold (cheese, canned or frozen fruit juices and vinegar) or mold relatives (baker's yeast, brewer's yeast and mushrooms) may bother the mold-allergic person. Mold sensitivity also suggests that your child may suffer from yeast-connected health problems. (See Section F.)

POLLENS

Plants of all types produce pollens. Yet, the relatively heavy yellow, powderlike pollen particles found in flowers rarely cause allergy because they don't float freely in the air. By contrast, the lighter tree, grass and weed pollens are easily carried by the wind, sometimes for hundreds of miles. Common troublemakers include ragweed, Bermuda and Johnson grasses, oak, elm and other trees.

The pollens that bother your child depend on where you

live. Spring and summer pollen seasons often overlap, especially when there's lots of rain. However, in the autumn, pollen-producing ragweed and other weeds are usually killed by the first frost.

FUR AND FEATHERS

Any pet with fur or feathers can provoke allergic symptoms in sensitive people. Common culprits include cats, dogs, horses, rabbits, mice, hamsters, gerbils, parakeets and farm animals. Feathers, fur or animal hair in pillows, quilts, furniture or clothing may also cause symptoms.

INHALANTS MAY AFFECT BEHAVIOR

Do particles your child inhales contribute to his behavior problems? The answer may be yes, if his nervous system symptoms increase during a particular time of the year. For example, I've seen children whose behavior and attention span deteriorated in the fall. Although some of these youngsters were bothered by obvious hay fever, in others respiratory symptoms were mild. The explanation is that the allergic reaction to the pollen affected mainly the nervous system.* This relationship was confirmed when the child's hyperactivity and other nervous system symptoms improved following allergy

*In 1927 I. S. Kahn, M.D., described a number of overactive, irritable and "incorrigible" children whose symptoms were clearly triggered by sensitivity to pollens.[1] In 1942 L. Sternberg, M.D., told of a patient who experienced incapacitating drowsiness each year during ragweed season even though he showed no associated respiratory symptoms. Moreover, symptoms subsided following treatment with pollen extract.[2]

testing and the administration of appropriate pollen extracts.

More often I've seen children whose behavior became worse on damp days or when they visited grandmother, because molds the child was breathing in grandmother's musty old home, or which showered down on damp days, affected his nervous system.

While I've found that foods cause behavioral changes more frequently than inhalant allergies, testing for inhalant sensitivity and treating the child with appropriate extracts or vaccines can play an important role in helping him.

19

How to Help Your Inhalant-Sensitive Child

ENVIRONMENTAL CONTROL

Reducing exposure to dust, molds, pollens and animal danders should always form the first line of defense against allergic substances that your child may be breathing.

Although you can't remove all of the inhalant particles your child breathes, you can reduce their number by using an electronic air cleaner. Such a filter-cleaner removes molds, house dust and pollens from the air. The best models use high-efficiency particulate air (HEPA) filters. Some units with charcoal filters also remove chemicals.

Choose an electrostatic air cleaner that produces less than .01 parts per million ozone gas (ozone might bother the chemically sensitive child). The unit should also remove more than 90 percent of particles from 10 to .01 microns in size.[*][1]

If possible, rent a room-sized electronic air cleaner for a month for your child's bedroom and see if it helps. With a doctor's prescription, you may include the cost of the filter in your medical deductions. Don't buy units with scented filters. The fragrance may aggravate your child's symptoms.

Here are other measures to reduce your child's inhalant exposures.

House Dust

1. In your child's bedroom
   a. Remove all carpets and rugs because they hold dust and mold and give off chemical fumes.
   b. Avoid heavy draperies, pennants and other dust catchers. Also remove stuffed toys, pets, flowers, plants and stuffed furniture or furniture made from odorous plastic materials. (Simple wooden chairs are best.)
   c. If possible, close and seal the heating ducts to keep out dust-laden air from the running furnace. Heat the room with an electric heater.
   d. Carefully clean the room at regular intervals. Don't use odorous chemicals.
   e. Get a cotton or sisal mattress (Simmons).
   f. Cover your child's mattress and pillow with a casing that doesn't bother him. Many allergic individuals are bothered by chemical fumes and odors, however, so stay away from foam rubber pillows and odorous plastic encasings. I recommend a special cotton, germ-resistant "barrier cloth."

      If your child is chemically sensitive, he may be bothered by pillow cases, sheets, pajamas and/or

---

*This technical information should appear in the brochure of the unit you're considering.

nightgowns containing synthetics. So I recommend 100 percent cotton.*

2. Change your furnace filters frequently.
3. Clean and vacuum your house while your child is away.

Molds

Molds thrive in cool, damp and poorly ventilated areas including refrigerators, refrigerator drip pans, garbage pails and the space under your sinks. To reduce your indoor mold population:

1. Clean mold-prone areas frequently with tolerated disinfectants.†
2. Keep air conditioners, humidifiers, dehumidifiers and vaporizers scrupulously free of mold. Follow the manufacturer's instructions, using only cleaning chemicals your child tolerates.
3. Check behind wallpaper and paneling and under carpets and carpet padding for molds. Carpets of all kinds (especially shag) encourage mold growth. Reduce molds by using cotton throw rugs. Wash them often.
4. Molds love every nook and cranny of your bathroom. They'll grow in your bathtub drain, on washcloths, damp towels and in any crevice. Keep your bathrooms as dry as possible. Use an exhaust fan to circulate fresh air. Scrub tiles and grout around tubs and showers with tolerated disinfectant. Don't leave damp, sweaty clothes in hampers, closets and drawers.
5. If your basement (especially one with a dirt floor) is damp, work to dry it out. Seal cracks in the walls or floor. Use a dehumidifier. Good ventilation and lighting also discourage dampness and molds.
6. Houseplants provide a haven for molds. Crushed rock on top of the soil around each plant will reduce the number of mold spores entering the air. However, if

*Pure cotton encasings can be obtained from The Cotton Place, P.O. Box 59721, Dallas, TX 75229. Another source of cotton fabric is The Janice Corporation, 198 Route 46 (APD), Budd Lake, NJ 07828.
†Use borax, vinegar, Zephiran (obtain from your pharmacy) or Impregnon.

problems continue you may need to give your plants away. In summer keep them outdoors.

7. Mattresses and other bedding sometimes become mold infested. You can usually lessen mold growth by washing mattress pads frequently.

8. Throw out old newspapers, books or magazines.

9. Houses in shaded areas or near rivers or streams grow more mold. You may also need to remove shrubs or vines planted close to your house. (Such plants retain moisture and encourage mold growth.)

If you don't know whether your house is moldy or not, obtain mold cultures and colony counts for several rooms by returning specially prepared samples to qualified labs.*

If necessary, reduce your child's exposure to molds outdoors by curtailing the following activities: raking and romping in leaves, mowing the grass, jumping in hay and playing in barns. If your child is really bothered by molds, pollens and other inhalants but loves to play outdoors, get him an allergy mask to try—even though it could make him self-conscious.

Pollens

Avoiding pollen exposure, especially during the height of the season, helps. Yet it's often inconvenient and hard to do. Staying inside, closing windows and doors, and using an air cleaner or an air conditioner usually helps. Roll up car windows and use your air conditioner. Ideally, escape to the mountains or seashore during the worst weeks of your pollen season.

Animal Danders and Hair

If you don't own a pet now, don't get one—unless it's a fish or a reptile! If you already own a pet who has grown to be an important and much loved member of your family, at least make your child's bedroom off limits. Better yet, keep the pet outside.

---

*Instructions for obtaining mold cultures can be obtained from Mold Survey Service, 2800 West Genesee Street, Syracuse, NY 13219.

Avoid stuffed animals or clothes with real fur. Don't use a feather pillow. Instead, stuff a pillowcase with cotton towels, blankets, or diapers.

ALLERGY VACCINES AND EXTRACTS

Consider allergy testing and treatment by a qualified physician if your child is bothered by inhalant allergies and environmental controls haven't helped.

Most children with respiratory allergies show positive skin tests on allergy testing. These children can usually be helped by allergy vaccines. In my own practice, I carry out such testing and prepare treatment extracts based on my test findings. Here's a brief report on a child in whom the inhalant pieces of the puzzle played a major role in causing his hyperactivity:

Seven-year-old Sammy Smith, one of my hyperactive patients, experienced trouble "settling down," especially during the first few months of school. During that time, his nose was congested and he sneezed a lot. He also complained of headache and couldn't sit still in his classroom.

On testing with the major inhalants, Sammy showed strong reactions to ragweed, plus milder reactions to molds and spring grasses. A mixture of allergy extracts was prepared based on my test findings. Sammy's mother was told how and when to give the vaccine.

With the administration of these allergy injections, plus a comprehensive program of management, Sammy's hyperactivity, attention span, respiratory allergies and other symptoms improved remarkably.

Should your child be tested and treated for inhalant allergies? My answer will usually depend on the severity and seasonal pattern of his symptoms. It will also depend on his response to other diagnostic and treatment measures, including elimination diets, good nutrition and the use of nutritional supplements. However, if he's bothered by troublesome respiratory symptoms—especially if they're seasonal—I feel that he should receive allergy skin testing and appropriate immunotherapy.

20

Do Chemical Exposures "Turn *Your* Child On"?

During my early years of practice, I knew nothing about chemical sensitivity and related health problems. My first awareness came in 1956, while visiting the brilliant allergy pioneer, Theron G. Randolph, M.D.

I got up one morning, bathed, shaved and doused myself with my favorite cologne. After breakfast I joined Dr. Randolph on hospital rounds. One of the first patients we saw was a lady with asthma. As we stood by her bedside, Dr. Randolph asked me to check her pulse rate. So I put my hand on her wrist and began to count. Within less than a minute, she began coughing, and in another minute or two she was wheezing. The odor of my cologne had triggered the attack.

I was "banished" and sent to my hotel to bathe and change clothes. Meanwhile, the nurse scrubbed the patient's wrist and Dr. Randolph administered medicine to terminate the asthma attack.

Needless to say, this was a learning experience I've never forgotten! And during the past twenty-eight years, I've seen countless other patients who show adverse reactions to chemicals they eat, breathe, or touch.

So getting rid of environmental chemical pollutants in your child's home, school and community helps you fit in another piece in your child's puzzle. As you know, chemicals can make you sneeze, cough, or cry. Yet you may be surprised to learn that they can also make your muscles and joints ache. Chemical exposures can also cause numbness, tingling and other nervous symptoms including irritability and hyperactivity.

Studies by William Rea, M.D., and others show that chemical exposures adversely affect a person's immune system.[1,2,3] Accordingly, the more chemicals your child is exposed to, the greater are the chances he'll show adverse effects.

If your child is troubled by chemicals, Dr. Rea's "barrel concept" may help you understand how chemicals affect your child.

Chemicals your child is exposed to resemble pipes draining into a rain barrel. The barrel represents his resistance. If heavy chemical exposure continues, the barrel overflows and symptoms develop. Infection may also cause a leak in the barrel, even when the barrel isn't full.

Many chemicals are normally present in your child's body, including sodium chloride (salt), potassium, calcium and magnesium. They're not the ones you need to worry about. In-

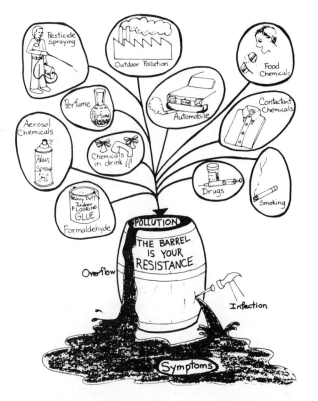

stead, pay attention to "foreign" chemicals that your child breathes, especially those derived from petroleum and related sources.

COMMON SOURCES OF CHEMICAL POLLUTANTS

Gasoline	Coal-burning stoves
Natural gas	Brass, metal or shoe polish
Diesel fumes	Floor waxes
Garage fumes	Wax candles
Cleaning fluids	Car roofs and roads
Nail polish	Asphalt pavements
Formaldehyde	Furniture polishes
Inks	Carbon paper
Typing stencils	Clothing dyes
Cosmetics	Disinfectants
Marking pencils	

Others include:

Phenol derivatives (carbolic acid or Lysol): alcohols, defoliants and household detergents

Rubbers: sponge rubber, foam-rubber pillows, typewriter pads, rubber-based paint, rubber tires, automobile accessories

Plastics: plastic upholstery, pillow covers, shoe bags, handbags, plastic folding-doors, plastic cement, adhesive tapes

Synthetic textiles: Dacron, Orlon, polyester, rayon, etc.

Paints, varnishes and shellacs

Insecticides: moth balls, insect repellants, termite exterminating materials, chlordane, lindane, parathion

Chlorine: chlorinated water, Clorox, bleaches

Pine: cedar-scented furniture polish, odors from knotty pine interiors and pine-scented household deodorants, bath oils, turpentine-containing paints

Fragrances: cosmetics, hairspray, shampoos, deodorants and after-shave lotions

Tobacco

Moreover, foods may be chemically contaminated in a number of different ways. For example, coloring is often added to hot dogs and to the rinds of fruits and vegetables. Fruits and vegetables may also be contaminated by insecticides or waxes derived from petrochemical sources. Sulfite sprays on vegetables (especially at salad bars) and potatoes have recently been noted to cause severe symptoms in susceptible individuals.

YOUR CHILD'S LEVEL OF CHEMICAL TOLERANCE

If phosgene, chlorine and other poisonous gases are released, everyone who breathes them will be poisoned. Illness from such chemicals is called "toxicity." By contrast, indoor and outdoor pollution from chemicals including formaldehyde, insecticides, weed killers, diesel fumes and other industrial odors may make some individuals sick, while others seem unaffected.

Whether or not your child develops symptoms when exposed to chemicals depends on these variables:

1. His inherited tendency
2. The load of chemicals he's exposed to
3. The load of other allergy troublemakers (foods, pollens, molds, etc.)
4. How well his immune system is functioning

CHEMICAL SENSITIVITY QUESTIONNAIRE

Do chemical exposures make your child feel sick, tired, nervous, depressed, irritable or spaced out? If you answer yes to two or more of the following questions, chemical sensitivity may play a role in causing his health problems.

1. Has your child ever been exposed to massive amounts of toxic chemicals?   Yes   No
2. Is he frequently exposed to toxic chemicals at school, home, or while pursuing hobbies?   Yes   No
3. Did his symptoms begin or worsen after moving to a new house, going to a new school or one undergoing renovations, or becoming involved in a new hobby?   Yes   No
4. Does your child seem more aware of chemical odors (particularly natural gas leaks) than other people? Is your child bothered by chemical odors that don't bother others?   Yes   No
5. Does your child crave the smell of certain chemicals?   Yes   No
6. Do you cook with gas or do you heat your home with a gas floor-furnace, open gas heaters, or kerosene heaters?   Yes   No
7. If you cook with gas, does your child's behavior deteriorate when he's in your kitchen?   Yes   No
8. Is your child worse when
    a. You're driving in traffic, riding on a bus, or in an area of high air pollution?   Yes   No
    b. You're pumping gas at a service station?   Yes   No

9. Does your child feel and act better in unpolluted places (in the country, the mountains or near the ocean)?   Yes   No

10. Does he show physical or behavioral symptoms when he has been exposed to
    a. A chlorinated swimming pool?   Yes   No
    b. Social gatherings where perfume and tobacco smoke abound?   Yes   No
    c. Chemical odors in a clothing or furniture store?   Yes   No
    d. Fresh paint?   Yes   No
    e. Pesticide sprays?   Yes   No
    f. Household chemicals?   Yes   No

If you answered yes to two or more of these questions, chemical sensitivity probably plays a role in causing your child's health problems. Reduce his exposure to chemicals, investigate yeast-related illness and take measures to strengthen his immune system.

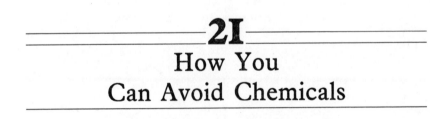

21
How You
Can Avoid Chemicals

We're polluting our planet with chemicals! These include automobile exhausts, industrial wastes, insecticides, weed killers, bathroom chemicals and many others. So unless your child lives in a bubble, he can't avoid many of the chemicals that can bother him. Yet, by learning about chemicals and steering clear of them, you can increase his chances of remaining well.

If you'll think about the term "outgassing," you'll get a clearer understanding of chemical sensitivity. *Outgassing* refers to the volatility of a material, its tendency to discharge molecules into the air.

Hard materials usually outgas less than soft materials. And natural substances less than synthetics. Marble and stone outgas less than other natural substances. Ceramic tile is the least volatile of the man-made materials. Soft plastics and polyurethane foam rank among the strongest outgassing substances.

HOME POLLUTANTS

"Clean up" your home so your child won't be breathing in a load of chemicals. Here are suggestions:

1. *Don't pollute your home with tobacco smoke.* Most hyperactive children are bothered by allergies. Sensitivity to tobacco commonly occurs in such children. Moreover, even if your child isn't allergic to tobacco, tobacco serves as a chemical irritant that your child's immune system must cope with.

Even if you confine your smoking to a room your child rarely enters, he will continue to be a "passive smoker." Here's why: Heating and cooling systems circulate smoke particles and contaminate the air in every room in your house. In addition, drapes, furniture, clothing and rugs become permeated with tobacco and provoke symptoms in the tobacco-sensitive individual.

So get professional help and give up the "filthy weed." You'll help your child and (as you already know) help yourself, too!

2. *Look under your sink.* Home janitorial supplies (laundry and dishwashing detergents, waxes, polishes, insect sprays, turpentine and other chemicals) often accumulate there. Dis-

card the products you don't need and transfer essential items, such as detergents, to glass bottles with tight-fitting caps. Store items you rarely use in your garage or storeroom.

3. *Check your bathroom, closets, drawers* and other areas of your house. If a "sniff" test reveals a strong or offensive odor, get rid of the troublemaker.

4. *Avoid perfumes, colognes, and scented soaps and cosmetics.* If you can't do without some of these preparations, ask your child to do the "sniff" test. Some perfumes and colognes bother sensitive people more than others. I've found that the strong colognes really bother me and many of my patients.

Ordinary Arm and Hammer baking soda helps get rid of chemical odors. You can use it as a dentifrice and an underarm deodorant. You can also add a tablespoon or two to your bath water. Ivory soap is tolerated by most people.

5. Choose cleaning chemicals carefully. Procter and Gamble now manufactures unscented Tide. Bon Ami is also unscented. Use Borax dissolved in water as a disinfectant. Don't use scented fabric softeners.

6. Avoid plastics since they outgas. A heated plastic lampshade can put out an odor that can cause headache, fatigue, irritability and other nervous system symptoms.

7. In the kitchen, use ceramic, glass or wooden bowls; cellophane bags instead of plastic wrap.*

---

*Cellophane doesn't contain "outgassing chemicals." Bags can be obtained from Erlander's, P.O. Box 106, Altadena, CA 91001.

8. Avoid other air-polluting chemical materials including sponge-rubber pillows, mattresses and seat cushions.

9. Most insecticides contain odorous, toxic chemicals that can aggravate your child's behavior and cause other health problems.

10. Avoid room deodorants and aerosol sprays of any type.

SCHOOL POLLUTANTS

Chemicals used in your child's school can contribute to poor performance by both children and teachers. One study of indoor air pollution at a public school found the following pollutants: aerosol sprays, insecticide sprays, paint enamel, lacquer sprays, fixatives, spray snow, spray plastic, solvent cleaner, germicidal cleaners, room deodorants, hair sprays, furniture polishes, disinfectants, deodorants and fungicidal sprays. The investigators found twenty-eight different chemicals in the supply closet, including some highly toxic products.[1]

Other things in a child's environment that bother some of my patients include copy machines, copied materials, newsprint, magic marking pencils, carbon paper, etc.

Laura comments:

Chemical pollutants at school gave one of my sons severe headaches. During one year new plastic classroom curtains made his life miserable for months until the odor finally subsided. Hairspray, perfumes and after-shave lotion have been particularly bothersome. It was embarrassing to ask his teachers not to wear perfume or after-shave lotion and approaching his peers was almost impossible. Several materials used in art, industrial arts and science classes gave him headaches and made him feel nauseated, spaced out and depressed. Bathroom disinfectants, cleansers and floor waxes also provoked headaches.

We were blessed with caring, helpful school personnel from nursery school on. I enlisted their help by writing letters,

initiating conferences and loaning appropriate allergy books.*
Not only did they cooperate in cleaning up the school environment, but they also helped the other children understand.

I hope your school personnel are cooperative. Try a low key approach followed by profuse thanks and appreciation for their efforts.

*The following books will help you and your child's teachers understand more about chemical sensitivities:

N. Golos and F. Golbitz, *Coping with Your Allergies* (New York: Simon & Schuster, 1979)

R. Mackarness, *Chemical Victims* (London: Pan Books, 1980)

R. Mackarness, *Living Safely in a Polluted World* (New York: Stein & Day, 1983)

T. G. Randolph, *Human Ecology and Susceptibility to the Chemical Environment* (Springfield, IL: Charles C. Thomas, 1962)

T. G. Randolph and R. W. Moss, *An Alternative Approach to Allergies* (New York: Bantam Books, 1982)

P. Saifer and M. Zellerbach, *Detox* (Los Angeles: Tarcher, 1984)

B. Small and B. Small, *Sunnyhill* (Goodwood, Ontario, Canada: Small Associates, 1980)

L. Stevens, *The Complete Book of Allergy Control* (New York: Pocket Books, 1986)

A. Zamm, *Why Your House May Endanger Your Health* (New York: Simon & Schuster, 1980)

These books are available in some stores and from Dickey Enterprises. 635 Gregory Road, Fort Collins, CO 80524.

Section F
YEASTS: ANOTHER CAUSE OF HEALTH AND BEHAVIOR PROBLEMS

22

The Yeast Connection:
A Medical Breakthrough

When I began my pediatric practice over thirty years ago, I knew nothing about the role of food allergies in making my patients develop nervous system symptoms. Then in the mid- to late fifties, I learned (much to my surprise) that a child's favorite foods could make him tired, peevish, grumpy, hard to manage and hyperactive. Then in the sixties and seventies I learned about nutritional deficiencies, environmental sensitivities and other factors that could affect the behavior of my patients.

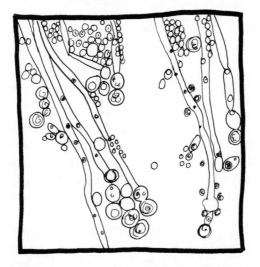

Not until 1979 did I hear for the first time about another cause of nervous system (and other symptoms) in my patients. And this cause, again much to my surprise, was the common yeast *Candida albicans.* This yeast is kin to other yeasts and molds and can switch from a single cell yeast form to a branching fungal form.

Candida normally lives on the interior membranes of every person's body and may cause minor infections* of the mucous membranes of the mouth (thrush) and the moist areas around the rectum. It also causes vaginal yeast infections.

Yeast infections of the mucous membranes have been recognized for centuries. Moreover, during my years of pediatric practice, I've successfully treated hundreds of patients with oral or vaginal yeast infections using simple medications which were dropped or painted on the membranes of the mouth or inserted by a suppository into the vagina.

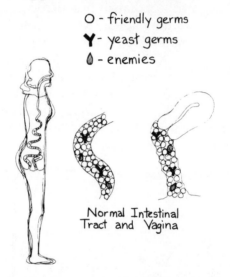

O - friendly germs
Y - yeast germs
● - enemies

Normal Intestinal Tract and Vagina

But until a few years ago, I looked upon the yeast *Candida albicans,* as a generally "friendly critter" that, at times, caused minor problems for some of my patients. And I had no inkling that this same yeast could play a role in making so many of my patients develop severe, persistent physical, mental and emotional problems.

Here's how I learned about "the yeast connection" to hyperactivity and other nervous system symptoms in my patients: In the summer of 1979, one of my patients brought me a reprint of an article by the Birmingham, Alabama, specialist

*Individuals with a weakened immune system may develop more serious and persistent *Candida* infections. Such infections are especially common in patients who have received immunosuppressant drugs following organ transplants or for the treatment of cancer or leukemia.

in allergy and internal medicine, C. Orian Truss, M.D.[1] This physician had become interested in health problems related to *Candida albicans* in the 1950s.

During the 1960s Dr. Truss found that many of his chronically ill patients with allergies, migraine headaches, depression and other health problems improved using a treatment program which featured a sugar-free, yeast-free diet and a safe, antifungal medication, nystatin. Other patients experienced relief when they were administered injections of a *Candida* extract. (Such patients were apparently allergic to *Candida albicans* and the extract appeared to neutralize or block *Candida-* [yeast] related symptoms.)

THE YEAST CONNECTION IS A VICIOUS CYCLE

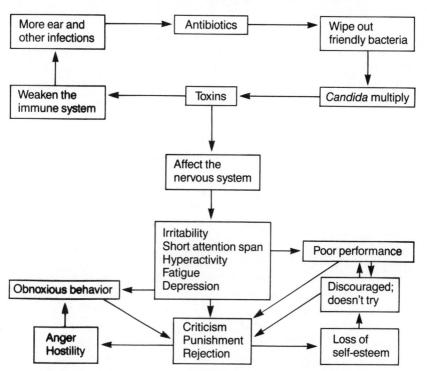

After reading the Truss paper, I phoned Dr. Truss, who gave me additional information about the yeast-human illness relationship. Here's a summary of the Truss hypothesis:

When a person is healthy and his resistance (immune system) is strong, *Candida* causes few problems. But when a person receives repeated or prolonged courses of a broad-spectrum antibiotic drug (such as, for example, amoxicillin, Septra, Bactrim, Keflex, and other antibiotics commonly prescribed for young children who have been troubled by repeated ear infections), yeast-related disorders may develop.

Here's what happens: Broad-spectrum antibiotics resemble machine guns shooting terrorists in a crowded airport. While they're killing enemies, they also kill friendly and innocent bystanders. In a similar manner, antibiotics knock out friendly bacteria on the interior membranes of a person's body while they're eradicating enemies.

When this happens, yeasts flourish and put out a toxin that affects various organs and systems in the body, including the immune system.

In his book, *The Missing Diagnosis,* in discussing the frequent use of antibiotics in children, Dr. Truss commented, "Unfortunately after the use of the antibiotic has been discontinued, the previous state of [good] health may not return. . . . Restlessness, discontent, and irritability often accompany the 'runny nose.' "[2]

Truss also discussed other health problems in children, including learning disabilities and depression and said, "At any age, but particularly in young children experiencing difficulty in school, this condition [candidiasis] is one worth considering.[3]

Recently, Allan Lieberman, M.D., a South Carolina pediatrician who has a special interest in environmental illness, commented:

> I treat many of my patients, including children with hyperactivity, behavior and learning problems, using a therapeutic trial of the anti-*Candida* program. The dramatic results I've obtained in many of my patients encourage me to continue this approach. I've found that children with recurrent respiratory and ear infections, and hyperactivity, seem to really benefit. So do children, especially teenagers, with chronic depression.[4]

Many studies reported by Gerald P. Bodey, M.D., and Victor Fainstein, M.D., from the Infectious Diseases Department of the University of Texas, clearly document the antibiotic-yeast relationship.[5] It would appear that the more antibiotics, the more *Candida* and the more *Candida* produced, the greater the amount of toxins.

Twentieth-century diets rich in sugar and refined carbohydrates also stimulate yeast growth. You've probably added sugar to bread dough to feed the baker's yeast so it will reproduce. Eating sugar and refined carbohydrates feeds the yeast in your child's digestive tract, making the *Candida* multiply and produce more toxins.

YEAST TOXINS

Many microorganisms ("germs") put out toxins. For example, before children were immunized against tetanus, many children suffered severe illness and death because of toxins produced by tetanus germs growing in a small and often insignificant wound.

I can remember one of my patients, when I was an intern at Vanderbilt, with a crusted-over sore on his knee—not the kind that a mother would ordinarily worry about. However, the child hadn't been immunized and severe tetanus ("lock jaw") developed. Although the boy recovered, he was a mighty sick youngster.

Also, when I was a medical resident at the hospital for contagious disease in Baltimore, I saw a number of patients with diphtheria. In the typical patient with this distressing infection, a thick white membrane develops on the surfaces of the throat. Throat soreness and severe laryngitis accompany the infection.

In addition, many diphtheria victims develop severe and sometimes fatal heart damage. The cause: Toxins released by the diphtheria germs in the throat are carried by the bloodstream to the heart.

Botulism, dysentery and "strep" germs also put out toxins. Yet, like most physicians, I had never heard of toxins being produced by the usually benign yeast *Candida albicans*.

However, research studies by a Japanese yeast and mold expert, Kazuo Iwata, M.D., have shown that *Candida* organisms also produce toxins that seem to affect the immune, endocrine and nervous systems.[6,7,8] In 1967, Kazuo Iwata and his coworkers in Tokyo, Japan, successfully isolated a potent, lethal toxin, canditoxin, from a virulent strain of *Candida albicans.* They later isolated several high and low molecular weight toxins from strains of *Candida albicans.*[9]

In an article published in 1977, Iwata stated, "Canditoxin produced unique clinical symptoms (in mice). . . . Immediately after . . . intravenous injections (of toxin) the animals exhibited ruffled fur and unsettled behavior. This progressed . . . to paralysis of the extremities."[10]

More recently, Iwata reported his findings at the December 1983, Birmingham conference, "The Yeast-Human Interaction . . . 1983."

At a subsequent conference on "The Yeast-Human Interaction" in San Francisco, in March 1985, Steven Witkin, Ph.D. of Cornell University Medical College, described studies in which he reported defects in cellular immunity associated with *Candida albicans* infections. And in an article published in the summer of 1985, he stated:

Reports that immunological . . . abnormalities have been reversed following successful anti-fungal . . . therapy for *Candida* infection lend credence to the idea that these abnormalities can arise as secondary consequences of fungal infection.[11]

Also at the San Francisco conference, John M. Whittaker, a veterinarian, commented:

Candidiasis is probably today's most overlooked disease in swine production. Overgrowth of yeast in the digestive tract often follows the promiscuous use of treatment with antibacterial drugs, including sulfa drugs. Such therapy wipes out many of the beneficial bacteria that hold *Candida* and other fungal invaders in check. Piglets with *Candida*-related health problems experience many symptoms, including irritability, skin disorders and respiratory disease of various types.

So it's easy to understand, then, how yeast toxins may be related to hyperactivity, irritability and learning problems in children, even though positive proof of this relationship hasn't yet been established.

There is still more support for the yeast connection to a wide variety of health disorders. Since 1982, C. Orian Truss, M.D., has been carrying out research studies. In these studies, Dr. Truss selected a group of adult patients with *Candida*-related health disorders.

He studied both amino acids and fatty acids and found significant abnormalities in both of these important nutrient substances in his patients with yeast-related disorders.[12] In a group of normal individuals who were studied at the same time, the amino acid and fatty acid levels were normal. Similar findings have been reported by Leo Galland, M.D.[13] Both investigators feel that abnormalities of amino acids and fatty acids affect many parts of the body, including the nervous system.

Although all the *t*'s aren't crossed and the *i*'s dotted, these studies show clearly that usually benign yeast can play a part in contributing to health disorders of many types in both children and adults.

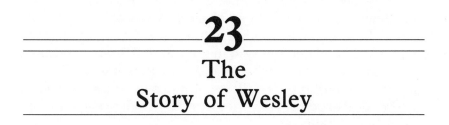

23
The
Story of Wesley

Three-year-old Wesley was referred to me in August 1982, for evaluation of his hyperactivity, irritability, peevishness and behavior problems of all sorts. His mother said, "This child is driving me up the wall. I don't know how much longer his father and I can take it. He doesn't sleep, he's always on the go, he tears up his toys and wears out his furniture."

Before Wesley's parents came in for a checkup, they filled

out several questionnaires, which I reviewed. I also spent a long time going over his entire history. Here are some of the things I learned.

Wesley was born in August 1979 and weighed eight pounds at birth. His parents both enjoyed general good health. Except for several episodes of vaginal yeast infections in pregnancy, his mother's health during pregnancy was good. Moreover, her labor and delivery were normal.

At the age of two months, Wesley developed a yeast infection (thrush) in his mouth and a yeast-related diaper rash. In spite of treatment with antiyeast medication, the rash in his mouth and diaper area persisted for over a month. Yet, his health was otherwise good during the first three months of life.

At three months, Wesley developed an ear infection, which was treated with a ten-day course of antibiotics. At the age of four months, he was treated for another ear infection and again for thrush. During the next two years, Wesley had repeated—almost continuous—ear infections. During each flare-up, he was given broad-spectrum antibiotic drugs, including ampicillin, amoxicillin, Ceclor, Gantrisin, Septra and Bactrim.

Between the ages of eighteen months and two years, Wesley showed more and more characteristics of the "terrible two's." In addition, his mother noted that eating sugar-containing foods caused nervous system symptoms. He would become unusually aggressive, irritable and hard to please, and would cry almost constantly. Similar symptoms were also triggered by chemical exposures of various kinds, including colognes and after-shave lotions.

Between the ages of two and two and a half, his nervous system symptoms continued, and included disturbed sleep and long-lasting temper tantrums. These symptoms were so severe that the family was referred to a clinical psychologist for consultation. The psychologist requested the parents to give Wesley a lot more attention when he behaved well and to ignore his bad behavior. Yet such techniques didn't seem to help. And during the following year, Wesley's ear infections and nervous system symptoms continued.

On August 17, 1982, I saw Wesley for the first time and prescribed a yeast-free, sugar-free diet and nystatin. Supplemental nutrients were also prescribed, including zinc, linseed oil and vitamins.

In a visit a month later, Wesley's mother reported, "He is like *an entirely different child.* Yet when he eats sugar or a yeast-containing food, his symptoms return."

Here are notes of subsequent follow-up visits taken from my office records:

October 15, 1982: Doing well. Sugar in any amount triggers symptoms. So do yeast and moldy foods. Nystatin being continued.

April 1, 1983: In for recheck. Wesley has been continued on diet and nystatin, but taking only small doses of nystatin two or three times a day. Symptoms still recur on eating sweets.

Recommendations: Tighten up on diet. Give 1/16 teaspoon of nystatin four times a day.

Follow-up visit, May 1, 1983: Comments by Wesley's mother:

Wesley has had a great month as far as his hyperactivity is concerned. He's been on the nystatin in full force and a sugar-free, yeast-free diet. We only had one outbreak of hyperactivity . . . this past Sunday . . . at a wedding anniversary celebration. He ate some cake and drank punch. That night he was in terrible shape.

I'm very sure that nystatin helps. Taking it on a regular basis four times a day has made a real difference as compared to taking it now and then. We've had a great month. Wesley is so much better. He sits down and looks at books, he can be taken places without tearing the place apart. He's very cooperative and things are running so smoothly.

Follow-up visit, November 22, 1983: Wesley's mother reported:

> Wesley had an excellent summer. Then we tried leaving off nystatin for five days in September. He became more hyperactive and developed an ear infection. No further problems in the last two months since we've continued his nystatin.

Wesley seems on the road to being a settled child—he eats whatever the rest of the family eats but limits sugar and yeast. Still taking vitamin C, nystatin and linseed oil.

November 27, 1984: Wesley's mother reported:

> Wesley is doing great. He still is taking nystatin twice a day. We tried leaving off the nystatin for a week and a half. His bad attitude and behavior returned by about the fourth day. In a couple of days he was running around in church, diving on his stomach and sliding from one pew to another—there was no stopping him. Back on the nystatin Wesley settled down. It is really amazing what a loving child he can be as long as he stays on nystatin.

July 7, 1985: Wesley is still doing well. No infections. Still takes nystatin.

Follow-up visit, April 9, 1987: Wesley's mother reported:

> Wesley's finishing the second grade and he's doing well. No problems with behavior and learning as long as he continues his treatment program which includes his special diet plus small doses of nystatin. Corn and sugar seem especially to cause problems. If he gets hold of sweets, I can tell it. He becomes overactive and doesn't concentrate. Also, I tried leaving off the nystatin again and he doesn't do as well when he doesn't get it. However, it takes only a small dose—no more than $\frac{1}{16}$ teaspoon twice a day.

24

Are *Your* Child's Problems Yeast-Connected?

Hyperactivity, behavior and learning problems may be related to toxins from the common yeast, *Candida albicans. Yeast-connected behavior disorders should be suspected in any child who has received repeated or prolonged courses of broad-spectrum antibiotic drugs.* And the diagnosis can be confirmed by the child's response to antifungal therapy.*

Here's a questionnaire that lists items in a child's history which suggest that his health problems may be related to yeast. The more questions answered "yes," the greater are the chances that your child's behavior and other health problems are yeast-connected.

Yeast Questionnaire

1. During the two years before your child was born, were you bothered by recurrent vaginitis, menstrual irregularities, premenstrual tension, fatigue, headache, depression, digestive disorders or "feeling bad all over"?   Yes   No
2. Was your child bothered by thrush?   Yes   No
3. Was he bothered by frequent or persistent diaper rashes?   Yes   No
4. Was he bothered by colic and irritability lasting over three months?   Yes   No
5. Are his symptoms worse on damp days or in damp or moldy places?   Yes   No
6. Has he been bothered by recurrent or persistent "athlete's foot" or chronic fungus infections of his skin or nails?   Yes   No

*Because *Candida albicans* lives in every person's body, cultures and skin tests for *Candida* don't usually help.

7. Has your child been bothered by recurrent hives, eczema or other chronic skin problems? Yes No
8. Has he received:
   Four or more courses of antibiotic drugs during the past year? Yes No
   Or has he received continuous (for a month or longer) "prophylactic" courses of antibiotic drugs? Yes No
9. Has your child taken prednisone, Decadron or other cortisone-type drugs? Yes No
10. Has your child been bothered by persistent or recurrent digestive problems, including constipation, diarrhea, bloating or excessive gas? Yes No
11. Does your child crave sweets? Yes No
12. Does exposure to perfumes, insecticides, gas fumes or other chemicals provoke symptoms? Yes No
13. Does tobacco smoke *really* bother him? Yes No

25

Treating Your Child's Yeast Problem

If my child's problems are *Candida*-related,
what do you advise?

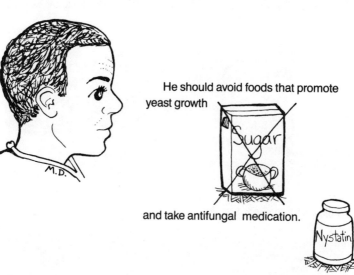

He should avoid foods that promote yeast growth

and take antifungal medication.

He should also avoid foods that contain yeast (as he may be allergic to yeasts).

After one week give him yeast or a yeasty food to see if he shows a reaction.

Later, give him sugar-free yogurt and garlic—both help control *Candida*.

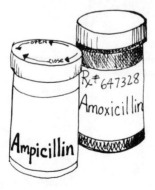

Whenever possible, avoid broad-spectrum antibiotics
and cortisone-type drugs.

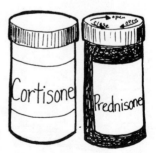

He'll also need to take other steps to improve his health.

26

Overcoming
Yeast-Connected Illness . . .
Questions and Answers*

Q: Tell me more about "the yeast connection." How do you go about making a positive diagnosis. Do tests help?
A: No . . . or not much. Here's why: *Candida* organisms are

*Adapted from *The Yeast Connection,* pp. 39–53.

present in everyone's body—your child's included. They live on his mucous membranes and in his digestive tract, even if he isn't troubled by digestive symptoms. Accordingly, smears and cultures that show *Candida* don't help.

Although immune system tests[1] may help in the study and diagnosis of adults with yeast-connected health disorders, such tests haven't helped in studying these disorders in children. Accordingly, diagnosis is based mainly on the child's history.

Q: If tests don't help, what do you do? How can you tell if my child's irritability, short attention span, hyperactivity and other health problems are related to yeast toxins? How can you rule out such a "yeast connection?"

A: When I see a hyperactive child, or any child with chronic allergic or other health disorders, who has received many courses of broad-spectrum antibacterial drugs, I put the child on an anti-*Candida* treatment program and note his response. I call this a "therapeutic trial."

Q: "Therapeutic trial?" Tell me more about it. . . . What does it consist of?

A: It's a treatment program designed to discourage the growth of *Candida* organisms in the child's body. The program consists of two main parts—a special diet and nystatin or other antiyeast medication. Let's talk about the diet first.

He'll need to avoid foods that encourage the growth of yeasts in his digestive tract—especially sugars and white-flour products. And because people with health disorders related to *Candida* are often allergic to yeasts and molds, I also recommend that raised breads, cheeses, mushrooms and foods containing yeasts and molds be avoided. Feature complex carbohydrates, especially vegetables and whole grains. You can also offer him a variety of other good foods, including chicken, turkey, fish and other seafood, lean meats, eggs and nuts.

Q: What foods should he avoid?

A: Candies, cake, ice cream, soft drinks and sugar-containing foods of all sorts. Also honey and maple syrup.

Q: No way! He's a sugar addict. He's even stolen sweets.
A: I'm not surprised. Sugar craving occurs commonly in children with the yeast problem. So what you're saying makes me suspect *Candida* even more.

Q: What about fructose, honey and corn syrup?* Are they as bad as ordinary table sugar?
A: Yes, and they encourage the growth of yeasts, just as rain makes grass, weeds and mushrooms grow.

Q: How about fruit juices and fruits?
A: Avoid juices, especially those that are canned or frozen, because nearly all contain yeast. Also, during the first ten days of the diet, avoid fruits. Here's why: Fruits and fruit juices are rich in fructose and other carbohydrates that may promote yeast growth. However, as your child improves, experiment with fruits and fresh-squeezed juices. If they don't cause symptoms, give them in moderation—especially on a rotated basis.

Q: Other than following the diet, what else do we need to do?
A: You can give your child foods and supplements that help control *Candida* overgrowth in your child's digestive tract. These include garlic and garlic products, and yogurt, especially home-prepared, fruit-free, sugar-free yogurt. Yogurt contains the friendly bacterium, *Lactobacillus acidophilus.* Powders and capsules containing these (and other) friendly bacteria can be obtained from health food stores.

As an antifungal food substance, caprylic acid is also available in health food stores. This short-chained saturated fatty acid obtained from coconut oil is marketed by several different companies under various brand names including Capricin, Caprystatin, Candistat–300 and Kaprystatin-A. Although these products are available without a prescription, I feel their use should be supervised by a knowledgeable physician or other competent professional.

Your child may also need a medication that helps eradicate or control yeast organisms in his digestive tract. Nystatin

*See also Chapter 29.

is the medication I usually prescribe for my patients with yeast-connected health problems.

Q: What kind of medicine is nystatin?
A: Nystatin is an antifungal drug that kills or arrests the growth of yeast and yeastlike fungi. Yet it doesn't affect bacteria and other germs.

Q: Is nystatin only available by prescription? What form does nystatin come in?
A: Yes. Only on prescription. Nystatin is manufactured by several drug firms and is available in 500,000 unit oral tablets and as an oral suspension containing 100,000 units per milliliter. These preparations are marketed by Lederle under the brand name Nilstat and by Squibb under the brand name Mycostatin. Generic preparations of nystatin are also available.

Still another form, chemically pure nystatin powder, is manufactured by the American Cyanamide Company (a division of Lederle Laboratories), Bound Brook, New Jersey 08805, telephone 1-800-LEDERLE. This powder is not usually available on prescription unless your physician has asked your pharmacist to order it.* I much prefer nystatin powder for my pediatric patients for several reasons: The liquid preparations contain sugar and are much more expensive than the powder. The tablets usually contain food coloring and other additives.

Q: Does nystatin often cause adverse reactions or side effects?
A: *Nystatin is an unusually safe medicine . . . as safe or safer than most drugs physicians prescribe for their patients.* According to the *Physician's Desk Reference* (which gives information on over twenty-five hundred prescription drugs), "Nystatin is virtually nontoxic and nonsensitizing and is well tolerated by all age groups including debilitated infants, even on prolonged administration."

Here's a major reason for the safety of nystatin: Very little is absorbed from the intestinal tract. Accordingly, it helps the person with yeast-related health problems by killing *Candida* in the digestive tract.

---

*A word of caution about nystatin powder: Most pharmacists stock a Mycostatin topical powder (Squibb). This powder is prepared for use on the skin and is not to be confused with the pure nystatin powder.

Nevertheless, nystatin disagrees with some patients and may cause digestive symptoms or skin rashes. In addition, some individuals develop other symptoms, including headache, fatigue and flulike symptoms, especially during the first few days of treatment. Fortunately, these symptoms usually subside within several days, even though the medication is continued.

Q: What causes these symptoms? Do they develop because of an allergy to the nystatin?
A: Although scientists haven't yet determined the mechanism of these reactions, many experts believe they occur when your body absorbs large quantities of killed yeast organisms.

Q: Could reactions to nystatin make it necessary for my child to stop the drug or change the dose?
A: Yes, but before I give up on nystatin, I instruct my patients to experiment with the dose, as the proper dose of nystatin must be determined by trial and error. Moreover, the correct dose varies from patient to patient.

Most of my patients improve when they take 500,000 units (one tablet or ⅛ teaspoon of the powder) of nystatin four times a day. However, some patients require two tablets or ¼ teaspoon of the powder four times a day. By contrast, occasional patients do well on a dose of ¹⁄₁₆ teaspoonful (or less) given four times a day.

Q: Do precautions need to be taken in handling and storing the powder?
A: Yes. The powder should be refrigerated.

Q: If nystatin helps my child, how long will he have to take it?
A: This will depend on his response. He may need to take it for many, many months . . . or until his immune system and nervous system return to normal. Some of my patients have required nystatin for a year or longer. Try to be patient.

Q: How can you tell if the immune and nervous systems are returning to normal?
A: By your child's response. If his behavior and other symp-

toms improve, try reducing the dose of nystatin. If he continues to do well, reduce it further, then discontinue it.

Q: Suppose the nystatin disagrees with my child or suppose his symptoms continue. Is there a medication other than nystatin which can be used?
A: Yes . . . ketoconazole . . . a drug that has been used extensively in both the United States and Europe for a number of years, rarely with serious reactions. It is marketed by the Janssen Company under the name Nizoral.

Nizoral is a potent, valuable drug. In certain ways it is superior to nystatin. It is absorbed from the intestinal tract and transported by the circulatory system to various parts of the body. So it not only kills yeast organisms in the digestive tract, it also helps eradicate them in other tissues.

Q: Why don't you prescribe Nizoral for all your patients with the *Candida* problem?
A: Because Nizoral, like any prescription medication, occasionally causes side effects. And a rare patient may show liver problems, especially if Nizoral is given in big doses for many months. According to a recent report by the FDA, "Serious liver injury was not observed in clinical trials before the drug's approval for marketing in the United States. It became manifest only when large numbers of persons began taking the drug."

During the first year of its use in the United States, approximately one hundred fifty thousand prescriptions for Nizoral were written. Three deaths have been reported in patients who had been taking Nizoral. However, these patients had severe, life-threatening disorders before the Nizoral was started. The FDA received reports of twenty additional patients who showed signs of minor liver irritation.

More recently, other observers have reported that Nizoral transiently inhibits testosterone production in men and also effects adrenal cortisol production. Moreover, the 1984 edition of the *FDA Drug Bulletin* had this to say:

The FDA has received several reports of allergic reactions to ketoconazole, some of which involved anaphylactic reactions after only one dose. The FDA is concerned that physicians be alerted to this possibility with ketoconazole.

Ketoconazole should not be used for systemic fungal infections that are not severe or for topical fungal infections. *However, the drug remains valuable therapy for serious systemic fungal infections provided patients are carefully monitored and the appropriate precautions are taken.* [2]

Q: Since Nizoral can cause side effects, is it worth the risk? And what can be done to lessen the risk?
A: Everything you do carries a risk. And fatal reactions have occurred from aspirin, penicillin and other drugs your child has taken. In spite of the possible side effects of Nizoral, I do not hesitate to recommend that it be tried in treating children with hyperactivity and related behavior and learning problems.

In discussing the side effects and risks of Nizoral, the warning section on the label prepared by the manufacturer states:

It's important to perform liver function tests . . . before treatment and at periodic intervals during treatment (monthly or more frequently), particularly in patients who will be on prolonged therapy or who have a history of liver disease.

Dr. Allan Lieberman commented:

Over half of my patients with hyperactivity and chronic allergic disorders improve on anti-*Candida* therapy, and I've found Nizoral to be an extremely effective drug in treating these patients. Here's the treatment regimen I use:

Nizoral, 200 mg tablets, once daily for five to seven days. (Dose: ¼ tablet for children under 44 pounds; ½ tablet for children 44 to 88 pounds; one tablet for children 88 pounds and over.) I prefer Nizoral as a starting drug as it seems to cause fewer die-off reactions. Moreover, because it is absorbed from the digestive tract into the blood stream it reaches yeasts in parts of the body other than the intestines.

Admittedly, Nizoral may cause adverse and/or toxic reactions, especially if used for many weeks and months. However, the severity of the health disorders experienced by hyperactive children is such that I feel that the risk of giving the medication is far less than the risk of the physical and psychological disturbances that go along with the attention deficit disorder. [3]

Q: What else besides diet and medication will my child need to take care of in order to overcome his yeast problem?

A: Molds and yeast are kin to each other. So you should lessen his exposure to molds. (See Chapter 19 for suggestions for reducing your child's mold exposure.)

Q: What about *Candida* vaccines? Could such a vaccine help my child?

A: Possibly. In some of my patients, the yeast vaccine has worked like a miracle in relieving symptoms. Apparently it helps by stimulating the immune system.*

Yet, the vaccine disagrees with other patients and the dose may be difficult to regulate. In the past year I've received a number of reports from both patients and physicians describing the effectiveness of homeopathic (extremely weak) dilutions of *Candida* extracts. Although I don't understand how or why they work, I have found that such extracts have seemed to help a number of my patients. In my own practice, I sometimes use the vaccine and I sometimes don't. However, if your child needs yeast vaccine, you should find a doctor who is experienced in using *Candida* extracts.

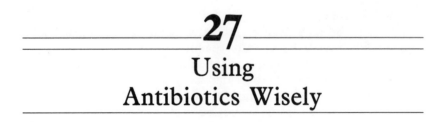

27

Using Antibiotics Wisely

Since the beginning of time men, women and children have died or suffered from severe illnesses caused by tiny bacteria. These troublemaking germs include: *streptococci* (the

---

*Moreover, several reports in the medical literature document the effectiveness of immunotherapy in treating people with *Candida*-related health problems.[4,5]

cause of "strep throat," tonsillitis, scarlet fever and other more serious health disorders), *pneumococci* (a cause of lobar pneumonia and meningitis) and *staphylococci* (the germ that causes boils, styes, "blood poisoning," lung, kidney and brain abcesses). And there are many others.

Then, beginning about fifty years ago—quite by chance— Sir Alexander Fleming, an English physician, discovered the "wonder drug" penicillin. Derived from a common mold, this remarkable substance kept "strep," pneumonia, "staph" and other bacteria from multiplying, allowing the body's immune system and other defenders to conquer them. The course of many previously devastating illnesses was shortened. Countless lives were saved.

Soon after penicillin was discovered, scientists discovered and produced dozens of other germ-fighting substances, including streptomycin, the tetracyclines and the sulfa drugs. These new "magic bullets" (as the broad-spectrum antibiotics were sometimes called) attacked and wiped out families of bacteria that penicillin didn't affect. Yet, like a machine gun or a bomb, they killed friendly germs along with enemies.

Happily, if such antibiotics aren't given repeatedly or for long periods of time, when the drugs are discontinued (in a week or so) the friendly germs usually return and no apparent long-lasting health problems develop.

However, following the lead of medical pioneer C. Orian Truss, M.D., I've observed that repeated courses of broad-spectrum antibiotics can cause yeast overgrowth in susceptible individuals. So I feel I should discuss with you my thoughts about antibiotics.

WHAT SHOULD YOU DO IF YOUR CHILD GETS SICK WITH A FEVER?

1. *Remember, most fevers in children (perhaps 80 to 90 percent or more) are caused by viruses.* Viral infections are usually "self-limiting." (This means your child's immune system conquers the infection without the help of medication.) And *viruses aren't affected by currently available antibiotics.*

2. *Watch your child.* Keep him at home. Give him fresh air, small amounts of water, clear soup and nourishing whole foods including fruit, bananas, oranges, oats, rice, rice crackers and chicken. Let his appetite be his guide. *Avoid foods and beverages that contain sugar and food coloring.*

3. *Give him vitamin C, as much as he can take without causing diarrhea or stomach cramps.* * Get vitamin C powder, 4000 milligrams per teaspoon. Add a teaspoon to a glass of water or juice. Let him sip on it every fifteen to thirty minutes. You may find he'll tolerate one-half to two or more teaspoons— 2000 mg to 10,000 mg or more—each day.

4. Sucking on zinc gluconate tablets, 15 mg, every one to two hours (for two to four days), may increase your child's resistance to infection and help him get well sooner.[2]

5. *If your child looks or acts "really sick" or complains of:*

a. Severe or persistent ear pain
b. Persistent or severe sore throat
c. Severe hoarseness, asthma, croup, shortness of breath, persistent cough or other respiratory difficulty
d. Persistent abdominal pain, vomiting, diarrhea
e. Severe headache, neck stiffness, convulsions, delirium
f. Unusual or severe skin rashes

*I've been especially impressed by the observations and reports of double Nobel Prize winner Linus Pauling, Ph.D., and Robert Cathcart, M.D., which indicate that vitamin C stimulates the immune system. If you'd like a copy of Dr. Pauling's report, "Vitamin C and Infectious Diseases," you can order it from Executive Health Publications, 9605 Scranton Road, Suite 710, San Diego, CA 92121, for $3.00.[1]

g. Urinary burning and frequency, flank pain and backache

take him to your physician at once.
    If after examining your child your physician finds no evi-
dence of a bacterial infection, do not "twist his arm" and de-
mand an antibiotic.*

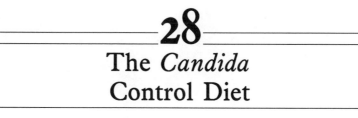

28

The *Candida* Control Diet

FOODS YOUR CHILD CAN EAT†

All fresh vegetables:

Asparagus	Cucumbers
Beets	Eggplant
Broccoli	Green peppers
Brussel sprouts	Greens:
Cabbage	Beet
Carrots	Collard
Cauliflower	Kale
Celery	Mustard
Corn	Spinach

---

*Note to physicians: If I feel an antibiotic is indicated in treating a respiratory or skin infection, I nearly always first use penicillin V, penicillin G or erythromycin. These antibiotics do not wipe out the normal intestinal flora, encouraging the growth of *Candida albicans.* And if I prescribe a broad-spectrum antibiotic, I always give ny-statin along with the antibiotic to discourage yeast overgrowth.
†Avoid any food that provokes an allergic or adverse reaction.

Lettuce
Okra
Onions
Parsley
Parsnips
Peas, beans and
   legumes

Radishes
Squash
Sweet potatoes
White potatoes
Zucchini

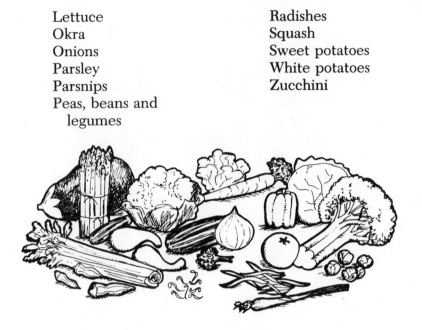

All fresh fruits:
   Apples
   Apricots
   Avocados
   Bananas
   Berries:
      Blackberries
      Blueberries

   Raspberries
   Strawberries
   Grapefruit
   Grapes
   Lemons
   Mangos
   Melons

Nectarines
Oranges
Papayas
Peaches

Pears
Pineapples
Plums
Tangerines

Meats and eggs (any but bacon, sausage, ham, hot dogs or luncheon meats):

Red meats
  Beef
  Lamb
  Pork
  Rabbit
  Veal
  Wild game

Poultry
  Chicken
  Cornish hens
  Duck
  Eggs
  Goose
  Pheasant and
    other game
    birds

Quail
Turkey
Seafood
  Clams
  Crabs
  Lobster
  Oysters
  Salmon,
    mackerel, cod,
    sardines
  Shrimp
  Tuna
  Other fresh or
    frozen fish that
    is not breaded

Beverages:
  Water
  Milk*

*Because of my experience, milk allergy occurs commonly in hard-to-raise children and because milk, including skim milk, is rich in lactose (milk sugar), I recommend that milk be eliminated during the first eight to ten days of the diet. If your child improves, let him drink milk again and note his reaction. If it doesn't bother him, he can drink milk in moderation.

Whole grains (cereal grains, bread and muffins containing no yeast, honey or sugar):

Barley

Corn (stoneground, unenriched cornmeal, popcorn)

Millet

Oats (long cooking oatmeal)

Rice (brown rice, rice cakes, puffed rice, brown rice flour)

Rye (rye flour, rye crackers)

Wheat (whole wheat flour, cream of wheat, Shredded Wheat)

Nuts, seeds and oils* (unprocessed):

Almonds

Brazil nuts

Cashews

Filberts

Pecans

Pumpkin seeds

Oils (unprocessed):

Corn

Linseed

Safflower

Soy

Sunflower

Walnut

Butter

---

*Most commercially available nuts and seeds have been processed and contain additives. Most commercially available oils have been heated and processed. So get unprocessed nuts and seeds and unrefined oils from a health food store. (You can offer him any nuts except peanuts and soy nuts.)

FOODS YOUR CHILD MUST AVOID

Sugar and sugar-containing foods:
  Sugar and other quick-acting carbohydrates, including sucrose, fructose, maltose, lactose, glycogen, glucose, mannitol, sorbitol, galactose, monosaccharides and polysaccharides. Also avoid honey, molasses, maple syrup, maple sugar, date sugar and turbinado sugar.

Packaged and processed foods:
  Canned, bottled, boxed and other packaged and processed foods usually contain refined sugar, hydrogenated or partially hydrogenated fats and oils and other hidden ingredients.

Avoid yeasty foods for the first seven to ten days of your child's diet. Then do the yeast challenge. If he's allergic to yeast, you'll need to continue to avoid yeast and mold-containing foods indefinitely. However, if he isn't allergic to yeast, you can rotate yeast-containing foods into his diet in moderation.

Here's a list of foods that contain yeast or molds:

Breads, pastries and other raised bakery goods

Cheeses:
  All cheeses, including Swiss cheese, cottage cheese, cream cheese and especially moldy cheeses such as Roquefort. Prepared foods, including Velveeta, macaroni and cheese, Cheezits and other cheese-containing snacks. Also buttermilk, sour cream and sour milk products.*

Edible fungi:
  All types of mushrooms, morels and truffles.

Fermented beverages:
  Alcohol, cider and root beer.

*Many individuals tolerate fruit-free, sugar-free, homemade yogurt.

Foods You Must Avoid

Sugar and Sugar-containing foods

Yeast Breads and Pastries

Condiments

Malt Products

Processed and Smoked Meats

Dried and Candied Fruits

Leftovers

You Must Also Avoid

Fruit Juices

Melons

Edible Fungi

Cheeses

Yeast

Miscellaneous Foods

Coffee, Teas and Herbs

Antibiotics

Vitamins Containing Yeast or Sugar

Malt products:
    Malted milk drinks, cereals and candy.

Condiments, sauces and vinegar-containing foods:
    Mustard, ketchup, Worcestershire sauce, Accent (monosodium glutamate); steak, barbecue, chili, shrimp and soy sauces; pickles, pickled vegetables, relishes, green olives, sauerkraut, horseradish and mince meat. Also avoid sprouts. Vinegar of all kinds and vinegar-containing foods such as mayonnaise and salad dressing. (Freshly squeezed lemon juice may be used as a substitute for vinegar in salad dressings prepared with unprocessed vegetable oil.)

Processed and smoked meats:
    Pickled and smoked meats and fish including sausages, hot dogs, corned beef, pastrami and pickled tongue.

Coffee and tea:
    Regular coffee, instant coffee and teas of all sorts, including herb teas.

Fruit juices:
    Canned, bottled, or frozen, including orange juice, grape juice, apple juice, tomato juice, pineapple juice. (Exception: freshly prepared juice.)

Dried and candied fruits:
    Raisins, apricots, dates, prunes, figs, pineapple.

Melons:
    Watermelon, honeydew melon and especially cantaloupe.*

*Porous skin of cantaloupe is especially apt to be contaminated with mold. However, careful washing before cutting may enable melons to be tolerated.

Nuts:

> Peanuts and peanut products usually contain mold. So do pistachios.

Left-overs:

> Molds grow in left-over food unless it's properly refrigerated. Freezing is better.

Vitamins and minerals:

> B complex vitamins, selenium products (unless labeled "yeast-free" and "sugar-free").

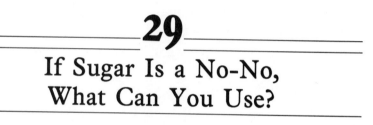

29

If Sugar Is a No-No, What Can You Use?

If *Candida* plays a role in causing your child's health problems, avoid sugar, because sugar feeds yeasts and promotes their growth. Sugar may also trigger symptoms in children who do not have *Candida*-related illness.

During the past twenty years, I've seen dozens of hard-to-raise children whose mothers commented, "My child craves sugar. He'll cheat, lie or steal to get it. *When he eats sugar, he's like a different person.* He becomes overactive, aggressive and irritable."

Yet, because children desire sweetened foods which taste good, I'm sure you'd like to know how you can safely sweeten your foods and beverages. Here are my comments on sweeteners, including some you can use and others I do not recommend.

ASPARTAME

In July 1981, the Food and Drug Administration finally approved the use of *aspartame,* a new low-calorie sweetener. This product is two hundred times sweeter than sugar, but contains only one eighth the calories found in sugar. The product tastes like sugar, but contains no saccharin or other artificial sweetener.

Aspartame can be found on supermarket shelves under the brand names NutraSweet or Equal.*

One packet of Equal has the sweetness of two teaspoons of sugar, but supplies only four calories. It costs about four cents per packet, so it's much more expensive than saccharin. Also, it can't be used in baking because high heat for long periods of time causes chemical changes in the amino acids, eliminating the sweet taste.

Aspartame was discovered in 1965 when a chemist wet his finger to pick up a piece of paper and noticed a sweet taste. The compounds he was working with were two amino acids—aspartic acid and phenylalanine—found naturally in proteins.

*Small amounts of fillers in Equal may bother the very sensitive: corn sweetener (dextrose) in the packets and milk sugar (lactose) in the tablets.

Although neither of these compounds alone tastes sweet, combined they're very sweet.

Since the discovery of this product in 1965, more than a hundred scientific tests for its safety have been conducted. Yet researchers continue to study its safety.

Most scientists feel aspartame is safe for "normal persons," as it's made of two normal food ingredients (amino acids) that have been joined together.[*,1] So when it goes into your body, it's like a tiny bit of food, rather than a synthetic chemical.

Yet, controversy surrounding its safety still continues. For example, R. J. Wurtman, M.D., of M.I.T., has reported that disturbances in brain chemistry affecting mood and behavior may occur if large amounts of aspartame are ingested.[2] Allergist Anthony Kulczycki has linked allergic reactions (hives, itching and swelling) in two patients to their aspartame consumption.[3] And many of my patients complain that eating aspartame-sweetened foods gives them headaches, dizziness and depression. If aspartame provokes symptoms in your child, avoid it. If he tolerates aspartame, use it sparingly.

LAURA COMMENTS:

My children and I don't tolerate sugar, honey or saccharin. Using a few packets of aspartame *occasionally* doesn't provoke our symptoms, yet lets us sweeten a bowl of oatmeal or enjoy a glass of lemonade.

Although I don't recommend routinely giving your child soft drinks, he may tolerate the new soft drinks sweetened with NutraSweet (especially uncolored, cola-free, caffeine-free ones like 7-Up, Slice or Sprite) *in small quantities on special occasions.*

Like any other food or additive, *aspartame may cause adverse effects in sensitive individuals.* So if it disagrees with your child, avoid it.

---

*Individuals who suffer from phenylketonuria, an amino acid metabolism disorder, should avoid aspartame.

SACCHARIN*

Foods and beverages containing saccharin must be labeled with the following warning: "Use of this product may be hazardous to your health. This product contains saccharin, which has been determined to cause cancer in laboratory animals."

In spite of this label, I prefer saccharin to sugar for patients with yeast and sugar sensitivities. When used in limited quantities, I feel it is relatively safe. Moreover, a study in a leading medical journal comparing patients with bladder cancer to a similar group who had no cancer, showed no evidence that the cancer patients had consumed more saccharin than those who did not have cancer.[4] Nevertheless, the Council on Scientific Affairs of the American Medical Association recommends "careful consideration of saccharin use by young children and pregnant women."[5] On rare occasions, saccharin has provoked physical and mental symptoms in my patients. If saccharin bothers your child, avoid it.

FRUITS

Some of my patients with yeast-connected illness tolerate complex carbohydrates, including apples, bananas and pineapple. If your child is such a person, Karen Barkie's cookbook, *Fancy, Sweet, and Sugar-Free* (New York: St. Martin's Press, 1985) should interest you. It's full of recipes for sugar-free, fruit-sweetened foods.

Others among my patients develop symptoms when they eat fruits. For example, the mother of one of my patients recently commented:

> Terry has really been doing well the last six months except when he eats sugary treats. And eating fruits high in natural

*Packets of saccharin contain corn sweetener (dextrose) but liquid saccharin preparations such as Fasweet and Sweeta do not.

sugars, like bananas, raisins, grapes and apples (particularly if he eats them without any protein foods) makes him restless, overactive and uncooperative.

Because fruits are rapidly metabolized and converted into simple sugars, they may promote yeast growth. Accordingly, I advise my adult yeast-sensitive patients to avoid them during the first three weeks of their treatment program. Then most of my patients with yeast-related problems find they can eat fruits in moderate amounts. Even though I limit fruit intake in my adult patients, I do not restrict fruits in my pediatric patients unless they provoke symptoms.

HONEY AND PURE MAPLE SYRUP

Over the years, many parents of hard-to-raise children have reported, "Cane sugar disagrees with my child. It 'turns him on' and makes him irritable and overactive; yet he tolerates honey or pure maple syrup."

If your child tolerates honey and pure maple syrup, it's okay to give them to him occasionally. But, if his health problems are yeast-connected, he should avoid these sweeteners. Honey and maple syrup, like sugar, promote yeast growth.

FRUCTOSE OR HIGH-FRUCTOSE CORN SYRUP

Fructose has received a great deal of publicity. It's sweeter than cane and beet sugar in cold liquids and is now used in many commercially sweetened foods. Yet I don't recommend it. Here's why: Like sucrose (table sugar), the fructose found in commercial foods is a refined "empty calorie" carbohydrate. No vitamins and minerals. No fiber. And none of the enzymes or other health-promoting nutrients found in fructose-containing bananas and other whole fruits.

Still other reasons: Commercially available fructose is usually made from corn, and corn frequently provokes allergic reactions; also, fructose or high-fructose corn syrup feeds yeasts in the digestive tract. Avoid it.

Section G

NUTRITIONAL, METABOLIC AND BIOCHEMICAL FACTORS THAT MAY AFFECT YOUR CHILD

30

What Is
a Good Diet?

Almost without exception, to help your hard-to-raise child you'll have to put the allergic pieces of his puzzle into place. Sensitivities to foods, chemicals, molds (and other inhalants) may be causing some of his symptoms. While you're working to help your child's allergies, however, you'll need also to look at his nutrition.

If your child isn't troubled by allergies, you'll find that the nutritional pieces of his puzzle lead the list of those that must be identified and put into place.

Your child's body resembles an amazing chemical factory and warehouse. It manufactures, processes or stores over a hundred thousand different chemicals. To make these chemicals your child imports only about fifty raw materials, chemicals it can't make by itself or in sufficient quantity: ten essential amino acids, two essential fatty acids, twenty to thirty minerals, a dozen or so vitamins, water, glucose and fiber. If your child doesn't take in enough of these raw materials and absorb them adequately, his "factory" can't function optimally. And some of his assembly lines may perform erratically or shut down.

Amino acids are the building blocks of proteins. Your child needs an adequate supply of all the essential amino acids for growth and development. He also needs amino acids to produce hormones, enzymes, immunoglobulins and neuro-transmitters. Neurotransmitters are critical because they form the chemical links between nerve cells in the brain. So abnormal levels of neurotransmitters may lead to depression, hyperactivity, anxiety and other nervous system symptoms.

Essential fatty acids are the building blocks of fats. They perform two critical roles in your child's body: They form an important part of the cell membrane that controls the flow of nutrients and wastes into and out of his cells. They're also the precursors for prostaglandins, a group of powerful hormone-like chemicals that control many types of body functions. Essential fatty acid deficiencies may cause your child to develop both physical and mental problems.

Minerals are inorganic nutrients that perform many important tasks in your child's body, including formation of teeth and bones and regulation of body fluids. Minerals participate in many biological reactions.

Vitamins are specific organic compounds that your child requires in his diet in tiny amounts. Vitamins help regulate nearly all of his metabolic reactions.

Water is not only the most abundant nutrient found in the body, but it is also the most critical. Although your child might live for several weeks without food, he could survive only a few days without water. Water transports nutrients and wastes throughout the body. It is essential for digestion, absorption, circulation, excretion and maintaining body temperature.

Your child's body in certain ways resembles an automobile. It won't "run" if it doesn't have the proper fuel. Just as gasoline furnishes energy to your car, glucose, a simple sugar, furnishes fuel for all of the cells of your child's body, including, especially, his brain. When your child eats potatoes, oatmeal, bananas, and other vegetables, grains and fruits, the complex carbohydrates in these foods are digested and broken down to form glucose. Glucose can also be made from proteins and fats but this conversion may cause side effects.

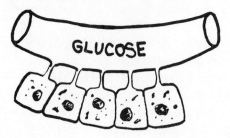

Fiber or roughage is the strandlike, stringy material that holds plants together. Because fiber can't be digested by the stomach or small intestine, and because it absorbs moisture, it adds bulk to digested foods and stimulates muscles in the digestive tract. So your child needs fiber to enable him to eliminate waste products and to keep him from becoming constipated. Research studies by the British physician Denis Burkitt, carried out in Africa, show that many diseases of Western civilization, including cancer and heart disease, occur less frequently if the bowel "transit time" is shortened.

Here are dietary guidelines I give all my patients (and their families). You may need to alter these suggestions to avoid symptom-provoking foods.

1. Fresh *vegetables* are important to any good diet, especially vegetables that aren't contaminated with poisonous chemicals (see also Chapter 7, p. 35), and vegetables that are raw or aren't overcooked. Vegetables provide vitamins, iron, calcium, trace minerals, complex carbohydrates and fiber. Vitamin A-rich vegetables include carrots, pumpkin, squash, sweet potatoes, spinach, broccoli and other dark green vegetables. Tomatoes, green pepper, potatoes and dark green vegetables are good sources of vitamin C. Beans, including kidney, navy, pinto and red beans, are good sources of essential fatty acids.

2. *Grains,* including whole (unrefined) wheat, rye, oats, rice, barley, millet and corn, supply B vitamins, vitamin E, iron, magnesium, trace minerals, complex carbohydrates, incomplete protein and fiber.

3. *Fruits,* especially fresh fruits, are excellent sources of vitamins A and C, minerals, complex carbohydrates and fiber. Vitamin A-rich fruits include cantaloupe, watermelon, peaches, apricots, mangos, papayas and oranges. Citrus fruits, cantaloupe, watermelon and strawberries are excellent sources of vitamin C.

4. *Nuts and seeds* are delicious, ready-to-eat foods rich in

essential fatty acids, iron, calcium, potassium, B vitamins, vitamin E, complex carbohydrates, incomplete protein and fiber. Two words of caution: Do not give your children under the age of four whole nuts and seeds. They can choke on them. And discard "runt" nuts as they're apt to contain harmful toxins.

5. *Eggs,* a popular and readily available food, are a superb source of many essential nutrients, including complete protein, minerals and vitamins A, B_{12} and D. If high blood cholesterol or heart disease run in your family, your physician may wish to measure your child's blood cholesterol and limit his intake of eggs to three per week. Boiled or poached eggs are better for your child than fried or scrambled.

6. *Dairy products* are especially good when they are low in fat—skim milk, unsweetened low-fat yogurt and low-fat cheese (including low-fat cottage cheese and farmer's cheese). These foods provide complete protein, vitamins (especially A, D, riboflavin and B_{12}) and minerals (especially calcium).

7. *Unrefined vegetable oils* can be obtained from health food stores . . . vegetable oils that haven't been treated with high heat. These oils provide essential fatty acids and vitamin E.

8. *Lean meat* (especially fish, chicken and turkey) supplies complete protein, vitamins and minerals. Cold-water fish such as salmon, mackerel and herring are rich sources of essential fatty acids.

If he is to be well nourished your child must eat good foods. Equally important, he must avoid bad foods. Cut down especially on animal fats (hamburger, bacon, beef, sausage, luncheon meats), salt, sugar and white-flour products. Use whole rather than processed and packaged foods. In preparing fruits and vegetables, cook them less and eat more of them raw. Bake, broil, or boil your meats; avoid frying and browning.

Your child needs protein if he is to grow and develop properly. Yet, nutrition authorities are now saying that Americans of all ages—including children—are consuming more protein than they need.

In the March 1987 issue of the *Nutrition Action Health Letter,* in an article, "Overdosing on Protein," Elaine Blume said: "According to government statistics, on the average, infants and children in the United States consume about twice the RDA (Recommended Daily Allowance) for protein."

In discussing our "passion for protein," she continued: "In the 1970s, Frances Moore Lappe's best-selling *Diet for a Small Planet* contributed to the protein mania—it had thousands of people painstakingly combining peanuts and sunflower seeds or bulgur and garbanzo beans in an effort to make sure that they met their daily protein quota."[1]

But in a revised edition, published in 1982, Lappe offered different advice. Referring to the earlier book, she wrote: "In combatting the myth that meat is the only way to get high quality protein, I reinforced another myth. I gave the impression that in order to get enough protein without meat, considerable care was needed in choosing foods. Actually, it's much easier than I thought."

Jane Brody of *The New York Times* said in her book, *Jane Brody's Nutrition Book:*

> Even if you have no interest in vegetarianism, there's no reason why you should have animal protein at every meal or even every day. . . . We'd all be better off if we stopped thinking of vegetables and grains as merely side dishes to embellish a chunk of animal protein. . . . Vegetables can be an important source of protein for everyone.[2]

"You should eat breakfast like a king, lunch like a prince and supper like a pauper." Although the rush of getting parents to work and children to day-care centers, kindergartens and schools puts pressure on families, *hard-to-raise children must be given a good breakfast.* To do this, get up thirty minutes earlier in the mornings and allow time for a good breakfast. Trouble? Yes, but well worth it.

The late Dr. Charles Shedd achieved outstanding success in managing children with behavior and learning problems. An important feature of his program was a good breakfast.

MEAL SUGGESTIONS FOR A GOOD DIET*

Breakfast

Fruits:
•Fresh fruit or fruit juice (whole fruit is *much* better). (Avoid fruit punches or fruit "drinks"—mixtures of sugar, corn syrup, fructose, food coloring, flavoring and water!)
•Cooked fruits including baked apples are acceptable. So are prunes, apricots and other dried fruits if your child isn't allergic to yeasts and molds.
•Include one or more servings of citrus fruits each day.

Whole grain cereals and breads:
•Steel-cut (or other whole grain) oats, whole wheat, barley or brown rice cereals (usually found at health food stores). Regular Quaker pure oat cereal is also acceptable.

Less desirable are refined oat products, especially those that contain sugar or other additives. One or two table-spoons of pure bran, especially wheat and oat bran (usually found in health food stores) will provide extra roughage and help prevent constipation and other health problems. Fresh or frozen fruit and a tablespoon or two of chopped almonds, pecans, walnuts (or other nuts) can also

*You may need to alter these suggestions to avoid symptom-provoking foods or to adhere to a rotation diet.

be stirred into the hot cereal just before removing it from the stove.

•Whole grain bread contains vitamins, minerals, trace elements and fiber. (White bread lacks many of these important nutrients and often contains sugar, corn syrup, hydrogenated or partially hydrogenated fats and preservatives.)

Other dry cereals:

•Nutri-Grain, Shredded Wheat, Grape-Nuts, Cheerios and cornflakes may be acceptable for occasional use. Yet I prefer the whole grains. Here's why: Cheerios and cornflakes contain added sugar; Shredded Wheat contains the preservative BHT, and Grape-Nuts contains malt and yeast.

•Many of the highly advertised-bran containing cereals, including All-Bran, are loaded with sugar. However, I like and recommend the new sugar-free, salt-free Shredded Wheat 'n Bran.

Sweeteners:

•Honey and pure maple syrup in small quantities* are better than sugar-containing jams and jellies. Look for sugar-free, color-free, corn-free preserves and fruit spreads in your health food store. Your child will love them.

Butter:

•Avoid margarine, because it's loaded with hardened vegetable oil. Use butter instead—but don't overdo it.

Eggs:

•Boiled or poached, especially.

---

*If your child's behavior problems are yeast connected, avoid all sugars, honey, and maple and other syrups.

Meat:
    •Hamburger (ground, lean) patties, pork chops, turkey, chicken, sardines or other fish. I especially recommend sardines packed in sardine oil, because this oil contains essential fatty acids. Although you may not have thought of these meats as "breakfast foods," give them a try. *Avoid bacon and other processed breakfast meats.*

Lunch, Including School Lunches

Whole grain breads or crackers

Sandwich fillings:
    •Sliced chicken, turkey or water-packed tuna; sugar-free, pure peanut butter or cashew butter.
    •Sugar-free jams and jellies.

Unprocessed nuts

Fruits:
    •Apples, oranges, peaches, nectarines, bananas or grapes may be packed in lunch boxes. Your child will also enjoy small containers of unsweetened applesauce, frozen fruits (sweetened with fruit juices) and pure fruit juices.

Fresh vegetables:
    •Celery, carrots, cherry tomatoes and other vegetables may also be packed in your child's lunch.

Hot lunches:
    •For a hot home lunch, try a barley casserole and load it with vegetables—you can also add morsels of meat or chopped nuts, or soups and stews prepared with homemade broth, meats, vegetables and seasonings.

Dinner

Meat:
    •Chicken, turkey, fish, lean beef, lean pork, lamb, and wild game.

Vegetables:

•Raw and cooked vegetables of all sorts (don't over-cook). Salads using vegetables, fruits, and meats, poultry, or fish. Pure unrefined vegetable oils can be used for making salad dressings.

•Avoid premixed dressings that contain sugar, partially hydrogenated oils and other additives.

Whole wheat bread or rolls

Fruits:

•Fresh fruits make delicious salads and desserts while satisfying your child's sweet tooth.

Snacks

Fruits, pure juices, raw vegetables, unsweetened yogurt, nuts (children under four should not be given whole nuts), sugar-free peanut butter, whole wheat toast, pretzels or crackers.*

WHAT IS A BAD DIET?

If your child and your family are eating significant amounts of animal fats, hydrogenated or partially hydrogenated vegetable oil, sugar, soft drinks, candy, salted foods, white flour products and the highly advertised snack, junk and processed "convenience foods," you're eating a bad diet.

---

*Read labels carefully. Many boxed crackers labeled "natural" or 100 percent whole wheat, such as Triscuits are loaded with unhealthy (hydrogenated or partially hydrogenated) fats or oils.

Nutritionally Poor Food, especially Sugar, White Flour and Hardened Vegetable Oil.

Such foods lack vitamins, minerals, essential fatty acids, amino acids and fiber and often contain excessive amounts of phosphates and salt. If your child fills up on these "junk foods," he won't have room left for nutritious foods.

Sugar, pure granulated white sugar, is a particular bad guy. It is produced and refined from sugarcane and sugar beets. I like sugar-sweetened foods and so do my grandchildren and just about everyone else in the world.

But sugar is loaded with "naked calories." No fiber, complex carbohydrates, vitamins or minerals. Studies show that the average adult American is consuming over 120 pounds of refined sugar a year. Many children are taking in that much or more from carbonated beverages, punches, candies, cakes, ice cream and dry cereals. What's more, sugar is hidden in many other foods ranging from salad dressings and canned peas to catsup.

A special word on cereals: Many cereals featured (and heavily promoted) on children's television programs contain 40 percent or more sugar. *A fourteen-ounce box of such a cereal may contain fifty or more teaspoons of sugar.* In my experience, sugar is a major cause of behavioral disorders in children, including hyperactivity, inappropriate drowsiness and short attention span.

How do you get children to cut down on sugar? It isn't easy. Yet it can be done according to Carol F. Smith, a physical education specialist on the faculty of the San Antonio Texas Northside Independent School District.

Carol has devised a unique plan for creating an awareness of excess sugar consumption by students and their families. Moreover, she has instituted a statewide nutritional project in the schools called the Triple Threat Challenge.

I visited with Carol in July 1987, just as this book was going to press and she said, "This program works! Studies I've carried out with the help and cooperation of school personnel have indicated a definite relationship between sugar intake and behavior."* If you'd like more information about this program, send a long, stamped self-addressed envelope to Carol F. Smith, Ph.D., 8202 Meadow Forest, San Antonio Texas 78251.

If your hard-to-raise child is a "junk-food addict," you must "clean up" his diet. If he is to enjoy good physical health, he must eat good nutritious food from a variety of sources. Equally important, he requires such good food if he is to settle down, concentrate and get along with his parents, siblings, schoolmates and teachers.†

---

*Note to physicians: Analysis of behavior inventories used in the project were statistically significant at the 0.001 level of confidence.
†Two recent books by Sara Sloan (the food service director of the Fulton County [Atlanta], Georgia, public schools for thirty-one years) are loaded with practical information that will help you prepare and feed your children good foods they'll eat and like. Their titles: *The Brown Bag Cookbook*[3] and *The Care and Feeding of Healthy Kids.*[4] If you can't find them in your bookstore, you can order them from Nutra, P.O. Box 13825, Atlanta, GA 30324.

3I
A Guide to Vitamin Supplementation

I f you write to the Department of Nutrition of the American Medical Association and ask about the vitamin and mineral requirements for your hard-to-raise child, you're apt to be told, "If your child eats a good diet, he doesn't need supplemental vitamins."*

That statement undoubtedly may have been true for our ancestors who ate only unrefined foods. Yet vitamin deficiency diseases, including scurvy, beriberi, pellagra and rickets, caused a tremendous amount of suffering and millions of deaths in our ancestors until the last century.

Scurvy, for example, commonly affected sailors and soldiers on long voyages and campaigns. Yet no one knew why. According to Linus Pauling:

> The idea that scurvy could be prevented by proper diet developed only slowly. In 1536, the French explorer Jacques Cartier discovered the St. Lawrence River and sailed upstream to the site of the present city of Quebec, where he and his men spent the winter.
>
> Twenty-five of the men died of scurvy and many others were very sick. A friendly Indian advised them to drink tea made of the leaves and bark of the *arbor vitae* tree—the treatment was beneficial. The leaves of this tree were later shown to contain about 50 milligrams of vitamin C per 100 grams.[1]

*In a report, *Vitamin Preparations and Dietary Supplements as Therapeutic Agents,* published in the April 10, 1987, issue of *The Journal of the American Medical Association,* the Council on Scientific Affairs commented, "Application of sound dietary practices should eliminate any need for supplemental vitamins after infancy in essentially all healthy children." However, they state, ". . . In situations in which an individual is unable or unwilling to eat an adequate diet, the physician must decide whether vitamin supplementation is necessary. . . . All health practitioners should repeatedly emphasize a properly selected diet for the primary basis for good nutrition" (*JAMA,* 257:1929-1936, April 10, 1987).

Subsequently, Captain James Cook, the famous English explorer, and Dr. James Lind, a Scottish physician in the British Royal Navy, found that limes and other fresh fruits and vegetables kept sailors from developing scurvy. Yet they didn't know it was the vitamin C in these fresh foods that made them effective.

Cure for another vitamin deficiency disease, beriberi, was also discovered through chance observations by a young Dutch physician, Christiaan Eijkman, beginning in 1886. Subsequent investigations by Eijkman and others showed that a substance that could be isolated from unpolished rice kept pigeons (and other poultry) and people from developing severe diseases which affected many parts of the body, especially the nervous system and the heart.

In the next several decades, many other investigators studied the nutritional value of foods, including the English biochemist F. Galland Hopkins. In 1929, Hopkins and Eijkman were awarded the Nobel Prize for their nutritional investigations. Later studies by many investigators showed that the antiberiberi nutrient was vitamin B_1.

Credit for coining the word *vitamin* goes to Casimir Funk, a Polish biochemist working in the Lister Institute in London. In 1911, Funk published his theory of vitamins and suggested that four such substances are present in natural foods and serve to protect people against beriberi, scurvy, pellagra and rickets. He coined the word *vitamine* from the Latin word *vita* (life) and a chemical term, *amine,* a member of a class of nitrogen compounds.*

Although modern nutritional and medical scientists now know a lot about vitamins, your difficult child's problems might be related to less than optimum amounts of vitamins,

*For a full discussion of how vitamins were discovered, get a copy of Linus Pauling's *How to Live Longer and Feel Better* (New York: W. H. Freeman Company, 1986).

in spite of your efforts to feed him good foods. Here's why:

1. *The pollution of our planet.* Vegetables, fruits and grains grown on chemically treated soils are often contaminated with lead, cadmium and other toxic substances, including insecticides and weed killers. These substances may displace or compete with good minerals (such as zinc) and interfere with the metabolism and utilization of other nutrients. Other chemical pollutants, including polychlorinated biphenyls (PCB's), herbacides and insecticides, may increase your child's vitamin requirements, especially his need for vitamin B_6.[2] Sulfur in acid rain blocks the uptake of selenium by plants.

2. *The "mining" of our soils.* Soils of many American farms aren't as good as they used to be. Raising the same crops on a farm or in your vegetable garden every year and not replacing organic materials with compost or manure depletes the soil. Also, improper land use leads to soil erosion and loss of the topsoil. Foods grown in such soil often lack vital nutrients.

3. *The trail from farm and garden to your child's stomach is long and complex, and foods lose vital nutrients along the way.* Drying, canning, freezing, processing, boxing, shipping, standing, storing and cooking all cause vital nutrients (like vitamin C and B complex vitamins) to be lost.

4. *Your child may not be eating a wide variety of good foods.* In discussing this subject with his patients, Vancouver physician Saul Pilar, M.D., had this to say:

> You want the best school, the best teachers, the best books, the best clothes, the best sports activities for your child. How about your child's nutrition? Are you going to give him a better chance or are you going to give him another handicap—suboptimal nutrition? If you want your child to have A+ marks, don't give him a C− diet, please![3]

I share Dr. Pilar's feelings and give the parents of my own patients similar advice. Yet your child may dislike the good foods you put on his plate or put in his school lunch box. Moreover, he's brainwashed by hundreds of deceptive television food ads each week. When you send apples, bananas, tuna and whole-grain bread to school with him, he may swap them for a Twinkie or a serving of sugar-coated cereal.

Because of these factors, I feel that with a rare exception Americans today should take nutritional supplements, including vitamins, minerals, trace elements and essential fatty acids. My belief is based on the clinical and research studies of many American scientists, including Roger Williams, the discoverer of two important B vitamins—folic acid and pantothenic acid.

Moreover, Dr. Williams has repeatedly emphasized that each person is biochemically unique.[4] This means that your child's requirements for a particular nutrient may differ significantly from those of your neighbor's child.

SCIENTIFIC STUDIES OF THE EFFECTS OF VITAMIN SUPPLEMENTS ON HARD-TO-RAISE CHILDREN

Before trying to answer the question "What vitamin supplements should I give my child?" I'd like to tell you about some of the experiences of other professionals who have been working with hard-to-raise children.

More than fifteen years ago, Arnold Brenner, M.D., a Maryland pediatrician, found that the behavior of one of his three-year-old hyperactive patients improved following the administration of large doses of vitamin B_6.[5] So he began to try different B vitamin preparations on other hyperactive children.

Some of his patients improved dramatically when he gave them large doses of vitamin B_6—100 to 400 mg per day. When the vitamin was discontinued, their hyperactive, wild and disruptive behavior would return. He found, however, that the hyperactivity in other patients was accentuated when they took large doses of vitamin B_6. But some of these patients would improve when they were also given vitamins B_1, B_{12} and other B vitamins. We now know that insurance doses of all vitamins should be given before increasing one vitamin alone.

In analyzing the Brenner studies, I found that his observations support those of Roger Williams: Children are *biochemically unique* and a vitamin preparation that helps one child may not help another, and in still a third child, it may aggravate his symptoms. Brenner also noted that a number of his patients required supplementation with zinc, magnesium and other minerals to maintain their improvement.

In a series of studies first reported in 1971, Mary Coleman of Washington noted that serotonin, a "brain chemical," was found in abnormally low levels in the majority of a group of hyperactive emotionally disturbed children she was studying.[6] Coleman and other observers found that large doses of B_6 raised the blood-serotonin levels and relieved the symptoms in a number of their hyperactive patients. Subsequently, they carried out a small double-blind study contrasting the effects of Ritalin and B_6 and they noted that there was a trend that suggested that B_6 might be as effective as or more effective than Ritalin.[7]

In another double-blind study Bernard Rimland, Ph.D., director of the Institute for Child Behavior Research,* Enoch Calloway, M.D., and Pierre Dreyfus, M.D., of the University of California, found that a group of autistic children who received vitamin B_6 showed significant improvements in behavior.[8] Rimland has also observed that a nutritional program which features larger doses of all the B vitamins plus other nutritional supplements appears to play an important role in helping many hyperactive patients.[9,10,11]

Still other studies by Derrick Lonsdale, M.D., formerly of the Cleveland Clinic, show that some children require larger than usual doses of vitamin B_1 and that such children are vitamin B_1 dependent. Moreover, blood studies described by Dr. Lonsdale help identify these children.[12]

*4182 Adams Avenue, San Diego CA 92116.

Ira Fritz and associates used a similar program in studying and treating a group of hyperactive patients. They found that dietary changes plus nutritional supplements helped all the children in their study. Included in their treatment program were large doses of vitamin C and the B complex vitamins.[13,14]

Another scientific study by Harrell and associates reported increases in the IQ of sixteen retarded children who were given nutritional supplements. This study group of children were given large doses of C and B complex vitamins plus other vitamins, minerals and small amounts of natural thyroid extract.[15]

In spite of a good diet plus supplements, your child may still show a deficiency of one or more vitamins. Such a deficiency might be caused by diminished absorption, which may be present in the child with food allergy or a yeast-related health problem. Children with chronic health problems, including behavior problems, are apt to be deficient in vitamins A, B_{12}, folic acid, niacin and thiamine.[16] In evaluating a child's nutritional status, I sometimes order a blood test to determine blood-vitamin levels. For about $150, Vitamin Diagnostics, Inc., c/o Herman Baker, Route 35 and Industrial Drive, Cliffwood Beach, NJ 07735, will analyze a blood sample for twelve vitamins.

VITAMIN SUPPLEMENTS

Vitamin A. In his article "Using Vitamin A Safely," Donald R. Davis, Ph.D., of the University of Texas, had this to say: "Vitamin A toxicity must rank as one of the most minor public health and nutritional problems. An average of five or fewer cases of hypervitaminosis A have been reported annually in the United States."[17]

Davis further stated that, in his opinion, prescription and nonprescription drugs commonly used by Americans cause thousands of times more problems than vitamin A overdosage. Moreover, such so-called vitamin A toxicity cases cleared promptly when doses were lowered. He also pointed out that blood studies show that about 10 percent of the U.S. population has low or deficient serum vitamin A levels.

How much vitamin A can you safely give your child?*

In my own practice, I generally recommend that my pediatric patients take 2500 to 5000 units of supplemental vitamin A, and I occasionally recommend larger doses for a few weeks or months if they're bothered by recurrent respiratory problems, patches of dry, bumpy skin on their arms or legs, and are exposed to environmental pollutants.

Good Sources of Vitamin A

Liver
Eggs
Cheese, butter and milk
Yellow, orange and dark-green vegetables (carrots, broccoli, squash, spinach, pumpkin and sweet potatoes)
Apricots, peaches, strawberries, mangos and papayas

Vitamin B Complex. There are many members of the B vitamin family, including B_1, B_2, B_3, B_6, B_{12}, folic acid and pantothenic acid. These play important roles in many complex biochemical and metabolic reactions in the body. Moreover, they act as a team, although, as we've already discussed, some children may require more of one of these B vitamins than do other children. In working with hyperactive and other hard-to-raise children in my practice, I nearly always recommend more than the minimal daily requirements of the B vitamins and I usually recommend from 10 to 25 mgs of each member of the B complex family.

Good Sources of B Vitamins

Liver
Whole grains
Wheat germ
Brewer's yeast
Dark-green leafy vegetables

*If a blood test shows that he is vitamin A deficient, you may need to give him 10,000 to 20,000 units of vitamin A for a few weeks if so directed by your physician.

Based on experiences of the investigators I've referred to, larger doses may be appropriate in some youngsters if supervised by a physician who is experienced and knowledgeable in orthomolecular medicine.* So there are alternatives to giving a depressed, irritable or overactive person a foreign drug, as for example an "upper" or "downer": brain functions may improve if the proper amounts of natural molecules, including vitamins already present in the brain, are increased or decreased according to the unique requirements of a particular person.

Vitamin C. Dr. Pauling and a California physician, Dr. Robert Cathcart, have stressed the role of large doses of vitamin C in strengthening the immune system and helping people fight infection and enjoy better health.[18,19,20,21]

And in individuals with viral infections they recommend "mega" (huge) doses of vitamin C (5000 mgs to 10,000 mgs or more each day). The precise dose is arrived at using "the bowel tolerance test." Here's a summary of the Pauling-Cathcart recommendations for administering the vitamin C in carrying out the test:

Vitamin C powder (ascorbic acid) is obtained from a pharmacy or health food store. One level teaspoon of the powder, containing 4000 mgs of vitamin C, is added to a glass of water or fruit juice. One or more glasses of the vitamin C mixture is sipped during a twenty-four-hour period. If diarrhea, excessive gas, abdominal pain or other digestive symptoms develop, smaller amounts of the vitamin C mixture should be given. If larger doses of vitamin C are used, the dose should be gradually reduced over a period of several days to lessen the chances of a temporary vitamin C deficiency.

In my own pediatric practice, I've used vitamin C in doses of 1000 to 3000 mgs per day in dozens of my patients with infections. Occasionally I've used even larger doses.

Do such doses help shorten the course of infection? I think they do, and they appear to be perfectly safe—and a lot safer

---

*About fifteen years ago, Linus Pauling coined the word "orthomolecular." *Ortho* means to straighten (e.g., the orthodontist straightens teeth). Pauling used the word *orthomolecular* to convey the idea that many chronic mental disorders could be corrected by "straightening" the concentration of molecules in the brain.

than many other remedies used in treating colds and other viral infections.

Good Sources of Vitamin C

Citrus fruits
Tomatoes
Strawberries
Melons
Green peppers
Potatoes
Dark-green vegetables

Vitamin D. Vitamin D is known as the sunshine vitamin because it's produced when sunlight strikes the skin. Vitamin D is one vitamin that has been subject to overdosage in the past. A vitamin supplement for children should not, except under rare occasions, include more than 400 IU's of vitamin D_3. Moreover, in children who live in parts of the country where they spend a lot of time outdoors in the sun year-round, even smaller amounts may be desirable.

Good Sources of Vitamin D

Sunshine
Milk
Egg yolks
Liver
Tuna and salmon

I usually prescribe supplemental vitamins in combination with minerals. The preparations I use are always free of chemi-

cals, food coloring, sugar, starch and yeast. I also recommend synthetic vitamins because I feel they're identical to natural ones and much cheaper. Most so-called natural vitamins are synthetic and deceptively labeled. However, I prefer natural vitamin E (d-alpha-tocopherol).

The preparations I recommend for my hyperactive hard-to-raise patients contain the recommended daily allowances of vitamins A, D and E, and much larger doses of the water-soluble B vitamins, usually 10 to 25 mg (or more) of B_1, B_2, B_3, B_6 and pantothenic acid, and 25 to 50 mcg of vitamins B_{12}, plus 300 to 1500 mg of vitamin C. For convenience' sake, I usually prescribe or recommend a vitamin preparation that also contains minerals (in daily amounts of 10 to 15 mg zinc, 50 to 100 mcg chromium, 5 to 10 mg manganese, 50 to 200 mcg selenium).

Preparations I recommend include: Vital Life's vitamin and mineral preparation (this product is available from Vital Life Company, P.O. Box 618, Carlsbad, CA 92008); Basic Preventive Junior (this chewable supplement is available from Professional Nutritional Products, P.O. Box 31, Trout Dale, VA 24378); or Super Nu-Thera Nutrient Powder (this preparation is available from Kirkman Laboratories, P.O. Box 39289, Portland, OR 97208).

You may also use comparable vitamin and mineral preparations manufactured and distributed by other companies, including:

Bob's Discount Pharmacy, 2800 South 18th Street, Birmingham, AL 35209; Bronson Pharmaceuticals, 4526 Rinetti Lane, La Canada, CA 91011-0628; Freeda Vitamins, Inc., 38 East 41st Street, New York, NY 10017; Nutri-Cology, Inc., 400 Preda Street, San Leandro, CA 94577; and Willner Chemists, Inc., 330 Lexington Avenue, New York, NY 10016.

SAFETY

In discussing nutritional supplements and their safety Jeffrey Bland, Ph.D., a nutritional biochemist and authority on nutrition education, commented:

Recently John Hathcock of Ohio State University, a member of the Food and Nutrition Board that established the 1980 recommended daily allowance (RDA), evaluated the safety of vitamin supplements for children. It would appear that the safety factor for the vitamins range anywhere between ten times the RDA for vitamin A to as high as 1000 times the RDA for vitamin C.

The range of safety is quite large and I feel that parents can, with confidence, give children larger than the RDA using the ranges that Hathcock has established.[22]

When supplements are prescribed by a knowledgeable physician, the amounts may vary widely from what I've outlined in this chapter. And his experience, expertise and clinical judgment will override my recommendations.

Finding such a professional isn't always easy, and vitamin supplements (like food allergies and yeast toxicity) continue to be ignored or rejected by many professionals. Nutritional supplements are rapidly gaining credibility and respectability. Robert A. Good, M.D., Ph.D., chairman of the department of pediatrics at the University of South Florida, commented recently, "An explosion of new information shows that the proper combination of nutrients . . . will help fortify the body's immune system and help in fighting disease."[23]

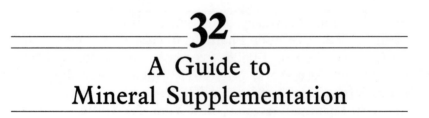

32

A Guide to Mineral Supplementation

If you want to help your hard-to-raise child, you must make sure that he receives an adequate supply of many different nutrients. Minerals, like vitamins, help his brain and other parts of his body function properly.

Calcium. First, I'd like to talk about the familiar mineral calcium—the most plentiful mineral in your child's body. Calcium plays a part in blood clotting, formation of bones and teeth, wound healing and normal cell function. Since your child's body is made of cells, calcium is needed everywhere in his body. If your child doesn't receive enough calcium, he may experience tooth decay, irritability, insomnia, poor posture, muscle cramps, retarded growth and many other symptoms.

Diets that are loaded with hamburgers, sweets, potato chips, soft drinks and french fries leave little room for an adequate intake of calcium-rich foods.

GOOD CALCIUM SOURCES

Milk, cheese, yogurt
Green leafy vegetables
Sardines
Citrus fruits
Dried peas and beans
Nuts and seeds
Whole grains

Although cow's milk, yogurt, cheese and other dairy products furnish significant amounts of calcium, many children dislike milk and others develop adverse reactions when they drink milk. Unless a child takes in a lot of dairy products, greens or sardines, chances are he isn't getting enough calcium.

The usual child needs 500 to 1000 mg of calcium a day. It's available in many different forms, including calcium carbonate, calcium gluconate and calcium lactate. Calcium is often combined with other nutritional supplements including magnesium and other minerals and vitamins.

Magnesium. Overconsumption of phosphorus and phosphate-containing foods may lead to a magnesium deficiency. Beef is especially high in phosphorus. So are food preservatives and soft drinks. Saturated and hardened fats also contribute to magnesium loss. Also, soft water (prevalent in many parts of the country, including the Mississippi and Ohio river valleys) contains less calcium and magnesium than hard water.

Another reason why people become magnesium-deficient

is because of chronic yeast infection. According to Leo Galland, M.D., "Many *Candida* patients seem to develop their nutritional problems after exposure to antibiotics. Some behave like magnesium sieves."[1]

In assessing magnesium status, laboratory tests don't help much. So we base our diagnosis on the history, a deficient diet, plus other symptoms including fatigability, muscle cramps, irritability, poor concentration and depression. Although food allergy, a chronic yeast problem, calcium deficiencies and vitamin deficiencies may contribute to some of these symptoms, when these symptoms are prominent I always consider the possibility of a coexisting magnesium deficiency.

This deficiency (and an associated calcium deficiency) can be evaluated by doing what we call Cvostek's test. You can look for a positive Cvostek's sign in your child rather simply. All you have to do is to tap lightly in the hollow of his cheek, halfway between the bottom of his ear and the corner of his mouth. If the top of his lip beneath his nose twitches, grimaces or jumps, the test is considered to be "positive" and usually indicates a magnesium deficiency.

A positive Cvostek's sign seems to be seen more often in people who live in industrialized societies and especially in people with chronic allergic problems.

GOOD SOURCES OF MAGNESIUM

Whole grains
Nuts and seeds
Beans
Sea foods
Fresh vegetables and fruits
    (especially melons, oranges and bananas)

Many magnesium preparations are available, including magnesium oxide, which is readily available and inexpensive. Because calcium and magnesium deficiencies are often combined with vitamin and mineral deficiencies, I usually prescribe a multivitamin-mineral supplement containing magnesium. The magnesium requirement is 3 mg per pound or about 150 mg per day for a fifty pound child. Some children require even more magnesium. I do not recommend dolomite and bone meal supplements containing magnesium because they may be contaminated with lead and other toxic minerals. Too much magnesium can cause diarrhea, which limits absorption. If this happens, you can reduce the dose. Also, if your child develops muscle cramps while taking magnesium and they haven't been present before, he may need less magnesium and more calcium.

Sodium and potassium. These minerals are found in such large quantities in so many foods that it is rarely necessary to supplement your child's diet with either of them. Sodium (as you probably know) is found in ordinary table salt and it's added to so many foods I worry about too much sodium rather than too little. Since a high sodium intake plays a role in causing high blood pressure, go easy on the salt shaker—especially if heart and blood vessel disease runs in your family.

Potassium and sodium have what might be called a "seesaw" relationship. When too much sodium is taken in, your child's body tends to lose potassium. To maintain normal potassium levels offer your child good foods, especially fruits, and limit his salt intake, except in hot weather.

TRACE MINERALS

Your body needs some minerals in such tiny amounts that we call them "trace minerals." You may be surprised when you read the list of these minerals, which you're more apt to associate with bulldozers and mine shafts than with human nutrition. These trace minerals include chromium, zinc, selenium, copper, cobalt, manganese, molybdenum and silicon. Trace elements resemble supporting actors in a theatrical production who play small but vital roles.

Not long ago, scientists thought many of these minerals acted as poisons. Now, research has proved them to be essential and valuable, but—in excess quantities—dangerous.

Here are examples of how unbelievably small our requirements are for two trace minerals, chromium and cobalt: The estimated typical daily intake of chromium is 200 micrograms. A microgram is one millionth of a gram and it takes thirty grams to make an ounce! The daily need for cobalt, a constituent of vitamin B_{12}, is between 100 and 150 *nanograms*. A nanogram is one billionth of a gram!

These different trace elements interact within your child's body. For example, copper and zinc compete, and if he absorbs too much zinc, he'll develop a copper deficiency. Zinc also interacts with manganese and iron. And arsenic, that classic poison, may help his body use and absorb zinc.

Zinc. According to Michael Hambidge, M.D., of the University of Colorado, and other researchers, many children lack sufficient zinc. Moreover, Hambidge's studies show that zinc-deficient children tend to have impaired taste, poor appetites, slow growth and impaired resistance to infection.[2]

GOOD ZINC SOURCES

Milk
Liver
Shellfish
Wheat germ

Chromium. Hambidge and his co-workers also found that the concentration of chromium in the hair of juvenile diabetics was much lower than in children who don't have diabetes.[3] Other researchers have noted the importance of chromium in glucose and carbohydrate metabolism.

GOOD CHROMIUM SOURCES*

Brewer's yeast
Meat products
Cheese
Whole grains

Iron. As you know, iron is needed to keep your child from developing one type of anemia. It combines with protein and copper to form hemoglobin. It also helps supply oxygen to muscles and is involved in protein metabolism. Iron also keeps lead from being absorbed into the blood and helps eliminate lead from the body. Symptoms of iron deficiency include anemia, constipation, fatigue, muscle weakness and memory impairment.

GOOD SOURCES OF IRON

Liver and other organ meats
Lean meats
Legumes
Whole grains
Eggs
Green leafy vegetables
Shellfish

Children require 10 to 20 mg of elemental iron a day and iron is often included in the vitamin and mineral preparations I prescribe.

Selenium. This mineral plays an important role in many metabolic processes, especially in strengthening the immune

*If a child is allergic to yeast and is on a yeast-free diet, I recommend a chromium supplement (100 to 150 mcg daily).

system and in combatting what has been described as "free radical pathology."

Jeffrey Bland, Ph.D., pointed out recently that although we need oxygen to survive, oxygen through its active molecular forms (such as peroxides, superoxides, hydroxyl radical and excited state oxygen) can initiate what are known as "free radical reactions."[4]

Although many free radical chemical reactions occur normally in the body and are necessary for health, other reactions appear to damage tissues. Substances which protect the body from free radicals are called free radical scavengers, or antioxidants. In addition to selenium, these include vitamin C, vitamin E, beta-carotene and glutathione.

GOOD SOURCES OF SELENIUM

Whole grains
Seafood
Nutritional yeast
Wheat germ
Broccoli
Cabbage
Tomatoes
Garlic
Liver
Eggs

In prescribing selenium supplements, I generally recommend 50 to 75 mcg per day. Selenium supplements (derived from yeast) are available in tablets. A nonyeast derived, liquid form, sodium selenite, is made by Nutri-Cology, Inc., 400 Preda Street, San Leandro, CA 94577. A few sensitive patients react adversely to moderate doses of 25 to 200 mcg. The liquid selenium can be given by the drop (about 2 micrograms per drop) and gradually increased as tolerated.

Manganese. Manganese is needed for many different functions in the body, including proper functioning of the nervous system and the immune system. Symptoms of manganese deficiency include hyperactivity, incoordination, growth disturbances and digestive disturbances.

GOOD SOURCES OF MANGANESE

Peas, beans
Nuts
Liver
Bananas
Spinach
Sweet potatoes
Brown rice and other whole grains

MEASURING TRACE MINERALS

Your child's trace elements can be measured using blood, urine, hair, sweat and tissue samples. Each method has strengths and weaknesses. Blood shows the status of trace elements only at the time the blood is drawn. Urine shows what your child's body is excreting, not what is stored. Tissue biopsies are rarely practical. Sweat studies appear interesting but are not yet widely available. While hair analyses aren't perfect, they're cheap and easily obtained.

So you should consider asking your doctor to order a hair analysis as long as you don't get too carried away with the findings.* Recently, Elmer Cranton, M.D., hair mineral analysis expert, commented:

A careful review of the published scientific literature indicates that there are only ten elements that have been proven by two or more research studies to be clinically significant in hair: cal-

*Physicians interested in carrying out such studies can obtain further information from Doctors Data, 30 West 101 Roosevelt Road, West Chicago, IL 60185; MineraLab, Inc., P.O. Box 5012, Hayward, CA 94540; Omega Tech Laboratory, P.O. Box 1, Trout Dale, VA 24378.

cium, magnesium, zinc, copper, chromium, nickel, arsenic, lead, mercury and cadmium.[5]

     Properly interpreted hair studies may provide information about your child's toxic mineral levels, especially lead, cadmium, copper, aluminum and mercury levels. (See also pages 200–206.)

Hair analysis also helps identify individuals who consistently eat foods that lack needed "good minerals," especially zinc. Hair analysis may also provide useful information about other essential minerals, including chromium and selenium. Blood and urine studies can be used to confirm abnormal levels.

However, reported hair levels for sodium, potassium, phosphorus, iron and other "good minerals" are probably not accurate, due to a variety of factors. Hair calcium and magnesium results may be unreliable or misleading. If your child's hair analysis shows low levels for five or more minerals, he may not be absorbing the minerals he takes in. Causes of such problems include insufficient stomach acid or pancreatic enzymes, food allergy and thyroid deficiency.

Since interpreting hair analysis is complicated, find an experienced professional to help you.

In summary, Jeffrey Bland, Ph.D., commented:

> As we learn more about the important role that these trace elements play in human health it becomes obvious that there is a great need for sensitive, convenient, and inexpensive methods for screening patients for their trace element status.[6]

I feel that hair testing gives me a convenient and reasonably inexpensive way of studying the mineral status in my patients, especially of toxic minerals. Yet I will admit that it isn't a panacea that gives me perfect answers.

Would you like to learn more about trace minerals, including both the good ones (like zinc and chromium) and the bad ones (like cadmium)? Then go to your library and check out copies of the easy-to-read books by the late Henry Schroeder, M.D., Ph.D.[7,8] Dr. Schroeder served as head of the Trace Element Laboratory of Dartmouth College for many years. And along with Walter Mertz and other trace element researchers, Dr. Schroeder points out that cardiovascular disease, cancer, diabetes and other chronic diseases may be connected to as yet undiscovered trace element imbalances.

Minerals, like vitamins, essential fatty acids, complex carbohydrates and essential amino acids, are needed to make your child's brain and body function properly. He can best obtain them by eating a wide variety of good foods. But just as with vitamins, I recommend an "insurance policy": a mineral-containing supplement.

33

Toxic Minerals

LEAD

The air, soil and water of our planet have been polluted with lead. Today, any American child can suffer from lead toxicity. In an article in the July 24, 1981, issue of *The Wall Street Journal,* staff reporter Nancy Nusser had this to say:

> Long perceived as a peril facing only ghetto dwellers, lead poisoning has started turning up in the homes of the affluent. . . .
> A Washington couple, who live in a posh section of Capitol Hill, found that their normally agreeable three-year-old had suddenly turned cantankerous, a symptom of lead poisoning. The child had swallowed enough toxin from sucking on a lead-painted gate to cause slight learning disabilities.[1]

In another report, in the May 27, 1982, *Wall Street Journal*, Michael Waldholz wrote:

> More than a decade after lead poisoning was first recognized as a major childhood health problem, it appears to be more widespread, more serious and more difficult to prevent and treat than anyone first suspected.
>
> While few lives are lost to lead poisoning . . . the study, by the National Center for Health Statistics, found "at least 50% more" children than expected with chronically high lead levels. . . . The big casualty: mental capacities.
>
> "Lead won't kill these kids," says Devra Lee Davis, Director of the Environmental Law Institute in Washington. "It will make them a little dumber, make life a little harder. And for many of them, life's already tough. Elevated levels of lead just drains the quality of their lives."[2]

Lead toxicity can cause headaches, vomiting, fatigue and behavioral problems such as hyperactivity and shortened attention span, as well as more serious health problems.

Too much lead in the body also affects learning. Herbert L. Needleman, M.D., and associates at the Children's Hospital and Medical Center in Boston, studied two groups of children. Fifty-eight were found to have relatively high lead levels in the dentine of their teeth, while one hundred had lower dentine lead levels. The children with higher lead levels scored significantly lower on the Wechsler Intelligence Test for Children-Revised (WISC-R) than those with low lead levels.[3]

In another study Rhonda Folio, Ed.D., Ph.D., Mike Marlowe, Ph.D., and other researchers analyzed hair samples from a group of children with developmental problems. They found that a group of mentally retarded children (cause unknown) had significantly elevated hair levels as compared to a nonretarded group.[4]

In yet another study, by Arthur Sohler, Ph.D., Marcus Kruesi, B.S., and Carl Pfeiffer, M.D., Ph.D., one thousand psychiatric outpatients were evaluated for lead levels. In their discussion, these researchers said that lead appears to be more easily absorbed in children and is retained to a greater degree.

They believe that in hyperactive children lead levels (in the blood) of 25 mcg percent may be suspected of causing psychiatric symptoms.[5]

Notwithstanding the observations of these researchers, none of the thirty hair tests I've obtained on my hyperactive patients have indicated abnormal lead levels. However, the effects of lead toxicity are so devastating I'll continue to look for it—especially as it's reversible if found in time.

To learn more about treating children with lead toxicity, I asked Sidney Baker, M.D., of the Gesell Institute, how he treats patients with abnormal levels of lead and other toxic minerals. In responding, Dr. Baker said:

> I first "clean up the diet." In doing this, I recommend a broad variety of foods obtained from different sources. Ideally, such foods should be grown on good soil, uncontaminated with insecticides, industrial chemicals or "fall-out" from automobile exhaust. Also, the soil should have been fertilized by natural or organic substances, including compost, animal manure and other natural substances.
>
> In my pediatric patients with higher than normal levels of lead, and who do not require immediate treatment with drugs, I also recommend the following nutritional supplements:
>
> a. Elemental zinc, 60 mg a day (especially important in those with high hair copper and low serum zinc or other measures of zinc deficiency)
>
> b. Calcium, 1 to 1½ grams daily (1000–1500 mg)
>
> c. Magnesium, 500 mg daily
>
> d. Selenium, 100 mcg daily
>
> e. Vitamin B[6], 200 mg daily
>
> f. Vitamin C, 4000 to 5000 mg daily (in the adult patient). Children may take a little less or they may be able to take this same dose. If more vitamin C is taken than can be tolerated, it will generally cause loose stools.
>
> All of these nutrients help the body unload and get rid of some of the toxic minerals.[6]

In a leaflet entitled "What Every Parent Should Know About Lead???" distributed by Tennessee Technological University (TTI) the following sources of lead are cited:

Leaded gas	Fertilizers
Newsprint and colored ads	Tobacco smoke
Certain pottery	Certain cosmetics
Lead pipes	Polluted air,
Hair dyes	water, dust and dirt
Leaded glass	Lead-based paint
Pewterware	Some pencils
Pesticides	Certain plastics
	Some toothpaste tubes

Lead exposure (from paint chips, newspapers and comic books printed with red or other inks containing lead) can be especially hazardous to a child who sucks his thumb or keeps his fingers in his mouth.[7]

Here are suggestions for reducing your child's exposure to lead (adapted from the TTI leaflet):

1. Get rid of the lead sources around your house and yard. Or keep your child away from them.
2. If you live in an industrial area, vacuum your home frequently to lessen your child's exposure to lead-containing dust.
3. Keep your child indoors during peak traffic hours— especially if you live near a heavily traveled street or road.
4. Watch your child's "hand or mouth" activities. Make sure he washes his hands before eating—especially after looking at colored funny books or magazines.
5. Carefully wash or peel apples, oranges and other fruits and vegetables that have been exposed to pesticides, weed killers and other chemicals.
6. Keep your child indoors during crop dusting or spraying operations.
7. Provide your child with a good diet containing a balanced group of minerals. (Good minerals including calcium, magnesium and zinc help crowd out lead and other toxic minerals.)
8. Don't let your child play around abandoned housing, dump sites or a commercial dump.
9. Take a look at your child's toys and hobbies. Throw out

fish sinkers, gunshell casings, metal toy soldiers or old cans that are probably lead contaminated.

CADMIUM

According to the late Henry Schroeder, M.D., most Americans are taking on a heavier load of cadmium, a toxic mineral. Schroeder pointed out that body levels of cadmium and zinc are related. When a person takes too much cadmium into his body, it depresses zinc levels.[8]

Moreover, in carrying out hair tests on hyperactive children in my own practice, I've found elevated cadmium levels in several youngsters. Sources of cadmium include cigarette smoke, water from galvanized pipes, paint pigments, evaporated milk and the fumes from rubber tires.

During the fall of 1983, I visited Ellen Grant, M.D., a British physician who has carried out a number of studies on children and adults with migraine, food sensitivities and other disorders caused by environmental substances. In our conversation, Dr. Grant commented:

> Some British investigators studied a group of hyperactive children and they found abnormally high hair cadmium levels in many of the children. Moreover, high levels of toxic metals are often found in children who are deficient in zinc.[9]

COPPER

Carl Pfeiffer, M.D., Ph.D., of the Brain-Bio Center in Princeton, New Jersey, has long been interested in the role of excessive copper in contributing to nervous system problems. Discussing this subject with me a few years ago, Dr. Pfeiffer commented:

> In my opinion, many Americans are taking in too much copper. Studies show that excessive amounts of this metal may contribute to hyperactive behavior in children and schizophrenia in adults. Moreover, zinc and copper are closely interrelated.

When your body takes in too much copper, it drives the zinc down (and vice versa).[10]

More recently, Dr. Pfeiffer reported:

We find high levels of copper and lead in hyperactive children . . . in agreement with reports by many other investigators. A high copper intake increases lead toxicity so children exposed to both lead and copper suffer a double whammy—or even triple—when one considers that zinc deficiency is also rampant in the lower socioeconomic groups where high blood lead is common.[11]

Copper toxicity can cause all kinds of symptoms, from fatigue, irritability and joint pain, to behavior problems, learning disabilities and mental diseases.

During the last decade I've seen several patients whose hair copper level was elevated. After ruling out hair contamination from external sources (shampoos, swimming pools), I gave parents the following instructions:

1. Check at home and see if you have copper pipes.
2. If the water pipes in your house are made from copper, flush them for two minutes each morning before drinking the water or brushing your teeth with it.
3. Don't use copper-lined pots, pans or other vessels for cooking and storing food.
4. Drink bottled mineral water or have a water filter installed in the kitchen of your home so that the water used for drinking, cooking and making ice cubes is uncontaminated.
5. Avoid nutritional supplements containing copper.

I also suggest children with high hair copper levels follow the nutritional program outlined by Dr. Baker. This program features a good diet and nutritional supplements including zinc, which helps to "drive abnormal amounts of copper from the body."

MERCURY

The finding of high hair mercury concerns me. In patients with high hair mercury levels, I feel that a second hair test, carried out by a different laboratory, following careful washing and rinsing of the hair, is indicated. Moreover, I also ask the patient to use a simple soap, such as Ivory, in washing hair for several weeks prior to carrying out the second hair test. Ideally, the hair should be washed in spring water or filtered water.

If a second hair analysis also shows an elevated mercury level, I recommend a good nutritional program (good diet and supplemental vitamins and minerals). I also consider the possibility of mercury pollution from industrial sources or from eating fish from mercury-contaminated waters.

Recently, a number of dentists and other professionals have reported mercury toxicity from silver amalgam fillings. These fillings contain more mercury than silver. Traditionally, silver fillings were thought to be inert once set in the teeth. Since saliva is an electrolyte capable of conducting a weak electrical current, these dentists report that the mercury leaches out of silver fillings causing a wide variety of mental and physical symptoms.[12,13,14]

If your child's hair mercury is elevated and if his symptoms started after mercury-amalgam fillings were put in, removal of these fillings and replacement with other materials should be considered.[15]

ALUMINUM

I've read several articles about aluminum and its possible role in causing Alzheimer's disease and other types of brain damage. A number of the hair samples I've obtained showed elevated aluminum levels. Dr. Pfeiffer recently reports finding "elevated hair aluminum in a group of hyperactive boys and in a group with behavioral disorders or learning disabilities."[16]

Although physicians disagree on the importance of the

aluminum factor, I feel that reducing aluminum intake makes sense. So I tell my patients to avoid the following:

1. Aluminum cookware
2. Beverages in aluminum cans
3. Wrapping food in aluminum foil
4. Commercial baked goods that may be prepared with aluminum-containing baking powder
5. Aluminum-containing personal products, including deodorants, dentifrices and antacids

In discussing toxic metals, Dr. Pfeiffer recently commented, "The roles of lead, copper and aluminum in childhood disorders such as hyperactivity and other behavioral and learning problems warrant routine assay in every disabled child."[17]

I agree with Dr. Pfeiffer. Identifying and treating a toxic mineral problem in your hard-to-raise child could solve a significant piece in his puzzle.

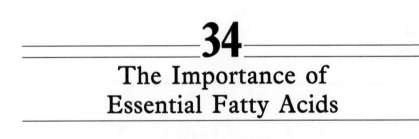

34

The Importance of Essential Fatty Acids

If you read your newspaper or look at TV, you've probably realized that you and most other Americans have been consuming too much fat—especially the saturated fats found in fatty meats, butter, whole milk, lard and coconut oil. It's hard to cut down on these fats unless you start baking, steaming, roasting and broiling your foods and begin eating more fish and chicken and less bacon, hamburger and pork products. Even when you eat low-fat chicken and fish in fast-food restaurants you may take in more fat than you get in hamburgers.

In addition to saturated fats you're also consuming a type of processed fat which is found in many commercial foods including margarine, Campbell's cream of celery soup, Triscuits, Wheat Thins, Zesta saltines and hundreds of other foods you find on your supermarket shelf. The fat I'm talking about is a bad fat and is described as hydrogenated or partially hydrogenated vegetable oil.

Hydrogenated or partially hydrogenated refers to the adding of hydrogen molecules to a fatty acid so as to make it more stable and less apt to break down. This chemical procedure is used to prolong the shelf life of many foods. Yet at the same time hydrogenation lessens your body's ability to handle fats.

Fats of all kinds contain over twice as many calories as proteins or carbohydrates (one ounce of fat contains 270 calories; one ounce of protein or carbohydrate contains 120 calories). Accordingly, a high-fat diet promotes excessive weight gain. In addition, many recent studies show that diets high in saturated fats result in abnormally high levels of cholesterol and triglycerides in the blood. Individuals on high-fat diets have now been shown to be more likely to develop heart disease, strokes, gallstones, diabetes and cancer.

With all of this publicity about the harm that fats do, along with most physicians I wasn't aware until recently that there are good fats as well as bad fats. Most Americans need a lot more good fats than they're getting. These good fats contain essential fatty acids (EFA's) and they cannot be manufactured by your body. Such fats are found abundantly in northern fish oils (salmon, cod, sardine and halibut) and in unrefined nut, seed and plant oils, including especially safflower, linseed, walnut, soy, olive and primrose oils.

New clinical and research studies by Donald Rudin, M.D.,[1,2,3] David Horrobin, M.D.,[4,5] and others show that deficiencies and imbalances of these EFA's may cause or contribute to many health problems, including schizophrenia, alcoholism, arteriosclerosis, arthritis, premenstrual tension, allergies and hyperactivity. Moreover, recent scientific studies by C. Orian

Truss, M.D., Sidney Baker, M.D., and Leo Galland, M.D., show that patients with yeast-related illness also show abnormalities in their fatty acids.[6,7]

FATTY ACID DEFICIENCIES AND CHRONIC HEALTH DISORDERS

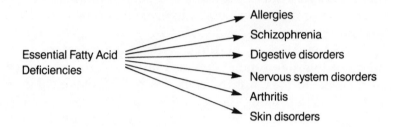

Essential Fatty Acid Deficiencies
- Allergies
- Schizophrenia
- Digestive disorders
- Nervous system disorders
- Arthritis
- Skin disorders

When you first start learning about fatty acids and how they work, you may be confused by a lot of big, unfamiliar terms. While there are many different types of fatty acids, only two, linoleic acid (LA) and alpha-linolenic acid (LNA), are considered *essential fatty acids* (EFA's). *Your child must consume these substances in his diet or take them in supplements because his body can't manufacture them.*

In your child's body, EFA's perform two critically important roles. *First,* they form the building blocks of the cell membrane that controls the flow of nutrients and wastes into and out of each cell.

Secondly, your child's body manufactures prostaglandins (PG's) from EFA's. Prostaglandins regulate many vital bodily functions. Although scientists first isolated PG's in the prostate gland (hence the name), these powerful chemicals are found in every body cell. Certain PG's play an important role in protecting you against heart disease, cancer, menstrual pain, arthritis and allergies.

In the last ten years prostaglandin research has blossomed. Some scientists predict that the impact of PG's in clinical medicine in the next decade will approach that of antibiotics thirty years ago.[8]

When we look at the chemistry of these EFA's, we find they are what we call "long-chain" polyunsaturated fatty acids.

They're composed of a string of eighteen to twenty carbon atoms . . . sort of like a string of pearls. Most of these "pearls" are linked by a single link, but two to six of them are hooked together by what we call "double bonds."

There are two series or families of EFA's, the "omega-6" EFA's, starting with linoleic acid (LA) and the "omega-3" EFA's, starting with alpha-linolenic acid (LNA). Your child's body uses these two EFA's to manufacture different PG series. So the two EFA families are not interchangeable.

EFA FAMILIES

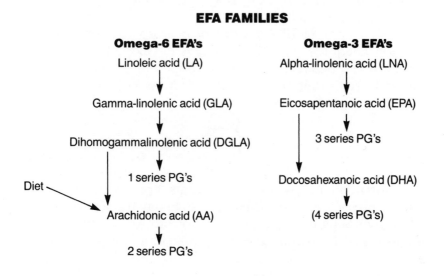

Omega-6 EFA's

Linoleic acid (LA)

↓

Gamma-linolenic acid (GLA)

↓

Dihomogammalinolenic acid (DGLA)

1 series PG's

Diet

↓

Arachidonic acid (AA)

↓

2 series PG's

Omega-3 EFA's

Alpha-linolenic acid (LNA)

↓

Eicosapentanoic acid (EPA)

↓

3 series PG's

Docosahexanoic acid (DHA)

↓

(4 series PG's)

OMEGA-3 OILS

Omega-3 alpha-linolenic acid (LNA) is found in linseed oil and in lesser quantities in soy, walnut and wheat germ oils. Salmon and other northern fish oils are rich sources of longer-chained omega-3 EFA's. Fish oils can also be purchased in concentrated capsules sold under several brand names, including MaxEPA.

Donald Rudin, M.D., an authority on EFA metabolism, concludes, "We have been systematically and selectively depleting the dietary availability of w-3-EFA (omega-3) by an estimated 80-90% during the past 50 years."[9] Dr. Rudin hypothesizes that modern food-processing and the overuse of omega-6 oils (corn, safflower, peanut and sunflower) have led to omega-3 EFA deficiency diseases characterized by mental, skin, immune or digestive symptoms.

Scientists have produced similar symptoms in laboratory animals. Six monkeys were reared on a standard laboratory diet. Corn oil (which contains almost no omega-3 EFA's) was the only source of EFA's. Instead of prospering on this supposedly adequate diet, the monkeys developed skin, bowel, immune and behavioral disorders. Supplements of linseed oil added to their diet corrected these illnesses.[10]

Nutritionally aware professionals are recognizing the effects of EFA's on our health and behavior. For example, Alexander Schauss, Ph.D., director of the American Institute for Biosocial Research, relates the case of a fourteen-year-old truant who responded dramatically to linseed oil when all other measures had failed:

> Tom was referred to our Institute for severe anti-social behavior. Both his parents and his school reported that Tom was "incorrigible, unmanageable, disrespectful, unmotivated, bored with everything, constantly eating junk food, and driving us nuts." Tom had been hospitalized on several psychiatric wards at a cost of over $11,000. Since he'd already appeared several times in juvenile court, his parents were very concerned he would soon find himself in a correctional institution.
>
> Although Tom had been studied extensively by psychiatrists and had undergone many medical tests, little attention had been given to his diet or metabolic state. We administered tests that showed several significant vitamin deficiencies. But Tom did not improve on vitamin supplements and a nutritious diet.

Finally, 3 tablespoons of linseed oil were added to Tom's daily supplements. Within 3 weeks, Tom had improved and continued to make excellent progress, returning to normal classrooms at school, making friends, and behaving appropriately at home.

Today Tom is a senior in high school with B and C grades. If you met him you would not for a second believe that he was considered destined to go to prison and "the worst behavior problem in his school system's history over at least 50 years" when we first saw him.[11]

OMEGA-6 OILS

Corn, safflower, sunflower oil and other oils from plants grown in warm climates contain significant amounts of linoleic acid (LA).

Reporting in *Update,* Leo Galland, M.D., relates the dramatic response of Jay, a twelve-year-old boy diagnosed as hyperactive who had been taking Ritalin for eight years.

Jay is allergic to many foods and showed two hallmarks of EFA deficiency: excessive thirst and dry skin. When his diet was enriched with raw safflower oil and his sugar intake reduced, his thirst promptly decreased, he became calmer, and was able to discontinue Ritalin.[12]

Some individuals lack the enzyme that converts LA into the next omega-6 family member, gamma-linolenic acid (GLA). Giving oil pressed from seeds of the evening primrose plant,* the only readily available source of GLA, bypasses this enzyme. Primrose oil is sold under several brand names in

*Primrose oil in high doses (twelve capsules per day) has made patients with temporal lobe epilepsy worse.

health food stores and pharmacies. Genuine primrose oil is expensive and the label should state "Efamol." Otherwise, the capsules may not contain GLA.

David Horrobin, M.D., of Nova Scotia, has directed many research projects using evening primrose oil. Dr. Horrobin commented to me in 1981, "Hyperactive children with clear-cut evidence of eczema, asthma and other associated allergic disorders are more apt to respond to EFA's than those who aren't bothered by such allergies."[13]

One study in England involved hyperactive children whose parents belonged to a hyperactive children's support group. In testing the idea that EFA supplements might help, the investigators gave twenty-five children two or three grams per day of primrose oil (four to six capsules, half in the morning and half in the evening). Half the children given the EFA supplement improved, some dramatically. For some children, this was given orally; for others, it was rubbed into the skin.

According to their report:

> A six-year-old boy with a characteristic history of hyperactivity, severely disturbed sleep and disruptive behavior at home and at school . . . was threatened with expulsion from school because of his impossible behaviour. . . . Three capsules (of the primrose oil) were cut open and the oil was rubbed into the skin morning and evening.
>
> The school was unaware of this, but after five days the teacher telephoned the mother and said that never in 30 years of teaching had she seen such a dramatic change in a child's behaviour. After three weeks the evening primrose oil was stopped and one week later the school again complained. The oil was then reintroduced with good effect.[14]

In an essay entitled "Fat Is Not Just to Hold Your Pants Up," Sidney Baker, M.D., had this to say:

> Too much of the wrong kind (of fat) is bad—but too little of the right kind is just as bad. In no other area of nutrition is the adage "you are what you eat" more true. . . . The key to the whole issue is that oils are not just the "padding" of your body, but are the structural core of the wall of each of the body's cells and the raw material for crucial hormones.[15]

So if you want your hard-to-raise child to look sharp, feel sharp and act sharp, and to enjoy good health, make sure that he gets adequate, balanced amounts of both omega-3 and omega-6 oils.

35

Your Child May Need "Oiling"!

DEFICIENCY SYMPTOMS

Your child may need more essential fatty acids (EFA's) in his diet (or as supplements) if he shows any of the following symptoms:

—Excessive thirst or insatiable appetite
—Dry, flaking skin; "chicken skin"—bumps on backs of arms, thighs or cheeks; calluses
—Brittle, soft or splitting fingernails

—Eczema
—Dry, unmanageable hair; dandruff
—Excessive or hard earwax; dry scaling in outer ear canal
—Asthma
—Multiple allergies

Your child may develop an EFA deficiency if:

—He doesn't eat enough foods rich in EFA's.
—His body doesn't produce enough of the enzyme needed to process EFA's.
—He isn't getting sufficient amounts of the co-factors (B vitamins, vitamin E, zinc, magnesium) that help his body convert one EFA to another.
—He eats margarine, crackers and other foods (especially snack foods) that contain hydrogenated or partially hydrogenated vegetable oils. Hydrogenation extends the shelf life of oils but *destroys* EFA's or distorts their molecular shape.

—He eats too much white flour and other processed foods. (Refining flour removes dietary fiber, vitamins and wheat germ increasing his need for EFA's.)
—He eats too much sugar, which increases his need for EFA's.

—He suffers from a chronic yeast infection, which may disturb his fat metabolism.

GUIDELINES FOR SUPPLEMENTING EFA'S*

If your hard-to-raise child shows signs of EFA deficiency, he may need to take oils rich in omega-3 EFA's or omega-6 EFA's or both. Without expensive, hard-to-interpret blood tests,† trial and error is your best way to determine which oils your child needs.

Keep in mind that giving the "wrong" oil or not giving the amount *your* child needs (either too much or too little) may temporarily aggravate his symptoms. Here's one way to proceed:

1. Purchase evening primrose oil capsules from your health food store. Begin with one capsule each day. At three-day intervals add another capsule up to a maximum dose of

---

*According to Dr. Rudin, EFA's sometimes enhance the action of drugs and megavitamins. As a result, side effects may occur. Reducing or stopping the drugs and megavitamins (with your physician's guidance) will usually relieve symptoms.
†Monroe Medical Research Laboratory, Route 17, P.O. Box 1, Southfield, NY 10975, telephone 1-800-831-3133, and Meridian Valley Clinical Lab, 24030 132nd S.E., Kent, WA 98042, telephone 1-206-631-8922, analyze plasma and red blood cell phospholipids.

two capsules three times a day. Most hyperactive children need one to three primrose capsules a day.*

Decreased thirst may occur within forty-eight hours of starting primrose oil. This is a good sign. Improvement in skin, food allergies and behavior usually takes from several weeks to several months. If your child improves at a given dose, maintain that dose.

Increased irritability, loss of appetite, acne or diarrhea indicate that your child needs less primrose oil. Reduce his dose.

2. If your child's thirst increases, if his skin gets drier or his behavior deteriorates when you give him primrose oil or safflower oil in any dose, he may need linseed oil instead.

Purchase linseed oil from your health food store. (Linseed oil found at your paint store contains harmful chemicals and should *not* be consumed.)

Start by giving your child one teaspoon of linseed oil each day at breakfast. After several days increase his dose to two teaspoons, then to three teaspoons. A few children need several tablespoons. To figure out your child's dose, evaluate his behavior, skin and thirst.

As I pointed out before, trial and error is the best way to determine which oils and what dose your child needs. Here are further suggestions:

3. Don't use rancid oils. When you open a bottle of linseed or safflower oil, check for a rancid smell or bitter taste. Then squeeze one capsule of 100 to 400 IU of vitamin E into the oil. Turn the bottle slowly several times to disperse the vitamin E, but don't shake it. Refrigerate the oil. Vitamin E and refrigeration help prevent spoiling.

4. If your child won't swallow primrose oil capsules or linseed oil, he'll absorb almost as much if you rub the oil on his skin.

5. Supplements of 25 mg vitamin B complex, 1000 mg vitamin C, 200 IU vitamin E (d-alpha-tocopherol), 5000 IU

---

*Some children will respond as well to safflower oil as they do to primrose oil. Safflower oil is considerably cheaper. Start by giving your child one teaspoon of raw safflower oil each morning at breakfast. If tolerated, gradually increase his dose to one or perhaps two tablespoons. To figure out his best dose, evaluate his behavior, skin symptoms and thirst.

beta-carotene, 3 mg per pound of body weight magnesium, 15 mg zinc and 75 mcg selenium help your child's body process EFA's.

6. Avoid or limit hydrogenated oils, partially hydrogenated oils, margarine, refined flour, processed foods and sugar.

If your child's symptoms are caused by an EFA deficiency, EFA supplements may help, sometimes dramatically. A few children start to respond within hours; others may require several months of EFA supplementation before improvement occurs.

LAURA COMMENTS:

EFA deficiencies were important pieces of "the puzzle" in my children—and other family members. Jack's eczema cleared up on oil of primrose, while Jeff's excessive thirst and dandruff decreased on linseed oil. And both children's irritability improved considerably.

EFA deficiencies may or may not be important pieces in your child's puzzle. *Watch his symptoms carefully and adjust his dose accordingly. Be patient!*

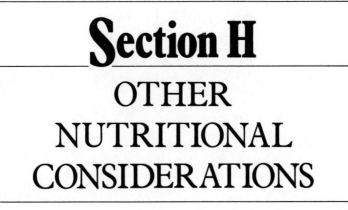

Section H

OTHER NUTRITIONAL CONSIDERATIONS

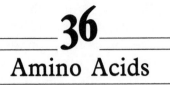

36
Amino Acids

When I was in medical school—a long time ago—like all of my peers, I learned that amino acids serve as the "building blocks" for proteins. Moreover, I memorized a long list of essential amino acids from my biochemistry textbook. Then, during my many years of pediatric practice, from time to time I read articles that discussed the amino acids. Among these were reports that said, "If you eat a good diet including meats, eggs, whole grains, seafoods, vegetables and nuts you'll get all the amino acids you need."

Beginning in the late 1970s and early '80s I read and heard more about amino acids—especially about amino acid deficiencies. Moreover, speakers at several conferences of the Association for Children with Learning Disabilities talked about these deficiencies.

Then seven or eight years ago I met Sidney M. Baker, M.D., of the Gesell Institute. During my conversations with Dr. Baker, he said, "If a child's body and brain are to function the way they should, he has to 'play with a full deck.' To do this *he must seek certain things and avoid others.* And amino acids rank high on the list of substances he needs."[1]

I also learned about the research studies of Jon Pangborn, Ph.D., of Illinois, the father of an autistic child. At a meeting in Winnetka, Illinois, of the Nutrition for Optimal Health Association (NOHA), Pangborn said that many children with autism and other severe behavior and learning problems show abnormalities in their amino acids.[2]

During the past several years I've obtained amino acid studies on a few of my patients. Yet in spite of these studies I often end up with more questions than answers. Nevertheless you may need to know more about amino acids—especially if your hyperactive, learning-disabled child continues to experience problems.

When your child eats meat, fish, eggs, legumes, oats, whole-grain wheat or any other protein-rich foods, his digestive juices and enzymes break the proteins in these foods into smaller units called peptides. Further digestion changes the peptides into even smaller units, the amino acids.

In discussing proteins, Gary Gordon, M.D., recently commented, "When we eat beef from a cow, it has to be broken down—just like taking an old building and taking all the separate bricks and then making it into a brand new building. That's what has to go on in our body."[3]

Your child builds his own proteins by linking amino acids together in various combinations. He needs amino acids to grow and develop—to build a strong and healthy body. He also needs them to make:

—Hormones and enzymes
—Neurotransmitters (to make his brain work as it should)
—Immunogobulins (to build and maintain his immune system)
—Other substances to promote wound healing and give him energy

Eight amino acids—isoleucine, leucine, lysine, methionine, phenylalanine, threonine, tryptophan and valine—are essential because the body can't manufacture them from other nutrients. Two other amino acids—arginine and histidine—are "semi-essential." The body can make them but not enough to meet its needs.*

Your child must eat foods containing these ten amino acids. *This is the only way he can get them.* Others can be formed from the essential amino acids when your child eats a good diet.

*For an excellent technical discussion of amino acids and their functions see Technical Memorandum Two, "Functions of Amino Acids," available from Bionostics, Inc., 4736 Main Street, Suite 10A, P.O. Drawer 400, Lisle, IL 60532.

Dietary Amino Acids

Meats, fish, poultry	Complete protein*
Eggs	Complete protein*
Milk, cheese, yogurt	Complete protein*
Grains	Incomplete protein (Deficient in isoleucine and lysine)
Seeds and nuts	Incomplete protein (Deficient in isoleucine and lysine)
Legumes	Incomplete protein (Deficient in methionine and tryptophan)
Other vegetables	Incomplete protein (Deficient in isoleucine and methionine)

*Complete protein contains balanced amounts of all essential amino acids.

So if your child skips breakfast, eats only potato chips for lunch and fills up on junk food, he's not getting enough essential amino acids and certainly isn't playing with a "full deck" of nutrients.

Your child must also consume amino acids in the proper balance. One advantage of animal protein (meat, fish, poultry, eggs and milk) is that it contains all essential amino acids, while legumes, grains, vegetables, seeds and nuts each lack several

essential amino acids. Nevertheless, combining foods lacking certain amino acids with others that are rich in those amino acids will provide all the essential amino acids. For example, combining legumes (rich in lysine and isoleucine, deficient in tryptophan and methionine) with grains, nuts or seeds (rich in tryptophan and methionine, but deficient in lysine and isoleucine) at the same meal will provide complete protein.

Yet amino acid problems may still develop even if your child eats enough, good-quality protein. Why?

—He may not be getting enough magnesium, zinc and vitamin B_6, nutrients needed to process amino acids.

—He may have a special need to obtain or avoid certain amino acids.

—He may not produce enough hydrochloric acid in his stomach or pancreatic enzymes in his pancreas to digest completely the proteins into amino acids.

Symptoms such as excess gas, bloating, chronic constipation or diarrhea, and undigested food in his bowel movements may indicate stomach acid or pancreatic enzyme deficiencies. If these symptoms do not correct themselves following treatment for food allergies and the yeast problem, your child's digestive functions may need further investigation.

Symptoms of many types have been linked to disordered amino acid metabolism. For example, you've probably heard of phenylketonuria (PKU). Babies born with this inborn metabolic error cannot metabolize phenylalanine, an essential amino acid, and will develop mental retardation unless they eat a special diet. Fortunately, all babies are routinely tested for PKU before leaving the hospital.

Other symptoms sometimes caused by amino acid abnormalities include allergiclike reactions to foods and chemicals, depression, chronic fatigue, headaches, attention deficits, lowered IQ and autistic behavior.[4]

The brain, especially, depends on adequate levels of amino acids circulating in the bloodstream. Brain cells called neurons manufacture neurotransmitters—chemicals that link one neuron to another. Here are examples: the amino acid tryptophan is converted into serotonin; another amino acid, choline, is converted into acetylcholine. In the same manner dopamine, norepinephrine and epinephrine come from the amino acid tyrosine. These neurotransmitters profoundly affect how your child thinks and behaves.

So neurotransmitter production depends on what your child ate at his most recent meal,[5] whether he assimilated and absorbed the necessary amino acids, and whether he has some special need to obtain or avoid certain amino acids.

During the past several years new blood and urine tests have been developed for over thirty amino acids and can now identify specific amino acid abnormalities.* Like the fatty acid studies, these tests are expensive and only a few physicians have gained experience in interpreting the results.

Yet in the hands of an experienced doctor these tests can be critical. Quoting Dr. Baker again:

> Disorders of amino-acid balance have been found in children with extremely severe disorders of development, behavior, or other body functions. As time goes by, more disorders of amino-acid metabolism will be discovered and children with milder and milder disturbances will be found to have errors of amino-acid metabolism as doctors learn to look for them.[6]

Chances are your child won't need these tests. But if he continues to experience problems, *blood and urine amino acid studies could help you find an important piece of your child's puzzle and put it into place.*

---

*Physicians interested in carrying out such studies can obtain further information from Bionostics, P.O. Drawer 400, Lisle, IL 60532 (Jon Pangborn, Ph.D., Director); Bio Science Laboratories, 150 Community Drive, P.O. Box 825, Great Neck, NY 11022, telephone: 516-829-8000; Monroe Medical Research Laboratory, Route 17, P.O. Box 1, Southfield, NY 10975, telephone: 914-351-5134 or 1-800-831-3133.

37
Hypoglycemia

During the past decade, dozens of books have been written about hypoglycemia, or low blood sugar. This disorder is said to cause weakness, fatigue, drowsiness, excessive hunger, jitteriness, impatience, nervousness and other nervous symptoms. Yet if you go to your physician with complaints of this sort and ask, "Do you think I could have hypoglycemia?" he's apt to say, "Probably not, because hypoglycemia is a *rare* disorder."

It's true that the "classic" type of hypoglycemia (as defined by most medical textbooks) doesn't occur commonly. This kind of hypoglycemia may develop following an overdose of insulin, or it may be caused by a tumor of the pancreas or glycogen storage disease of the liver.

However, along with a number of other physicians, I feel there's another form of low blood sugar, reactive or functional hypoglycemia.

Although physicians often disagree on the frequency and importance of this type of hypoglycemia, I feel you should know about it.

Normally when you eat (especially carbohydrates, starches, or sugars) you get a "lift" . . . especially if you feel tired or jittery. Along with this lift, your blood sugar rises. (It's sort of like stepping on the gas of your automobile or turning up the heat in your home.)

Blood sugar (glucose) is transported to all parts of the body including your heart, your muscles and your brain. Glucose furnishes fuel that enables your body to operate properly.

As your blood sugar (glucose) rises, your pancreas automatically releases a hormone (insulin) that helps metabolize (burn) the glucose and bring it down to its normal resting level. If you keep eating sweets and other refined carbohydrates,

your pancreas may overreact, and put out too much insulin, causing your blood sugar to drop to abnormally low levels. This makes you nervous, tired and hungry.

Insulin production by the pancreas is only one of the many automatic regulating mechanisms used in controlling your blood sugar level. For example, if you fast, you'll usually feel weak and hungry for a day or two. But your body soon adapts and begins to convert glycogen (a form of carbohydrate stored in your liver and muscles) into glucose. This normally keeps your blood sugar from dropping to abnormally low levels.

In discussing hypoglycemia, Drs. Emanuel Cheraskin and W. M. Ringsdorf, Jr., commented:

> The sugar-laden American diet has led to a national epidemic of hypoglycemia, an ailment characterized by irrational behavior, emotional instability, distorted judgment, and nasty personality defects. Almost 10 percent of the population is hypoglycemic.[1]

Cheraskin and Ringsdorf, and others who agree with them, blame hypoglycemia on the heavy load of sweetened snack foods and drinks and the white-flour products that Americans consume. Moreover, they feel that caffeine, tobacco and a variety of medications may also contribute to an unstable blood sugar level. And evidence from a number of sources suggests that it is not only what we eat, but what we *do not* eat that causes weakness, jitteriness and other hypoglycemic symptoms.

James Anderson, M.D., and associates of the University of Kentucky (who have studied the relationship of diet to diabetes and reactive hypoglycemia), have commented that if you want to regulate your blood sugar level, eat lots of vegetables, whole grains and other foods rich in complex carbohydrates and fiber.[2]

How is hypoglycemia diagnosed? What is a glucose tolerance test? In one of her books, *Allergies and the Hyperactive Child*, Doris Rapp, M.D., answers these questions. Here's a summary of what she said:

> The glucose tolerance test is a test to see if your blood sugar and insulin levels are properly balanced. . . . A blood sample is taken at the beginning of the test to see what your blood-sugar is at that time. You are then given a calculated amount of sugar solution to drink, depending upon your weight. At different intervals of time, for about five or six hours, samples of blood are taken to see what happens to your blood sugar level. . . .
>
> Normally, the level is about 80 or 90 mg% at the start of the test. . . . The blood level normally rises during the first hour of the test to about 130 to 220 mg%. During the final three hours of the test, the blood sugar gradually falls to the level it was at the start of the test.
>
> If the blood sugar level rises higher than normal and stays high for several hours, your pancreas may not be producing

insulin properly. You may have diabetes and need to take insulin. If your blood sugar rises just a little and then falls 20 mg% below the original level . . . it may indicate . . . functional hypoglycemia.[3]

But, hypoglycemia is tricky, very tricky. And confusing—very confusing. Here's why I feel this way.

Several years ago, I saw a fourteen-year-old youngster with food allergies who developed weakness, drowsiness and nervousness after eating potatoes. During the course of the study of her, glucose tolerance tests were carried out. When the standard test was performed (using glucose derived from corn), the test was normal. But when an equivalent amount of carbohydrate derived from potato starch was used, the test was abnormal and typical of hypoglycemia. Moreover, the girl developed her usual symptoms.

When I discussed this patient with Theron G. Randolph, M.D., he commented:

I'm not surprised. I've observed for many years that *what is commonly referred to as reactive or functional hypoglycemia is, in fact, a specific allergic reaction to a particular food.* So when a patient shows an abnormal reaction to the usual glucose tolerance test, chances are the person is allergic to corn since dextrose derived from corn is used in carrying out the test.[4]

Another physician who agrees with Randolph is William H. Philpott, M.D., who commented:

Testing . . . reveals the surprising fact that low and high blood sugar can be evoked by foods of *all* types, whether fats, carbohydrates or proteins. . . . [Moreover,] chemicals such as petrochemical hydrocarbons and even tobacco equally evoke abnormal sugar levels in susceptible persons. The foods causing these reactions are specific for each person. . . . The simple fact of the matter is that abnormal sugar levels in the body are caused by allergic-like reactions to specific substances.[5]

Here's more evidence that nervous system symptoms suggesting hypoglycemia are often caused by adverse or allergic reactions to specific foods:

In 1975, I carried out a study on twelve of my patients, whose parents had said, "Sugar makes my child hyperactive." Here's what I did:

I bought twenty-five pounds of cane sugar and twenty-five pounds of beet sugar. I gave each parent a two-pound bag of the two different sugars. One bag was labelled, "Bag A"; the other was labelled, "Bag B." Neither the parents nor the child knew which sugar was which. The parents were given detailed printed instructions for carrying out the study, for keeping a record of the child's hyperactivity and other nervous system symptoms, and a record of his diet.

A diary of the child's behavior was recorded for three days while he consumed a sugar-free diet.

The child was then given as much sugar as he wanted from "Bag A" for two days. Sugar was eliminated for two days. The child was then given as much sugar as he wanted from "Bag B" for the next two days.

Here's a summary of my results:

1. Several children became hyperactive on both the beet sugar and the cane sugar.
2. Several children reacted to neither sugar.*
3. Two of the children reacted to cane sugar and not to beet.
4. One child reacted to beet sugar and not to cane.

Although the study was a crude one, and possessed several flaws, my observations seemed to suggest that, in some children at least, the observations of Randolph and Philpott appear to be valid, i.e., *whether or not a person reacts to a particular sugar (or other food) may depend on the source of the food.*

---

*In speculating on why these children who once appeared to react to sugar did not react subsequently, the following possibilities occurred to me:

a. The parents' original observation that "sugar makes my child hyperactive" was an incorrect one. This could have been because of an erroneous observation by the parent or because the child was reacting to some other ingredient in sweetened foods such as food coloring, phosphates or other additives.

b. Because sugar had been eliminated from the diet for a period of many months, the child may have regained tolerance to the sugar that once bothered him.

c. Improvement in other nutritional, biochemical or metabolic factors.

Here's more. As a result of learning of the effect of yeast toxins on the nervous system I feel that sugar may cause behavior problems by promoting the overgrowth of *Candida albicans* in the digestive tract. Current research being carried out by *Candida* pioneer C. Orian Truss, M.D., shows that individuals with yeast-related health disorders show disturbances in carbohydrate metabolism.

A final word on hypoglycemia and its causes and manifestations.* In dealing with this subject I continue to have more questions than answers—especially when it comes to the mechanisms that may be involved.

Yet based on my clinical experiences in treating thousands of patients (including hundreds of hard-to-raise children) I know that *avoiding sugar and "cleaning up the diet" play a key role in controlling troublesome behavior.*

Whether these symptoms are caused by hypoglycemia (or some other mechanism) isn't important. What is important is that the child's body—especially his brain—be given fuel (foods and beverages) that will enable it to function properly.

38

Phosphates and Behavioral Disturbances

In 1978, Hertha Hafer, a biochemist from Mainz, Germany, published a book entitled *Phosphates in Food as a Cause of Behavioral Disturbances in Teenage Delinquents.* Here's a summary of Dr. Hafer's clinical observations:

*You can read more about this controversial and confusing subject in my thirty-two-page booklet *Dr. Crook Discusses . . . Hypoglycemia,* available in most health food stores or from Professional Books, Box 846, Jackson, TN 38302.

1. Foods containing phosphates and phosphoric acid play an important role in causing behavioral changes. Such foods depress the body's levels of calcium, magnesium and potassium, thereby upsetting the biochemical balance of the body. This imbalance produces irritability, overactivity and other nervous system symptoms.

2. Foods that contain high levels of phosphates include:

> Processed and packaged foods, especially convenience foods
> Foods containing ordinary baking powder (cream-of-tartar is okay)
> Processed meats
> Soft drinks
> Processed cheese and ice cream

Hafer's hyperactive son, Michael, improved on the Feingold diet. Yet when he ate German sausage (without artificial coloring or other additives described by Feingold), his nervous system symptoms returned. Since phosphates are added to German sausage, Hafer suspected the phosphates contributed to his hyperactivity.

So Hafer developed a special diet for Michael that excluded all foods containing phosphates as additives. Not only did Michael improve on this diet, but so did other hyperactive children.

Subsequently, a child psychiatrist, Brigitta Roy-Feiler, tested the effect of the phosphate-free diet on a group of hyperactive children. Reporting in *Academic Therapy*, Mildred M. Walker commented:

First, the child was placed on a 3-week diet which was strictly limited in phosphorus content. Then some of the children were given a capsule containing 75 mgs. of phosphate ion . . . and the remaining children received an identical capsule containing chopped cellulose. *All children receiving the phosphate showed typical MBD (hyperactive) behavior for 3 days.* Children receiving the placebo ("dummy" or blank capsule) had no reaction. . . . [The] results were analyzed by medical statisticians at a university who found them to be highly significant. . . .

Although the work of Hafer, Walker and Roy-Feiler points to the conclusion that the reduction of phosphate intake is a successful primary treatment of hyperkinesis, it is also possible to neutralize phosphate with liquid dolomite (a calcium and magnesium preparation) . . . and this has been found to be a useful supplementary treatment.[1]

Because the Hafer book hasn't been translated from German, I've seen few references to her work in English-speaking countries. Yet in discussing the "chemistry of healing" in an essay entitled "Magnesium and the Battle for Light," Leo Galland, M.D., talked about the importance of nutrients

of many sorts, including essential fatty acids, magnesium and calcium. In this essay, he especially emphasized the importance of an adequate magnesium intake, and he expressed concern over the excessive consumption of phosphorus. And he stressed:

> While phosphorus is an essential nutrient, excess phosphorus acts like a kind of intestinal sludge keeping both calcium and magnesium from being well absorbed. . . . One of the most alarming dietary changes in this country during the past decade has been the increasing consumption of soft drinks by teenagers. We take in more phosphorus than we can use.[2]

The Hafer and Galland observations provide important clues that may help you put one more piece of your hard-to-raise child's puzzle into its proper place. And because hamburgers, sodas (including the sugar-free ones), processed meats and other convenience foods are loaded with phosphates, avoiding or at least limiting them may be an important part of your child's treatment program.

Section I

MEETING YOUR CHILD'S PSYCHOLOGICAL AND EDUCATIONAL NEEDS

39

What Are
Psychological Vitamins?

Most hard-to-raise children irritate and frustrate their parents, siblings, teachers and just about everyone they come in contact with. Their overactive, meddlesome, annoying, unpredictable behavior understandably brings them criticism, punishment and rejection. As a result the self-esteem of these youngsters suffers. They often become frustrated, angry, irritable and depressed.

Such feelings cause them to strike out at those around them. So they become hostile, aggressive and destructive.

Every child is unique and not all hard-to-raise children follow the pattern just described. Yet all of these youngsters yearn for attention and recognition. And some become the "class clown" or the neighborhood prankster.

But regardless of which pattern these children follow, they're usually caught in a vicious cycle that repeats itself in ever widening circles. Although parents may possess the wisdom of Solomon, the patience of Job and show the kind of love described by Paul in the thirteenth chapter of Corinthians, the child's (and the family's) problems continue.

Happily I find that most of my difficult, overactive, unhappy, hard-to-handle patients feel better, look better and act better within a few days (or a few weeks) after an offending substance that has been disturbing their nervous system is removed. Others show a similar dramatic improvement when nutrients—for example, B vitamins, magnesium and the essential fatty acids—are supplemented.

Let's talk about another type of nutrient every person, including your hard-to-raise child, requires if he is to survive and thrive. I call these nutrients "psychological vitamins."

What are psychological vitamins? You can probably guess

THE MANY VICIOUS CYCLES

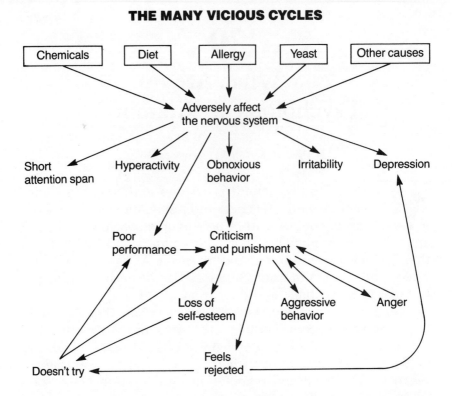

without my telling you. They include praise, recognition, smiles, hugging and other expressions of approval, affection or encouragement. They're what give you that "good feeling" when you do a task well and someone recognizes it, appreciates it and lets you know about it.

Your child must receive plenty of these psychological "vitamins" to develop self-esteem and self-confidence.

When he receives enough psychological vitamins, he can look in the mirror or at the world around him and smile. They bring him optimism, serenity and happiness. They help him like himself and other people and enable him to get along with his family, teachers, classmates and everyone in the world around him.

Accordingly, while you're changing your child's nutrition and other things in his biochemical, metabolic and chemical environment, you'll also need to provide him with psychological nutrients.

PSYCHOLOGICAL VITAMINS

Approval
Success
Recognition
Affection
Acceptance
Smiles
Love pats
  "Thank you." "Good boy." "Yes." "Let's play."
  "I'll read you a story." "Yes, I'll watch you."
  "You're so smart." "Isn't this fun."
  "You're somebody special."

Because your child may have experienced so many "battle scars" because of his often "obnoxious" and "unacceptable" behavior, you'll have to work diligently and consistently to make sure he gets these nutrients.

Here are suggestions.

1. *Smile at him and notice him* . . . especially when he's sitting still or staying out of trouble. As Spencer Johnson says in his books *One Minute Father* and *One Minute Mother,* "Catch him doing something right!"[1]

2. *Read to him.* Let him sit next to you on the couch (or

hold him on your lap if he isn't too big) and read to him. Or let him read to you.

3. *Give him simple jobs to do that will interest him and make him feel useful—things you know he can complete successfully.* Then when he finishes the task, reward him. A word of sincere praise will usually mean more than a tangible gift, although both types of reward can be appropriate.

For example, ask your child to help bring in the groceries, set the table or pick up newspapers and magazines from the floor of the family room. Praise him when he finishes a picture in his coloring book. Or play a game with him . . . one he can win at least half of the time.

As he becomes more confident, give him tasks that challenge him. But don't make them so hard that he'll become discouraged.

4. *Praise him.* Praising your hyperactive, irritable child, like watering a dry rose bush, will help him bloom.

Several years ago I read an article in *Family Weekly* entitled "The Importance of Being Praised." In this article freelance writer Jodie Gaylin stresses the role of praise in raising a happy, confident child. She makes these recommendations:

> *When you praise, be specific.* When Tommy builds a terrific tower out of blocks, don't just tell him what a good boy he is. . . . Instead, let him know what an impressive tower he built. And when he does something you don't approve of, the same rule applies. *Make sure it's the behavior, not the child, you condemn.*[2]

Don't go overboard and "overpraise." Too much praise can frustrate a child by setting goals he can't reach.

On the other hand, don't be "too honest." Don't expect your child to meet adult standards. You don't need to lie, just find what is praiseworthy.

Avoid loaded praise. Here are some examples.

"The picture is beautiful, but wouldn't it look better if you put the tree over there?"

"The ninety-eight on your math test is good. Next time try to get one hundred."

Such remarks make the child feel that he hasn't measured

up. So, incomplete, conditional or loaded praise doesn't encourage your child. Instead, it frustrates or angers him.

Be consistent. Some parents dish out praise only when they're feeling good. Base your praise on your child's behavior, not on your mood.

5. *Touch and hold your child as much as you can.* Touching lessens irritability, nervousness and anxiety. Moreover, I've read and heard reports that infants who are systematically handled, touched and stroked develop more rapidly that infants who did not receive such treatment.[3,4,5] A mother-to-be who has a caring person to hold her hand and stroke her brow or abdomen has been shown to have a shorter and less difficult labor.

In his book on touching, Ashley Montagu told of experiments in rats that showed:

> The more handling and petting rats received, the better they did in laboratory situations. . . . Equally remarkable was the influence of gentle handling upon behavioral development. And such handling produced gentle, unexcitable animals.[6]

What calms rats also seems to calm most humans. Many a parent of an unhappy, colicky infant has found that picking up her baby and holding him closely quiets him. And many a parent has found that rocking and holding an anxious, unhappy two-year-old (who may have been awakened by a bad dream or a clap of thunder) will soothe him and help him go back to sleep.

Several years ago, Arvin T. Henderson, M.D., and associates, from California, told of their experiences in treating twenty-four hyperactive children without drugs. These doctors said:

> Hyperactivity can be detected long before school age . . . even in infancy. We believe that hyperactive infants require more than the usual amount of holding, touching and soothing. We have now treated 24 hyperactive children with good results. Our treatment program consists mainly of massage for relaxation of muscle tension or talking to the child in a soothing tone.[7]

The observations of Henderson, Montagu and others fascinate me. I'm impressed by the growing amount of data that shows that hormones and other mediators, including endorphins, are manufactured in the body following touching and gentle handling. Although much remains to be learned about the mechanisms involved, I feel that *gentle touch will help your hyperactive child.*

6. *Be patient.* Try to think patient and happy thoughts (difficult though it may be!) when you're dealing with your child. Children watch their parents intently and can sense their parents' emotions. Even though you say pleasant words, if you're thinking, "I'd like to wring his neck," he'll read your body language.

Remember, your child doesn't want to appear dumb, lazy, stupid, clumsy or inept. And it'll take time for him to overcome the biochemical, nutritional, allergic and other imbalances that contribute to his annoying and frustrating behavior. So even though he doesn't immediately respond to the psychological vitamins you're giving him, don't be discouraged. They help—they really do!

40

Changing
Your Child's Behavior

Your child's behavior will often irritate and frustrate you. So your patience may wear thin. How do you handle it? What can you do?

As I've already pointed out, the chances are your difficult child will start improving when you identify the foods that bother him and remove them. He'll improve further when he eats a nutritious diet and takes nutritional supplements. Or when you lessen his exposure to pollutants in his environment, or start a treatment program to eliminate yeast toxins.

Yet, in spite of such treatment measures, all of your child's irritable, unpredictable behavior won't suddenly disappear. And your defiant, clumsy, impatient "Mr. Hyde" won't overnight turn into a cooperative, calm, patient "Dr. Jekyll." So don't expect too much too soon. Don't expect him to be your model child, his teacher's pet and the most popular child in your neighborhood.

Like all children (even those who haven't experienced problems) he won't always behave the way you'd like for him to behave. In managing your child, you can use principles of behavior modification that clinical psychologists have found to be effective.

In a fascinating program on *Donahue* in 1980, Marion Bailey of Animal Behavior Enterprises in Hot Springs, Arkansas, exhibited Pete, a remarkable parrot. Pete skated, rode a bicycle and pumped water from a miniature pump. After successfully performing each task, he gobbled a reward from Ms. Bailey's hand. She commented, "Pete works for peanuts." Ms. Bailey then presented other fascinating trained animals, including a chicken who had been taught to ring a bell three times to obtain food.

Ms. Bailey explained the rules she used to train these animals and to rear her children:

1. Reward your pet immediately. Although we use foods in rewarding our animals, you can use other rewards in both animals and children, including smiles or pats on the head.
2. Providing positive rewards is a powerful tool for changing behavior whether you're dealing with an animal, a child or an adult.
3. *You can get rid of unwanted behavior by ignoring it.* We call this "extinguishing" unacceptable behavior.
4. In rearing my children (who are now responsible adults), I found I never had to punish them. And in

training our animals, we never punish them. I feel the same principle holds true with children, almost 100 percent of the time.

During the discussion period, a mother in the audience asked, "Suppose my child runs into the street or starts to scribble on the wall, injure an animal or hit his baby sister. . . . What do you do then?"

Ms. Bailey responded:

> Obviously there will be occasions when you must limit your child and occasionally you may need to punish him. Yet you don't have to spank him. If and when you feel you must punish, do it at the right time. And the right time is when the unacceptable behavior is beginning.

Several years ago, I read of an experiment involving a nursery-school teacher who was trying to manage nine balky, misbehaving children.[1] The youngsters fought, scribbled on the walls, talked loudly and failed to pick up their belongings.

In the experiment, the children were divided into three groups:

Group A: Children in this group were punished and reprimanded each time they misbehaved. When they behaved well, no comment was made and no rewards were given.

Group B: The behavior of these children was ignored unless it was injuring another child or destroying property. But when a child in this group obeyed the rules, cooperated and was "good," he was rewarded with a smile or a love pat. In addition, he was given a token. After a child earned five tokens, he could exchange them for a small toy.

Group C: The children in this group were rewarded with praise, smiles and tokens for good behavior. But when they misbehaved, they were scolded and punished and tokens were taken away.

If you're like most people you'll be surprised when I tell you which group showed the greatest improvement: the Group B children, whose good behavior was rewarded and whose bad behavior was ignored.

Many similar experiments with both animals and humans show that you get the best results if you reward them when they do what you want them to do. Because people like rewards, recognition, praise and other psychological vitamins, they'll keep on doing the things that produce the rewards.

I'm not saying that you should ignore hostile, aggressive or destructive behavior. Certainly not. If your child is destroying property or infringing on the rights of others, stop him.

But if you want to teach your child to sit at the table, leave his baby sister alone or treat pets properly, you're more apt to succeed if you:

1. Set a good example
2. Establish clear-cut rules
3. Give him love and affection
4. Reward him when he's good, rather than nagging or punishing when he misbehaves

BEHAVIOR MODIFICATION—WHAT YOU DO AND HOW YOU DO IT

Carefully note how your child acts and where he stands *now*. Does he get up from the table at meals five times . . . or ten times? Does he drum or tap on his desk constantly, occasionally . . . or in between?

Also note the setting in which the problem behavior usually occurs.

To repeat, first describe your child's problem behavior and how often it's occurring.

Set a behavior goal. Establish both a short-term goal and a long-term goal. For example, if you want your son, Johnny, to sit at his desk and do his homework for thirty minutes, you must first teach him to stay at his desk for five minutes, then for ten minutes, fifteen minutes and so on. As he reaches each short-term goal, reward him.

In addition to smiles and compliments, you can use tokens (such as poker chips, stamps or stickers). As your child earns them, he can "spend" them later on for a toy or something else he wants.

For example, let's say you want your child to complete a tutoring class in reading. To reach this goal give him:

1. One token for going to visit the teacher before starting the program
2. One token for walking to the teacher's house each day

THE VICIOUS CYCLE OF DISAPPROVAL AND THE HAPPY CYCLE OF APPROVAL

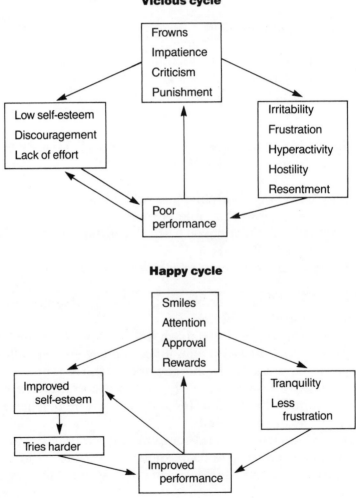

Vicious cycle

Frowns
Impatience
Criticism
Punishment

Low self-esteem
Discouragement
Lack of effort

Irritability
Frustration
Hyperactivity
Hostility
Resentment

Poor performance

Happy cycle

Smiles
Attention
Approval
Rewards

Improved self-esteem

Tries harder

Tranquility
Less frustration

Improved performance

3. One token for remembering to take pencil, tablet and other materials and getting started
4. One token for sitting in a tutoring session for thirty minutes
5. One token for staying in the class an hour
6. One token for not complaining during the session
7. One token for not crying during a session
8. A three-token bonus if he earns all seven tokens on a given day

As his behavior improves, he's to receive more compliments; his self-esteem will grow. As the weeks and months go by, his personality and behavior will improve. And rather than being trapped in a "vicious cycle," a "happy cycle" will develop.

PUNISHMENT

If you're like many parents, you worry about drug abuse, teenage pregnancy, vandalism and the rising crime rate among juveniles. You may have heard some self-appointed critic (usually a person with no children) say, "Such problems can be blamed on parents who don't know that if you spare the rod, you'll spoil the child."

I disagree with such a point of view. Although occasions will arise when you'll feel you need to punish your child, *punishment is a relatively ineffective method of discipline.* Here's why:

Punishment provides a child with attention for misbehavior. Since everyone wants attention, any attention—even negative attention (such as frowning at your child every time he misbehaves)—may be enough to keep the objectionable behavior going.

Usually, when you punish your child, especially when you spank him, you do it to appease your own anger or frustration. So you may find yourself punishing your child for your own sake, rather than for his.

When you punish a child (whether it's by laying your hand

on his bottom or by "chewing him out") he'll usually feel humiliated and rejected. When he's filled with these emotions he may not learn the lesson you're trying to teach him. This is not to say that you should never spank your child. For example, if you catch your four-year-old darting into the street, something he has been repeatedly warned not to do, you might give him a single, crisp swat on his bottom. But then, immediately afterward, give him a hug or love pat and tell him, "Son, I'm sorry I had to spank you, but you must not run into the street; a car could run over you." *Your purpose is not to punish your child, but to make such an impression that he won't repeat the dangerous behavior.*

I hope your child's behavior will so improve that you'll never have to punish him. But just in case you find punishment is necessary, here's a list of suggestions that may help you:*

1. *Punishment must be immediate.* Never threaten, never bribe. Never tell your child, "Daddy will get you when he comes home."

2. *The punishment must fit the crime.* If you send your child to bed for an hour when he spills a glass of milk, you're overdoing it.

3. *The most effective form of punishment varies from one child to another.* (For example, some children react with tears to a raised voice, others do not respond even to a hard spanking.)

4. *Do not discipline your child in front of his brothers, sisters and friends.* Discipline should be a private matter between you and your child.

5. *Isolation is one of the best forms of discipline.* It is especially useful in stopping attention-getting behavior like tantrums, yelling, hitting, or whining. If you ignore such behavior (hard as it is), the objectionable behavior will decrease. By isolating a child, you refuse to pay attention to the things he's doing that disrupt the household and annoy you.

Here are suggestions for carrying out isolation:

1. Tell your child what you're doing and why. For example, say, "Johnny, you must not hit Susie. Sit in the chair for five

*For further reading on this subject, see Dr. Fitzhugh Dodson's book *How to Discipline with Love,* especially pages 1–48.

minutes." Or, "Your crying is getting on Mommy's nerves. Go to your room for five minutes so I can't hear you. After five minutes you can come back to the playroom."

2. Immediate isolation in a room with the door closed, for no longer than five minutes, seems to work the best.

3. Once you decide to isolate your child, stick to your guns.

4. Don't place your child in a closet or darkened, frightening room. The isolation itself is the punishment.

5. Use a timer with a bell. Set the timer so your child will know when the isolation period is over.

6. Isolation or ignoring undesirable behavior often brings an initial increase in the behavior. Be patient and stick with it.

A final word. Punishment is sometimes called for. But use it sparingly. Remember you're more apt to change your child's bad behavior by rewarding him when he's good than by punishing him when he isn't.

41

Communicating with Your Child

Your Johnny comes home after a difficult day at school. His teacher had fussed at him because he'd fiddled with his pencil and didn't finish his work on time. She frowned at him every time he got out of his seat. Then at recess, he was the last one to be chosen by the captain for a baseball game.

So Johnny comes home from school feeling hurt, discouraged and angry. He wants to talk to you—to tell you how he feels. Yet, sometimes, in spite of your best intentions, he argues with you even though you're trying to help him. He

becomes angry when you try to find out what happened—what upset him.

Although there is no magic way or gimmick—no easy answer to Johnny's problems—communication specialists have found that there are right ways and wrong ways to communicate with your child. And how you ask questions can either help him or threaten him and put him down.

In his book, *Between Parent and Child,* in a chapter entitled, "Conversing with Children," the late Haim Ginott, Ph.D., commented:

> Parents are frustrated by dialogues with children because they lead nowhere. . . . As one mother said, "I try to reason with my child until I'm blue in the face, but he doesn't listen to me. He only hears me when I scream." . . .
>
> An interested observer who overhears a conversation between a parent and his child will note with surprise how little each listens to the other. The conversation sounds like two monologues, one consisting of criticism and instruction, the other of denials and pleading. The tragedy of such "communication" lies, not in the lack of love, but in the lack of respect; not in the lack of intelligence, but in the lack of skill.[1]

According to Dr. Ginott, to communicate effectively with your child requires:

> (a) that messages preserve the child's as well as the parent's self-respect; (b) that statements of understanding precede statements of advice or instruction.
>
> Eric, age nine, came home full of anger. His class was scheduled to go for a picnic, but it was raining. Mother decided

to use a new approach. She refrained from clichés that in the past had only made things worse: "There is no use crying over rained-out picnics." "There will be other days for fun." "I didn't make it rain, you know, so why are you angry at me?"

To herself she said, "My son has strong feelings about missing the picnic.... I can best help him by showing understanding and respect for his feelings." To Eric she said:

MOTHER: You seem very disappointed.
ERIC: Yes.
MOTHER: You wanted very much to go to this picnic.
ERIC: I sure did.
MOTHER: You had everything ready and then the darn rain came.
ERIC: Yes, that's exactly right.

There was a moment of silence and then Eric said, "Oh well, there will be other days."

His anger seemed to have vanished and he was quite cooperative the rest of the afternoon.[2]

I love Dr. Ginott's comments and discussion on this subject. In fact, *Between Parent and Child* ranks high on my list of favorite books. Get a copy. I know you'll enjoy it.

In discussing communication techniques with children, Fitzhugh Dodson, Ph.D., in his book *How to Discipline with Love,* discusses "the feedback" technique:

Children very desperately want us to understand how they feel. ... [Yet] many parents have not learned the importance of listening to their children and empathizing with them. The feedback technique can help parents overcome these barriers to parent-child understanding.

The essence of the feedback technique is simple. You are doing three things whenever your child expresses her feelings:

1. Listening carefully to what your child is saying
2. Formulating in your mind what your child is expressing
3. Feeding back to her in your own words the feelings she has just expressed to you[3]

Dr. Dodson also commented about the importance of allowing children to express negative feelings:

I believe that parents should allow their children to express *all* their feelings—positive and negative—through the medium of words. Unfortunately very few parents do allow their children to express their feelings in words. Particularly their negative feelings.[4]

And he recalls having his mouth washed out with soap for expressing a few negative feelings toward his mother!

By expressing his feelings, particularly negative feelings, your child is offered a "safety valve"—like the one on a boiler that keeps it from exploding. Because of the many frustrations a difficult child experiences, he's apt to develop all sorts of hostile and negative feelings. Your giving him an opportunity to talk about them will help him handle them.

Communication skills aren't something you're born with. You can learn them just as you can learn the right way to scramble an egg or hit a tennis ball. So if you're experiencing trouble talking to your child, try the "say it back" technique. It really works.

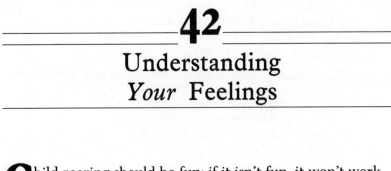

42

Understanding *Your* Feelings

Child rearing should be fun; if it isn't fun, it won't work. Parents should be able to laugh more than they cry.
—Lendon Smith, M.D.[1]

LAURA COMMENTS:

Raising any child tests the patience, wisdom and endurance of any parent. But parenting a difficult child challenges *all* of your inner resources. Surely, there must be a very special, quiet, peaceful nook in heaven some day for you and other weary parents! How can you survive in the meantime?

Understanding your feelings and recognizing that other parents feel the same way should help you cope. I haven't had a mother call me yet, who hasn't admitted in so many words, "I feel so guilty and incompetent. It must be my fault." Relatives, friends, neighbors and even her doctor often reinforce these feelings. Do you recognize any of the following characters in your life?

FATHER: "Something wrong with *my* son? Impossible! I acted the same way at his age and look how well I turned out!" or "You're just not strict enough. Spare the rod and spoil the child."

OR: "I come home tired after a long day at the office and you want me to deal with Johnny? Don't you know the constitution clearly states that fathers have the right to peace and quiet and time to read the newspaper undisturbed?"

OR: "Take the whole family off sugar? You gotta be kidding. What about my Twinkies and my colas?"

FATHER'S MOTHER: "Johnny's all boy, just like his father was." Or "Well, I only gave him *one* cookie. After all, what are grandparents for?"

MOTHER'S MOTHER: "I never had any trouble raising *my* children. What are you doing wrong?" Or "He was a perfect angel for me. Never cried or carried on at all. You should stay home more and give him extra attention."

FIRST PEDIATRICIAN: "Looks like a normal kid to me. See how well he's behaving in my office? Maybe you should get out of the house more or have you thought about having another baby? Every mother I see thinks her child is hyperactive."

SECOND PEDIATRICAN: "Yes, three-year-old Johnny certainly is overactive. But hang in there. Most of these kids settle down by puberty!"

FIRST NEIGHBOR: "You're just too hard on Johnny. What he needs is more tender loving care."

SECOND NEIGHBOR: "My Arthur was just like your Johnny. I finally found out what I was doing wrong. I just wasn't hitting him hard enough. You have to show Johnny who's boss!"

FIRST BABYSITTER: "Babysit . . . again . . . for you? You must be kidding. Johnny pulled the curtains down, dumped salt on the floor and tried to flush the cat down the toilet!"

SECOND BABYSITTER: "Johnny, a problem? Why he behaved better than most of the children I babysit. What a good kid."

TEACHER: "Johnny could learn if he'd only try. He can't sit still, doesn't listen and disrupts the whole class. Why can't you discipline him?"

It's no wonder you feel guilty. With friends, neighbors, doctors and relatives like these, who needs enemies? But *poor parenting rarely causes these behavioral disturbances.* Instead, these children make their parents look incompetent. As your child responds to Dr. Crook's program, you'll see for yourself what really causes your child's obnoxious and unacceptable behavior. So forget the guilt. You don't need that extra burden.

Do you feel angry? That's another normal reaction. You're mad at your child because he causes so much trouble and makes you feel like a failure. Although deep down in your heart and soul you know he doesn't really want to misbehave, you still feel he could stop if he only would.

You also may feel angry because you're wondering, "Why me? Why my child?" But you've probably found there's no good answer to these age-old questions.

If your child is hard to manage every single day, you probably feel desperate. How are you going to survive? Indeed, families with such a child experience great stress. Divorce occurs commonly.

One frustrated mother at the end of her rope wrote of her overwhelming despair and pain:

> My seven-year-old son acts up so much of the time I'm at my wit's end. In fact, I tried to give him to the Welfare Department. However, the doctor said that wouldn't help him so he is still with me. I'm taking strong tranquilizers so I can cope with him. I'm raising him alone and I desperately need help.

If you're physically and mentally exhausted, you may wonder where you'll get the strength to make the changes Dr. Crook recommends. I've been there. It's worth the time and effort! Don't forget your exhaustion may stem from the same biochemical problems your child is experiencing. If possible, put the whole family on the program. Everyone will feel better.

COUNSELING

Cleaning up your child's diet and avoiding foods he's sensitive to will usually help your child. Giving him nutritional supplements and reducing yeast toxins in his body will often help even more. And when these measures are combined with appropriate psychological vitamins, professional counseling will rarely be necessary.

But if your child continues to be bothered by behavior and learning problems, chances are you feel frustrated, discouraged, angry and depressed. In this sort of situation you and your family may need further help, someone to talk to—to share your feelings with—and someone to help you cope with the difficult problems you face.

You may need a counselor to outline behavioral management programs such as those previously described. Some counselors work mainly with the child, while others involve the whole family. A counselor trained in evaluating school problems may offer suggestions for helping the learning-disabled child at home and school.

How do you find such a counselor? Ask around. Start with your physician. Or ask your child's teacher or minister to give you suggestions. You might say:

> Our family is looking for a warm, competent counselor to help us deal with Johnny's behavior. We know food allergy and nutritional factors play important roles in causing his behavior problems. Accordingly, we must find a supportive, understanding counselor who's had some experience in these areas—or at least someone who has an open mind. Whom do you recommend?

Of course, counseling can be expensive . . . so expensive you feel you can't afford it. In such a case check with a local university or community health facility where charges are based on your ability to pay. Some health insurance plans pay for counseling, so check the provisions of your policy.

What should you look for in a counselor? And if you spend your time (and money) visiting a counselor, what criteria can you use to determine if he or she is the right one? Here are suggestions:

1. The counselor ought to be someone you like and can relate to. About the only way you can decide this is by making that first appointment and plunging in and getting started, If your hard-to-raise child and your spouse will also be working with this counselor—and I recommend it—then you'll want to consider their opinions, too.

2. The counselor you're looking for doesn't necessarily have to be knowledgeable about the biochemical aspects of your child's behavior. But he shouldn't reject this point of view. If he says, "Diet and hyperactivity? There's no proof that foods can make a child hyperactive. And a yeast connection to your child's behavior? That's a fad," then you'll want to find someone else. However, if he says, "I don't know much about

diet and behavior, but I'd like to learn more," you've found a counselor with an open mind.

3. At your first visit ask about the charges you can expect and if possible get an estimate of the number of counseling visits he or she feels will be needed.

4. The counselor should be a good listener. He should look interested and concerned. He shouldn't yawn, fiddle with his glasses, twirl his pencil or look bored. He shouldn't tell you all about *his* problems.

5. He shouldn't make you feel guilty; nor should he impose his own moral prejudices on you.

6. He should be someone with whom you feel comfortable sharing honestly your thoughts and feelings.

7. He shouldn't promise results but should always promise to try to help.

SUPPORT GROUPS

People all over the world who share common problems have found that they can help themselves and others with similar interests and problems by getting together and sharing information, experiences and feelings.

If your hard-to-raise child is bothered by foods and chemical sensitivities, see if there is a Human Ecology Action League (HEAL) chapter in your area. HEAL members are concerned about the effects of environmental chemicals and other allergens on their physical and mental health. For more information write to HEAL, 2421 W. Pratt, Suite 1112, Chicago, IL 60645.

If you feel that your child's symptoms are yeast connected, send a stamped, self-addressed envelope to the International Health Foundation, P.O. Box 1000RH, Jackson, TN 38302. They've put together a roster of support groups interested in *Candida*-related health disorders.

If your child is bothered by hyperactivity, a Feingold group could help you. These groups were started over ten years ago by parents who were following the Feingold diet. For more information write the Feingold Association of the United States, P.O. Box 10085, Alexandria, VA 22310.

Other suggestions: In some communities schools sponsor meetings for parents whose children are experiencing learning problems. Or check to see if your city has one of the over two hundred state and local chapters of the Association for Children with Learning Disabilities (ACLD). If your child experiences such problems send a stamped, self-addressed envelope to the Association for Children with Learning Disabilities, 4156 Library Road, Pittsburgh, PA 14234.

If you can't locate one of these support groups, subscribe to one or more supportive newsletters (see Appendix B: Other Sources of Information). Or start your own support group. All it takes is a few members and the word will spread. Posters, a notice in your newspaper or a TV announcement will attract new members. In helping others you'll help yourself.

So if your hard-to-raise child is driving you nuts, your guilt, anger, frustration and loneliness are normal feelings and should be expected. But if these feelings are overwhelming you and dragging you down, seek help and support from those who understand.

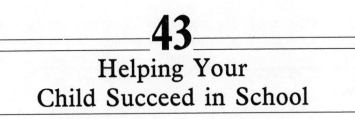

43

Helping Your
Child Succeed in School

SCHOOL PLACEMENT

School placement interests me for many reasons. I started the first grade on my fifth birthday. I didn't enjoy school or "set the woods on fire." In fact during my early years of school, getting my lessons done and avoiding criticism from my teachers was a real challenge.

However, gradually I caught up and made better than average grades in college. And when I got to medical school I was so scared and worked so hard that I ended up in the top 10 percent of my class. But if I had it to do over again I'd repeat the first grade; better still I'd start school when I was a year or two older.

During my early years of practice I was so busy treating sick children I devoted little time to youngsters with behavior and learning problems. Nevertheless (as you might guess), whenever I saw a seemingly immature youngster for a pre-school checkup, I'd usually say, "Even though Charlie's old enough to enter the first grade legally, let's study the situation carefully. Then you can decide whether to start him in the first grade this year or give him another year in kindergarten."

Then about fifteen years ago, I came across a book by Louise Bates Ames, Ph.D., called *Is Your Child in the Wrong Grade in School?* (New York: Harper & Row, 1967). I read it from cover to cover—almost in one sitting—and since then, I've reread it countless times. I was fascinated and delighted because I found an authority saying clearly and succinctly things I'd felt for a long time.

Dr. Ames emphasizes the following points:

1. *At least half of the school failures in the first grade could be prevented if children started school only when they were fully ready.*

2. *Children should be started in school (and subsequently promoted) on the basis of their behavioral age rather than their chronological age.* In other words, your child may be six years old and have an IQ of 125. However, if he behaves like a five year old and can't sit still, let him wait another year before he enters the first grade.

3. Before your child starts kindergarten (or school), give him a behavioral test or developmental examination. Such an examination helps you and his teachers decide whether he is truly ready. (See pages 261–262.)

4. Boys usually mature later than girls. While the average girl is ready for kindergarten when she's five, the average boy should be at least a half-year older.

5. Children who are started in kindergarten and school before they're ready do *not* usually "catch up" with the ready ones.

Dr. Ames comments, "I do not agree with . . . parents and educators who feel that most children fail in school because they do not try. . . . Rather than saying 'Johnny could do better if he only *would*,' we should say 'Johnny would do better if he only *could*.' "[1]

If your child isn't doing well in school, should he repeat the grade he's in? Quoting Dr. Ames again:

> Let's suppose . . . your child is already in school, is not doing well, and seems quite clearly overplaced. Should you have him repeat? Our answer would be a resounding "Yes." . . . The majority of children will accept the notion that they must repeat rather calmly if parents and school convey this information in a calm, unemotional way.
>
> Do not talk about failure. Instead present the position that parents and school *made a mistake* by starting the child in school before he was ready. Point out that *no wonder* he finds school so hard and doesn't like it and doesn't do well. Say that *isn't it lucky* you all found out in time so that now he can be in the first (second, third or whatever) grade again and this time it will be easy and fun.[2]

During over thirty years of pediatric practice, I've talked with hundreds of parents (including parents of children who were hyperactive and children who weren't). Some parents asked, "Is Timmy ready to start school?" Others wondered if David should repeat the first or second grade. *Almost without exception parents who delayed their child's entry into kindergarten or school by a year or decided to have their child repeat a grade have been pleased with their decision.*

How can you tell if your six-year-old is ready for school? What can you (or your physician) look for to tell you he *isn't* ready? What signals will let you know that he needs more time to mature?

Here's a simple readiness checklist I've used for many years that has helped parents in my practice answer the question, "Is my child ready to start in the first grade?"

Readiness Checklist for Starting School

GENERAL:

1. Is a girl		Yes	No
2. Objects to being away from mother		No	Yes
3. Plays well with other children		Yes	No
4. Can be trusted with small amounts of money		Yes	No
5. Has attended kindergarten		Yes	No
6. Can cross the street by himself		Yes	No
7. Looks forward to going to school		Yes	No
8. Will be six years and three months old, or older, when school starts		Yes	No
9. His kindergarten teacher feels he's ready to start in the first grade		Yes	No

HEALTH:

1. Speaks distinctly with no impediment		Yes	No
2. Has had a serious or prolonged illness		No	Yes
3. Feels good most of the time		Yes	No
4. Has a serious physical or emotional handicap		No	Yes
5. Complains often of headache, stomachache or leg ache		No	Yes
6. Is frequently overactive, restless or irritable		No	Yes
7. Complains of being tired		No	Yes

INTERESTS:

1. Likes to draw and color		Yes	No
2. Likes to look at books		Yes	No
3. Likes to play games		Yes	No
4. Likes other children		Yes	No

ABILITIES:

1. Can print his name, or one or two simple words		Yes	No
2. Can draw a square readily		Yes	No
3. Can draw a triangle		Yes	No
4. Can repeat four digits		Yes	No
5. Can repeat five digits		Yes	No

6. Can repeat one of these sentences without a mistake: "Johnny likes to eat ice cream with his baby brother." "Mary has lots of fun playing dolls with her big sister."　　　Yes　No

7. Can draw a man with twelve (or more) of the following features: head, two eyes, nose, mouth, ears, hair, arms, legs, fingers, neck, clothing, length of trunk greater than breadth; mouth, nose and eyes in more than one dimension, hair better than scribble, shoulder indicated, correct number of fingers shown.　　　Yes　No

I've used this simple questionnaire hundreds of times in evaluating a child's readiness for the first grade. *No absolute number of items automatically divides children into those who are ready for school and those who aren't.* But if I see five, six or more answers in the right-hand column I usually advise parents to wait a year before starting him.

OTHER TESTS

The late Eric Denhoff, M.D., of Providence, Rhode Island, described a number of simple nervous system tests that can help physicians, other professionals and parents identify nervous system signs and symptoms that may interfere with your child's ability to meet the demands placed on him in school.

Although, ideally, these tests should be carried out by a physician or other experienced professional, you can test your own child. If he performs poorly, you'll increase his chances of succeeding in school if you delay his school entry for a year.

1. Balance: See if your child can stand (with a reasonable degree of steadiness), with his eyes closed, for fifteen seconds.

2. Coordination:
   a. Ask him to hold his arms straight out in front of him for five seconds (with his eyes open).
   b. Let him rest for a few seconds and then ask him to hold his arms over his head for five seconds.
   c. Ask him to hold his arms straight out in front. Then ask him to turn them over and back smoothly four times.
3. Fine coordination: Tell him to close his eyes and touch his little finger to the tip of his nose. See if he does this test smoothly.
4. Motor-Speech: Ask him to open and close his mouth smoothly five times.
5. Eye Movement Test: Have him sit down and look straight ahead. Then hold a pencil ten inches in front of his eyes. Move the pencil first to one side and then to the other, then up, then down. Finally, move it up to the side, and then down to the side. Notice how well he follows the pencil.
6. Take a coin, key or button and put the object first in his right hand, then in his left. Then ask him, "Which hand is the quarter in?" Repeat the test several times and make sure he can tell his left hand from his right.

According to Dr. Denhoff, 95 percent of 355 normal children, ages six to seven and a half years, passed the tests listed above successfully. He commented, "Children who cannot pass these items likely will fail the first or second grade."[3]

If your hard-to-raise child experienced problems during his preschool years and is improving on a better diet and a comprehensive program of management, you're relieved—even delighted. Nevertheless, go slow and don't push. Regardless of your child's calendar age, the best time for him to begin school is when he's truly ready.

READING PROBLEMS

Your hard-to-raise child may experience problems sitting still, paying attention and concentrating. As a result, he may not read well. Yet, in my opinion, many American children—·including intelligent, calm, attentive children—do not read well because of the way they're taught.

My older brother Joe learned to read when he was four. My Aunt Lucy, who lived with us, taught Joe to read using intensive phonics. He learned the sound of the letters; so he took to reading as a duck takes to water.

Before I got to the reading age, Aunt Lucy married and moved away. So I learned to "read" by listening to Joe and looking at the pictures in my first primer. In this way I was able to recognize the size and shapes of several dozen familiar words. But no one taught me phonics.

In discussing my reading problems my mother commented:

> You would sit with me and try to read a book other than your primer. When you came across a word you didn't know, you'd say, "Give me my *Baby Ray Primer* and I'll tell you what the word is." Then you'd go back to the book and were able to recognize the word that had previously baffled you; *but using this system you weren't learning to read.*

Then at some point my mother sent me to a tutor who used intensive phonics. I can even remember the big phonics book I used—especially a picture of Harry who was running hard and out of breath and making the "h" sound. I also remember the picture of the dog used to emphasize the "d" sound. I'd go to this teacher every day and be drilled in phonics, and she'd praise me and reward me as I improved. Soon I learned to read, and in a few months, reading was no longer a problem for me.

I'd just about forgotten about my reading problems and during my early years of practice I wasn't especially interested in or involved with children with these problems. Then along with many of my pediatric peers I gradually learned that illiteracy in the United States had reached epidemic proportions and that reading ability had continued to decline in our public schools.

Somewhere along the way I read and reread Rudolf

Flesch's books, *Why Johnny Can't Read* and *Why Johnny Still Can't Read*. According to Flesch:

> Learning to read is like learning to drive a car. You take lessons and learn the mechanics and the rules of the road. After a few weeks you've learned how to drive, how to stop, how to shift gears, how to park and how to signal. You've also learned to stop at a red light and understand road signs. When you're ready, you take a road test, and if you pass, you can drive.
>
> *Phonics-first works the same way. The child learns the mechanics of reading and when he's through, he can read.* . . .
>
> With phonics first, the child is first taught the letters of the alphabet and what sounds they stand for.[4]

During the past fifteen years I've seen dozens of my patients overcome their reading problems using the same type of reading program that helped me. And I have realized that how reading should be taught resembles allergy, yeast-related problems and a number of other things I've discussed in this book. Moreover, I acknowledge that intensive phonic instruction may not suit every child. Yet, if your hard-to-raise child isn't a good reader, he needs help—lots of it. Here are my suggestions:

1. Set a good example for your child. If you want your child to read and to enjoy reading spend more of your own time reading.

2. Read to your child and let him read to you.

3. Learn more about reading and how it is taught. Get a copy of Flesch's most recent book, *Why Johnny Still Can't Read* (New York: Harper & Row, 1981) and a copy of Fitzhugh Dodson's book, *Give Your Child a Head Start in Reading* (New York: Simon & Schuster, 1981).

For even more information send a stamped, self-addressed envelope to the Reading Reform Foundation, 7054 East Indian School Road, Scottsdale, AZ 85261.

4. Tutor your child at home using one of these home teaching aids:

a. Listen and Learn with Phonics (available from Career Publishing, Inc., 905 Allanson Road, Mundelein, IL 60060). This home phonics-instruction kit contains illustrated books and audio tapes or records. Hundreds of families in my practice have used it with great success.

b. Word Hunt. This inexpensive card game has helped many of my patients—and my grandchildren—enjoy learning to read. Available from Bamberger Originals, 3557 Stoer Road, Cleveland, OH 44122.

c. *Professor Phonics Gives Sound Advice* and *Sound Track to Reading*. These unique books by Sister Monica Foltzer, M.Ed., of Cincinnati have been described as "the best, most economical, most enjoyable way for children to learn to read." I highly recommend them. Available from S.U.A. Phonics Dept., 1339 E. McMillan Street, Cleveland, Ohio 45206.

If your child doesn't read well he won't do well in his other subjects. As a result his self-esteem will suffer. He'll become frustrated, nervous and discouraged, adding to his other problems. Teaching him to read using intensive phonics instruction won't solve all his problems, but it might solve an important piece of his puzzle.

Section J
OTHER HELPFUL INFORMATION

44
Using Television Wisely

Most American children love television. So do their parents and grandparents. Several surveys show that the average American youngster looks at television twelve to twenty-five hours a week. Moreover, many children spend more hours looking at television than they spend in school. Certainly, they look at television more than they ride their bicycles, climb trees or participate in outdoor sports.

According to George Gerbner, dean of the Annenberg School of Communications at the University of Pennsylvania, "Children absorb what they see on telvision. . . . It becomes the norm against which they judge everything else in society."

In her recent book, *Raising PG Kids in an X-Rated Society,* Tipper Gore expresses concern about the messages our children are receiving through the media and gives parents suggestions for coping with them. Although most of Gore's concerns relate to pornographic lyrics found in rock music, she also expresses concern over TV programs that encourage suicide and that promote violence. In commenting on television, she had this to say: "Television is the most successful entertainment medium of all time with 98 percent of American households owning at least one set. Cable television now reaches some thirty-eight million homes; another two million households are on satellite dishes. The levels of violence on television have dramatically changed for the worse over the past five years.

"Television is a subtle teacher, welcomed into every home. Perhaps we need to step back from it to examine more critically some of the images that penetrate our consciousness from our new electronic hearth."

In her continuing discussion, Gore quotes Anna Kahn, a

former national president of the PTA, who pointed out that scientific studies are supporting the role of TV in causing unacceptable behavior in children. Kahn commented, "Teachers . . . observed . . . (that) child's play had become more violent and aggressive and that children seemed less sensitive to the pain that is a part of violence.

". . . The reality within the broadcast community is rooted in the pure market ethic. If it sells, it must be okay. Violence on TV is commercially successful."

In her book, Gore gives tips that will help you take action against those who are polluting the minds of your children. Included are the following resources:

American Academy of Pediatrics
141 Northwest Point Boulevard
Elk Grove Village, IL 60009

National Coalition on Television Violence
P.O. Box 2157
Champagne, IL 61820

Action for Children's Television
20 University Road
Cambridge, MA 02138

Like Tipper Gore, I'm concerned about the messages our children are receiving that promote sex, violence and suicide. I'm also concerned about TV ads that promote cereals (and other foods) that are loaded with sugar, food coloring and other nonnutritious substances. Moreover, Action for Children's Television (ACT) has expressed a similar concern and I've supported this organization for many years.

In the article "Kids and Television," Teresa Bell, a Jackson (Tennessee) *Sun* reporter, provided further information about ACT. This nonprofit organization was founded by Peggy Charren and three other mothers from Massachusetts nineteen years ago because they were disturbed about the lack of programming choices for children. Today, ACT has fifteen thousand members across the country and is supported by 150 national organizations ranging from the United Steel Workers of America to the American Academy of Pediatrics.

Action for Children's Television lobbies for quality children's programming and helps parents in the difficult job of selecting proper television shows for their children. In accomplishing this job, they've recently created a TV-planning calendar, published by E. P. Dutton, which helps them outline a monthly TV schedule.

The calendar, called "The Book for TV-Smart Kids," includes illustrated puzzles and games for choosing good programs and blanks for recording the choices. It's available in bookstores nationwide for $6.95.

According to Bell, Charren made other suggestions that will help parents and their children select better TV programs.

"Parents should stay well informed by reading and clipping current program and home video reviews. Keep up with news about the TV industry. Your familiarity with these things may persuade your children that you're not automatically against TV. Newspapers, TV columns and magazines are filled with facts about production deals, ad campaigns, audience ratings and the comings and goings of the stars.

"Set visible standards by your own choices—namely, a sense of quality and an interest in variety.

"Make it clear to your children where television fits into a list of family priorities. Writing choices down helps a great deal in setting TV priorities.

"Make sure children understand what takes precedence over TV: homework? exercise? sleep? daily chores? family excursions? Talk with your children about how they're spending their free time to see whether TV is crowding out other experiences.

"Set the home scene so that TV doesn't dominate. Don't put the set in a child's room where viewing is unsupervised or near the dining-room table where it curtails conversation.

"Don't use TV casually to punish or reward. Good behavior should not be equated with more television. However, if a problem is TV related, reduced viewing may be an appropriate remedy.

"When your child seems ready, help him figure out how

to cut back on his TV hours. A real incentive would be to offer him more time with you—doing things that are fun."

One way to devise a TV diet might be to rate shows (for example, Most Favorite—10; Second Most Favorite—9) and limit viewing to the shows with the highest ratings.

45

Other Factors That May Relate to Behavior Problems

ADOPTION

In my five-year study 18 (9.9 percent) of 182 new hyperactive patients were adopted, compared with 1 percent of my other patients. Other observers have also noted that adopted children are more apt to be bothered by hyperactivity.

Here are factors that *may* play a part in causing hyperactivity in adopted children:

First, children who are given up for adoption are usually born to teenagers. Such teenagers often live on junk food before and during pregnancy. These unmarried mothers are apt

to deny or conceal their pregnancy and do not usually receive good prenatal care, including good nutritional advice.

Moreover, mothers who aren't going to keep their babies may be more apt to smoke and consume alcohol and caffeine, and such substances, especially when taken in large amounts, may contribute to nervous system injury.

Finally, babies who are given up for adoption may not receive the touching, holding and other psychological nutrients essential for optimum development. Studies done by a number of workers indicate that infants who receive a lot of skin contact during the early days and weeks of life show significantly better development than infants who do not receive this sort of care.

EMOTIONAL FACTORS

Emotional factors can and do play an important part in causing nervous system symptoms in people of all ages. They can affect the behavior of children in a variety of ways. Moreover, occasionally, psychological or emotional factors may be the major . . . and perhaps the only . . . factor causing a child to be hyperactive, anxious or irritable.

For example, over ten years ago a young couple brought their son Eddie in for a checkup. Their complaint: nervousness and hyperactivity. Eddie was so "hyper" that his first grade teacher sent a note home to the parents saying,

> Eddie is ill at ease, nervous and jumpy. He doesn't pay attention or sit in his seat. Please take him to your doctor for a checkup. Based on my experience with other children, I feel Ritalin may help him overcome his hyperactivity, settle down and pay attention in class.

I gave Eddie a thorough examination and carefully reviewed his past medical history, his family medical history and his diet. There were few, if any, clues that would suggest allergy, and Eddie and his family ate much less sugar and junk food than most families.

But Eddie was obviously under stress, and I discovered what was contributing to his problem: The family had moved to a new community some six months previously. His father had a new job that kept him busy for long hours, so he was spending less time with Eddie and the rest of the family. A younger sister was receiving considerable amounts of attention and was competition for Eddie in the home. His mother—a perfectionist—had been putting extra pressure on Eddie at home and fussing at him when his grades and behavior were less than perfect.

So it was easy to see why at times Eddie appeared nervous, jittery and "hyper." After I conducted two counseling sessions with Eddie's parents, his father began spending more relaxed, one-on-one time with him. Both parents began to notice, pat, hug and smile at him more often. His mother and his teacher let up on the pressure they had been putting on him. Within a few months the hyperactive behavior vanished.

So psychological or emotional factors often play an important role in contributing to the problems of the hard-to-raise child. Yet, more often I see youngsters whose behavior problems are caused by allergic and nutritional factors that affect the nervous system, causing them to develop unacceptable behavior.

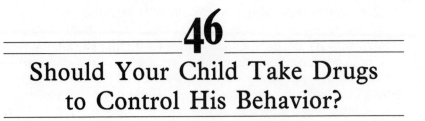

46

Should Your Child Take Drugs to Control His Behavior?

Although Ritalin and other stimulant drugs are still widely used in treating hyperactive children, I don't like to use them. When I have to resort to behavior modifying drugs, I'm admitting that I haven't been smart enough to identify the out-of-place pieces of the child's hyperactivity puzzle and to help parents put them in place.

Nevertheless, Ritalin and other medications can help control the symptoms in many hyperactive children. Moreover, I've used Ritalin in a few selected patients during the past fifteen years. However, as I've learned more about nutrition, food allergies and yeast-connected health disorders, I find I rarely need to use these medications.

Here are two examples of patients for whom I prescribed Ritalin.

Johnny, six and a half years old, came in with his distraught mother, Sara, who said, "I simply can't cope with this child's behavior any longer. Neither can his father. Moreover, Johnny's teachers are threatening to kick him out of school. They've 'had it,' too."

Johnny was "all over the office." He was the most "hyper" youngster I'd seen in a long time. Moreover, his mother appeared anxious, distraught and tearful. Devastated. When my nurse and I began talking about a carefully planned diet, Sara said, "I'm just not up to it at this time."

Because I felt that Sara wouldn't be able to do an elimination diet correctly or get the support and cooperation from other family members, I prescribed Ritalin. My nurse and I also gave her lots of warm reassurance. We said:

> Although we don't have a quick fix, we think we can help you. Here are some materials for you, your husband and your mother to read. Here's a prescription for Ritalin that will help Johnny settle down so they won't throw him out of school. Come back in ten days with your husband and mother and we'll talk about other ways of helping him.

Happily, within forty-eight hours Johnny was better. Much better. And as Johnny acted better at home, Sara's anxiety lessened. Moreover, Johnny's behavior and performance at school also improved.

In the weeks and months that followed, Johnny's family was able to plan and carry out an elimination diet and identify a number of food troublemakers, including artificial food colors, sugar and milk. These were eliminated and he was put on a good diet including nutritious, unprocessed foods plus vitamin and mineral supplements. He was also given lots of "psychological vitamins." After several weeks Ritalin was discontinued with no flare-up in symptoms. *In this patient Ritalin was used as a temporary "crutch," which enabled the family to settle down and deal with the causes of their child's problems.*

Here's another example: Sammy, an allergic child with two brothers and two sisters, was bothered by hyperactivity and a short attention span. With no father in the home, his mother experienced difficulty in taking care of her many responsibilities. And during a recent visit she said:

> I know that what Sammy eats plays a major role in contributing to his hyperactivity and other problems. If I could get him to stay on his diet and do all the other things I'm supposed to do, medication wouldn't be necessary. I do the best I can but I can't always control his diet. I've found that when Sammy's behavior gets out of bounds I can give him Ritalin for a few days or even a few weeks and it keeps him and our family from getting into even worse trouble.

Occasionally, I've prescribed other drugs including Cylert, Dexedrine, Tofranil and Benadryl. But I've used them much less often than I've used Ritalin.

However, some physicians prefer Cylert and use it just as much as they use Ritalin. Moreover, it seems to work just as well in some children. One problem with Cylert: Its effectiveness may not become apparent until a child has taken it for a couple of weeks.

Dexedrine, an amphetamine, has been available for some twenty to thirty years and I have used it occasionally. However, it curbs the appetite more than Ritalin.

Stimulant drugs affect the group of chemicals in the brain called "neurotransmitters." When these neurotransmitters aren't functioning correctly, hyperactivity, short attention span and other nervous system symptoms may develop. The role of stimulants in helping control hyperactive behavior was first reported by Charles Bradley, M.D., in 1937. In working with a group of disturbed hyperactive children, Dr. Bradley stumbled across an answer he wasn't looking for.

Here's what happened. In trying to calm these children, he prescribed a sedative, phenobarbital. To his surprise the phenobarbital had a reverse or paradoxical effect and made the children *more* hyperactive.

So Dr. Bradley concluded that if a sedative made children more hyperactive, a stimulant might calm them. So he gave these youngsters "pep pills" (amphetamines)—and they calmed down. He reported his observations in the medical literature[1] and stimulant drugs have been used by many physicians since that time.

Ritalin comes in 5, 10 and 20 mg tablets and in a 20 mg time-release tablet. When I feel Ritalin is necessary, I start with a small dose—usually 5 mg. It seems to work better when it's given on an empty stomach before breakfast and before lunch. A single dose usually lasts about four hours. Yet in some children a 5 or 10 mg morning dose may be effective until the school day is over.

When Ritalin works, it works in a hurry—in other words, you'll notice a difference in your child's behavior in a day or two. If in seven to fourteen days it hasn't helped, I'll usually increase the dose to 10 mg before breakfast and before lunch. Only rarely do I find bigger doses are needed.

About the side effects. Ritalin sometimes calms a child down too much—it makes him drowsy. It also curbs his appetite—although not nearly as much as Dexedrine. And in an occasional child, Ritalin increases hyperactivity.

278

About the long-term side effects. I've read reports in the medical literature indicating that Ritalin, especially in doses greater than 20 mg a day given for several years, may impair growth. However, experts who've studied this question don't always agree. One report I read said that it didn't impair growth while another report said it did. And another report said that Ritalin caused even more serious side effects including damage to the nervous system. However, such serious side effects appear to be rare.

I rarely prescribe Ritalin for children under the age of five or six. Also, Ritalin shouldn't be used if it causes persistent adverse reactions lasting more than a few days. These include a significant loss of appetite, headache, abdominal pain or depression.

Benadryl, an antihistamine, is commonly used to control allergic symptoms, and I've found it sometimes helps the hyperactive child. Moreover, I feel it's safe, especially for occasional use.

Tranquilizers and antidepressants including Mellaril and Tofranil have been used to control symptoms in hyperactive children by some physicians. However, I feel their use is rarely necessary in a child whose allergies, yeast problems and nutrition are appropriately managed.

I never use Ritalin or other stimulant drugs as a substitute for a more comprehensive treatment program. As Doris Rapp, M.D., the pediatric allergist and author of *Allergies and the Hyperactive Child* and *The Impossible Child,* comments:

> If you have a nail in your shoe which causes your foot to be sore, the cure is easy. Take out the nail. Putting ointments on the foot doesn't solve the problem. If your child is acting different when he eats certain foods, don't make him take drugs—stop him from eating the food that causes his abnormal behavior.[2]

Concern over the use of "behavior pills" to discipline unruly kids was discussed in the April 20, 1987, issue of *Newsweek.* This report pointed out that while Ritalin is an effective treatment for many hyperactive children, it doesn't help every rambunctious youngster. Yet drug officials in Atlanta have become concerned in the last year because they noticed, "an inordinate amount of Ritalin coming into the State; Georgia was using nearly three times as much as New York."

Moreover, a check of drug shipments showed that pharmacies in a few wealthy Atlanta suburbs accounted for 45 percent of the sales.

According to the article, one mother said her son's fifth grade teacher harassed her until she agreed to bring the child to a doctor who put him on Ritalin by day and an antidepressant by night. The boy's behavior did not improve, his grades slipped and he threatened to commit suicide.

In the discussion, the *Newsweek* article said, "In Georgia, parents and teachers hold each other accountable for excessive use of the drug. . . . Some teachers steer parents to doctors who are known to prescribe a sedative without asking too many questions. . . . School officials insist they are only doing their job. . . . There is enough blame to go around."

Andy Watry, executive director of the Board of Medical Examiners of Georgia, commented, "We're looking at a very complex problem. . . . The kids are not taking themselves to the doctor. Parents are taking them—because teachers are telling them to."

Watry's office will soon begin work with teachers, doctors and parents to unravel the chain of responsibility and control the spread of Ritalin.

This report shows that parents are beginning to worry about the use of medications in managing the hyperactive child. In my opinion, treating the hyperactive child resembles treating a person with headaches or high blood pressure. In each situation, medication may temporarily relieve a person's symptoms. *Yet medication should never be used on a long-term basis without attempting to identify and appropriately treat the cause.*

47

Mental Retardation, Autism and Tourette's Syndrome

Have you been told your child is retarded or autistic? Or has a study of his history, physical and psychological characteristics resulted in a diagnosis of Tourette's syndrome?

If the answer is yes, you've probably been told the causes of your child's problems are unknown and treatment rarely helps.

I certainly do not claim to have an answer for all—or even most children—who struggle with these problems. Yet I know, based on my own experiences and the reports of others, that some children with retardation, autism and Tourette's syndrome can be helped using the approaches and methods described in this book.

MENTAL RETARDATION

Many different factors can play a part in causing a child to be slow—even retarded. Some are well recognized and easy to identify, others remain obscure or unknown. Yet, I'd like to tell you about an exciting patient I followed for over twenty-three years. Here's a brief summary of his story:

Neil, a full-term, breast-fed youngster came in for his first visit with me in the summer of 1963. Although his mother was nursing him, he experienced allergic symptoms of all sorts, including rhinitis, irritability, wheezing and digestive problems. At the age of only a few months, his mother found that when she drank milk, Neil would wheeze. Yet, even though she changed her diet, problems of all sorts continued.

Neil was an unhappy, irritable, crying youngster. He

drooled and was hyperactive. He didn't walk until he was eighteen months old and his speech was delayed. Because of his multiple problems, he was seen in consultation by the Child Development Center at the University of Tennessee. Here's a summary of their report:

> Neil's current level of intellectual functioning is within the bor-
> derline or approximately dull-normal range. His greatest diffi-
> culties, aside from speech production, appear to be inattention
> and visual-motor skills. These difficulties suggest an organic im-
> pairment. . . . Diagnosis: mental retardation (mild).

Neil came back to see me again in 1967 at the age of four. His mother reported that he was drowsy and irritable. She was also concerned about his drooling, persistent nasal congestion and about his delayed development.

A physical examination showed no abnormalities except for nasal congestion and dark circles under his eyes. Because these manifestations indicated or suggested an underlying allergy, I prescribed the "cave man" diet at the conclusion of my evaluation. His response was immediate and dramatic.

Following food challenges, his mother noted that milk, chocolate, chicken and several other foods provoked symptoms. When these foods were eliminated, Neil's irritability, nasal congestion and other symptoms disappeared. During the ensuing months, Neil continued to improve to such a degree that he entered kindergarten and subsequently the first grade and did well. Infractions of his diet caused a prompt flare-up of his symptoms. Milk and chocolate were the major troublemakers. However, subsequently, peanuts were found to cause severe problems, even shock.

In late September 1986, I talked to Neil on the phone and here's the report he gave me: "Dr. Crook, I graduated from the University of Tennessee at Martin last year and I'm now taking postgraduate courses. I don't drink milk, eat chocolate, peanuts or chicken. Except for a little seasonal hay fever, I'm feeling great."

AUTISM

Autism puzzles and mystifies both parents and professionals. When you glance casually at an autistic child, he may appear "normal." Yet, his brain malfunctions in such a way that he seems "tuned out" from the world. He sometimes doesn't know who he is or where he is, and he often doesn't even recognize his parents. Although the condition is very rare, it can devastate the families of these children.

I first heard of this strange and bizarre disorder during my early years of practice in the 1950s. At that time experts in pediatrics and psychiatry felt autism developed in children whose mothers had "rejected" them.

I saw no autistic children in my practice until the early seventies. At that time, Dwane, a nine-year-old youngster with severe behavior and developmental problems, was referred to me for pediatric and allergy evaluation. In a letter Dwane's mother sent me, she said:

> Dwane, our fourth child, enjoyed good health during his first year and developed normally.
>
> Between one and a half and two years he began to "spin around" and look at his hands. At times he wouldn't notice us or his sisters.
>
> After the age of two, problems continued and became worse. He withdrew and behaved in a peculiar manner; his development slowed down.
>
> We took him everywhere looking for help. We were given advice of all sorts. Ritalin, Mellaril and other drugs were prescribed. Nothing has helped.

When Dwane came to see me, I reviewed his history and found that he had experienced relatively few illnesses, none serious. Not many antibiotic drugs. He showed some evidence of allergy, including nasal congestion (worse in the summer), bedwetting, bad breath, fatigue and dark circles under his eyes. His major complaints were: couldn't sit still, spaced out—like he was in another world, hummed and spun around.

A physical examination showed no abnormalities except

for nasal congestion and dark circles under the eyes. Because of Dwane's allergy history, at the conclusion of my evaluation I prescribed the "cave man" diet, a diet that avoided every food Dwane ate more often than once a week.

About five weeks later, Dwane's mother sent me the following report:

> After four days on the diet Dwane began to be more alert and less hyperactive; also less spinning. After seven days we added back the eliminated foods and noted the following reactions:
> Wheat and sugar: belligerence, antisocial behavior
> Corn: more withdrawn, talked to himself
> Eggs: clumsiness
> Since being on the diet, Dwane's social behavior is better. His nose has stopped running, he's less clumsy and is better coordinated. He's learned the entire alphabet and can now spell and read many words—something he couldn't do before.

Since Dwane lived over four hundred miles away, follow-up visits over the years have been conducted by mail and by phone.

On June 12, 1985, I received the following report:

> Dwane started public school in 1981 and graduated in 1985 with B's and C's. He's now enrolled in a trade school taking masonry and he rides his motorcycle every day. He cleans the kitchen and mows the yard. Although he's still somewhat a loner, he's involved in a local church and plays the organ for some events.
> He takes no medications of any type—only his multivitamin-mineral pill daily plus extra magnesium and B vitamins. He still avoids junk foods and doesn't eat wheat and corn or drink milk.

A few months after I began working with Dwane, a ten-year-old Nashville youngster, Ann, came to see me. Like Dwane, Ann experienced "peculiar" problems. Although normal at birth, during the second year of life she became "spaced out"—almost like an adult with schizophrenia. Then her speech regressed and a psychologist noted that her behavior was autistic.

She was examined by numerous physicians and other professionals over the next several years. Another psychologist who examined Ann made this report:

> At no time did Ann relate to me in any direct way. Sometimes she would respond, but only fleetingly and without any eye contact. . . . The content of her speech was meaningless and unrelated to anything going on in my presence. Most of the time she was echolalic. Her activity level would be described as hyperactive. All attempts at testing were a failure.

On the same "cave man" or rare food diet I had prescribed for Dwane, Ann improved significantly in one week. When foods were added back, her mother noted that sugar caused her to be moody and irritable; milk caused her to be irritable and spaced out; corn and wheat caused hyperactivity and hallucinations.

When these foods were avoided and a comprehensive program of management (including megavitamins prescribed by Alan Cott, M.D.) was followed, Ann showed remarkable progress.

I haven't seen Ann in a number of years, but in a recent letter to me, her mother had this to say:

> Ann has improved to a fantastic degree on a diet that avoids foods she's sensitive to and features nutritional supplements, including megavitamins and supplemental calcium, magnesium, manganese and zinc. She is fluent in Spanish and graduated from high school in May 1987. Ann will enter college this fall. We're very proud of her accomplishments.

My experience with these children convinced me that allergic, biochemical, metabolic and nutritional factors play important roles in causing severe developmental problems, including autistic behavior. Although I'd been able to identify some of these factors, others eluded me. Nevertheless, based on what I had learned from working with these children and their warm, caring parents, I knew that the "rejection theory" of autism should be discarded.

In the mid-1970s I first heard of the work of Bernard Rimland, Ph.D., the father of an autistic child and the founder of the National Society for Autistic Children, who studied two hundred autistic children in the early seventies. He found that megavitamins (especially large doses of vitamin B_6) plus magnesium helped many of these youngsters. Several years later (1978) he confirmed these observations in a scientific study, with the collaboration of E. Callaway, M.D., and P. Dreyfus, M.D.[1] Rimland's observations have also been confirmed by French researchers.[2,3]

My next exciting experience with an autistic child came in January 1982. At that time a central Tennessee couple brought their five-year-old son, Rusty, in for an examination and consultation. This child had experienced multiple health problems, including colic, recurrent colds, and ear infections and hyperactivity during the first year of life. Yet his development was normal and by one year he could say twenty words.

Soon after the age of one year, his developmental progression ceased. And by the age of two, mild autistic symptoms appeared and communication became an increasing problem.

Studies at a university medical center resulted in a diagnosis of "pervasive developmental disorder, with symptoms of autism."

At the time of his first visit, Rusty was put on the "cave man" diet. After following this diet for one week, he improved dramatically and became more responsive and cooperative. When foods were added back, especially mushrooms, wheat, corn and raisins, his symptoms returned, including staring spells, irritability and autistic behavior.

After challenging Rusty with mushrooms, his mother commented, "Rusty became hyper, wild . . . aggressive, ill; he cried and threw things. His pupils dilated. Yeast caused a similar reaction."

Because Rusty had received many antibiotic drugs and because his symptoms flared when he was challenged with yeast and mushrooms, I prescribed nystatin and a yeast-free, sugar-free diet. During the ensuing months Rusty continued to improve to a remarkable degree. Evidence of his dramatic improvement can be found in this report signed by three of his teachers:

> Institution of the treatment program has resulted in noticeable changes in Rusty's behavior. After two months, *Rusty's readiness for learning improved dramatically* . . . significant decrease in activity level and aggressive behavior, increase in attention span and response to commands, and less generalized irritability.

In a follow-up report in September 1986, Rusty's mother commented:

> Rusty continues to improve. Of course, he still requires special education, yet his verbal language has increased and he can carry on a conversation. He sets the table, helps me fold the laundry, swims, ties his shoes and is generally a cooperative and happy youngster. He took nystatin through December 1984 and continues to take his vitamins. We give him a rotated diet and he still must avoid mushrooms, dried fruits and sugar. Within ten minutes after eating any of these foods, he's "off the wall."

In December 1983, I learned of another child with severe developmental problems, including autistic behavior, who improved on anti-*Candida* therapy. The story of this child (Duffy Mayo) was described in an article by Don Campbell in the September 25, 1983, *Los Angeles Times.* It was also featured in an article by Nancy Baker in the February 1985 issue of *Good Housekeeping.*

Duffy, like Rusty, was a full-term healthy infant who enjoyed superior development during his first year and a half. However, because of recurrent ear infections he received many antibiotics. After the age of eighteen months his developmental progress ceased and autistic behavior appeared. He stopped talking, lost his vigor and began withdrawing. Some days he'd act depressed and stuporous. Other days he'd act restless and hyperactive. According to his mother, "he'd climb the walls."

His severe developmental problems continued in spite of his parents' efforts to find help. Then when he was three and a half, he saw Drs. Phyllis Saifer, Alan Levin and Cecil Bradley. These physicians put him on a program of antifungal medicine including both nystatin and Nizoral and a special diet. Duffy has improved dramatically, although he continues to show motor and comprehension problems.

After his experience in treating Duffy, Dr. Bradley, a psychiatrist, began seeing other autistic children whose histories closely resembled that of Duffy. At the October 1984 meeting of the American Academy of Environmental Medicine in Chicago, Dr. Bradley told of his experiences with fourteen such children. All of these youngsters showed normal development during the first year. Yet, all had experienced recurrent ear infections and had received multiple courses of broad-spectrum antibiotics. Then, like Duffy and Rusty, between the ages of one and two, each of these children began to regress and to develop autistic symptoms. Finally, all improved on special diets and antifungal medications.

TOURETTE'S SYNDROME

About a hundred years ago, a Frenchman, Gilles de la Tourette, described a group of children who showed peculiar convulsive movements. They'd grimace and make faces and jerk their arms and other parts of their body in a strange manner.

Along with these apparently unconscious gestures, victims of this disorder would make funny sounds, including a loud barking cough. At times when these sounds were enunciated more clearly, obscene words were heard.

Because Tourette's syndrome is rare, I saw only an occasional child with this disorder during my many years of practice. However, I recall John, a nine-year-old whose tic-like movements, "peculiar noises" and obscene words disappeared while on an elimination diet. Then, when the offending foods were eaten again, symptoms recurred. Subsequently, I tested this boy and found him to be sensitive to inhalants. On inhalant vaccine and dietary elimination, his symptoms were well controlled.

Then, at a meeting of the American Academy of Environmental Medicine several years ago, Marshall Mandell, M.D., of Norwalk, Connecticut, reported a number of patients like John, whose Tourette's symptoms were related to allergies and allergylike sensitivities. Although Mandell hasn't published his findings, he recently sent me several pages of notes. Here are excerpts from these notes:

> Because of two early experiences of food-related Tourette's syndrome (TS), I contacted the TS association several years ago and with their help, I was able to carry out comprehensive provocative tests on 26 individuals with this strange disorder.
>
> During provocative testing, numerous symptoms were triggered, including typical TS symptoms. Moreover, my testing demonstrated an 80 percent incidence of allergy in this group of children.
>
> During a series of symptom-duplicating tests, one patient showed typical episodes of facial and body movements. Moreover she reacted to many common substances present in her diet and environment.
>
> I saw this young woman over a period of several years, and as long as she stayed on an elimination diet and avoided exposure to chemicals, she remained clear of TS and required no medication.[4]

After receiving the report from Dr. Mandell, I phoned pioneer Chicago allergist Theron G. Randolph, and asked him about his experiences with Tourette's syndrome, Here's what he told me:

> Over the past fifteen or twenty years I've seen at least fifteen patients with Tourette's syndrome whose symptoms were related to environmental allergies. Because a problem of this sort is hard to handle on an out-patient basis, I've usually hospitalized these patients and put them on a spring water fast for five days.
>
> On such a fast, the tics of all these patients improved and in many they disappeared. Then, when foods and chemicals were introduced, the tics and other symptoms returned. So, in my experience, many and perhaps most cases of Tourette's syndrome are related to food and chemical sensitivities.[5]

Working with children with autism, Tourette's syndrome and other severe behavior and learning problems isn't easy. And I don't claim to possess a "quick fix." Yet, I feel that many of these children can be helped—often dramatically—by searching for and appropriately treating food allergies, nutritional deficiencies and yeast-related problems.

48

Miscellaneous Measures That May Help Your Child

AIR IONIZERS

The air we breathe contains molecules with positive and negative charges ("ions"). Research studies during the past several decades have shown that some people who

live or work in closed spaces and in environments containing more positive ions than negative ones develop a variety of symptoms. Typical manifestations include fatigue, headache, drowsiness, irritability, nasal discharge, burning eyes and cough.

One way to increase negative ions is to use an air ionizer. Jonathan Wright, M.D., of Kent, Washington, a family practitioner and author comments:

> The number of people who are sensitive to ionization of the surrounding air isn't known. . . . However, from observation in my practice, it appears to me that the proportion is significant and that air ion sensitivity is not rare or unusual.
>
> In practice it appears that the group most likely to benefit from negative ions are those who suffer from chronic respiratory tract allergy—hay fever, allergic sinusitis, allergic bronchitis, and asthma. . . .
>
> The response (to using an air ionizer) among my patients has been variable, but generally favorable.[1]

Albert Krueger, M.D., of the University of California at Berkeley, has studied the effects of negative ions on microorganisms, plants, animals and man for many years. Other researchers have noted beneficial effects of negative ions on asthma, burns, ulcers and nervous system diseases. Dr. Krueger comments:

> On balance, there appears to be substantial evidence that animals and man experience behavioral changes (depression, anxiety, irritability and sleeplessness) linked to shifts in the air ion milieu. How air ions evoke these changes remains a mystery.[2]

Whether a negative ionizer will help your child or not is uncertain. Such generators cost between $75 and $125 and are available from department and hardware stores. Further information on the effects of ions can be found in both the medical[3,4] and lay literature.[5]

ARTIFICIAL LIGHTING

Research in the new field of photobiology—how light interacts with life—shows that fluorescent lighting can cause physical and behavior problems in children and adults. Natural sunlight contains all the colors of the rainbow, but most artificial lighting contains only a few colors.

Richard Wurtman, Ph.D., a researcher at the Massachusetts Institute of Technology, who studied the effects of artificial lights on calcium levels of elderly nursing home residents, comments, "Little has been done to protect citizens against potentially harmful or biologically inadequate light. . . . Light is potentially too useful an agency of human health not to be more effectively examined and exploited."[6]

In the 1970s, researchers John Ott and Lewis Mayron carried out a study in the Sarasota (Florida) schools.[7] One part of their study consisted of movies that were made using time-lapse photography.

I saw some of the Ott-Mayron movies and their results were astonishing. Children with a tendency toward hyperactivity were studied in rooms with ordinary "full-spectrum" light; then the lighting was changed to the limited spectrum of fluorescent lights.

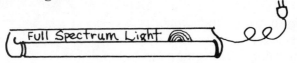

In the rooms with full-spectrum lighting, the children carried out their activities calmly and quietly, while under the fluorescent lights a number of them "climbed the walls" and bounced around the room like jumping jacks.

John O'Brian, M.D., of Fort Wayne, Indiana, a specialist in family practice and environmental medicine, commented:

I believe strongly that fluorescent lights adversely affect behavior and health while full-spectrum lighting is beneficial. We have changed all the fluorescent lights in our office to full-spectrum lighting. And we are encouraging our local schools to switch over, too.[8]

Interest in good lighting is increasing rapidly. In the Tuesday, November 13, 1984, issue of *The New York Times,* Jane Brody wrote an article called "Surprising Health Impact Discovered for Light."

According to Ms. Brody:

> Bright light in the visible spectrum affects the pineal gland's secretion of a hormone that regulates the human biological clock. Light therapy has been shown to influence reproductive cycles, sleeping and eating patterns and activity levels, and may be effective in treating seasonal depression.[9]

Experts encourage us to spend at least half an hour a day outside in natural light. In addition, they urge that we provide ourselves with the broadest spectrum of artificial light we possibly can. Special full-spectrum lights fit into standard fluorescent fixtures and can be purchased at garden supply stores, hardware stores, some lighting departments and health food stores.*

No presently available test will tell you whether fluorescent light contributes to your child's health problems (including hyperactivity, depression, recurrent colds or tooth decay). But it can't hurt to encourage your child to play outdoors, to replace ordinary fluorescent lights in your home with full-spectrum fluorescent bulbs and to make sure your child's school room contains similar lights. And if he improves, you'll have identified another piece of his puzzle.

---

*More information can be obtained by writing to the Duro-Test Corporation, 2321 Kennedy Boulevard, North Bergen, NJ 07047, and to Environmental Systems, 1140 Dillerville Road, Lancaster, PA 17604.

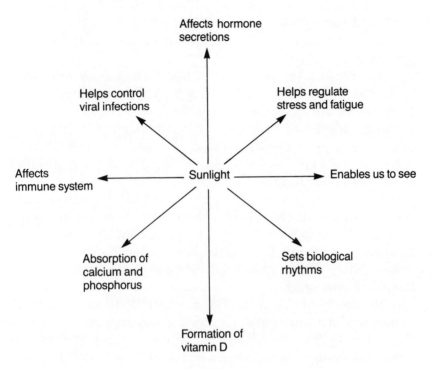

Affects hormone
secretions

Helps control
viral infections

Helps regulate
stress and fatigue

Affects
immune system

Sunlight

Enables us to see

Absorption of
calcium and
phosphorus

Sets biological
rhythms

Formation of
vitamin D

EXERCISE

Every day the press and media tell us, "Exercise! Exercise! It's good for what ails you. It'll make you feel better and live longer."

Yet today we live in an electronic, motorized, mechanized, televised, computerized world. In spite of the growing interest in fitness, jogging, aerobics and sports, we drive to work and our youngsters ride to school. And when our children aren't in school, they're apt to be watching TV and snacking.

An article in the January 26, 1987 issue of *Time* was entitled, "Getting an F for Flabby—U.S. Youths Come Up Short on Endurance, Strength and Flexibility." *Time* reporters commented, "It's the best kept secret in America today—the lack of youth fitness."[11] Declares former pro football coach George Allen, chairman of the President's Council on Physical Fitness in Sports, "It's a disgrace."

The article points out that one third of school-age boys and 50 percent of girls cannot run a mile in less than ten minutes. Moreover, due to tight budgets, physical education programs in school curriculums have often been reduced. And in many communities, the old ritual of playing outdoors after school has largely disappeared.

Moreover, in urban families in which both parents work, youngsters are often told to stay indoors because it's safer there. Finally, there's the lure of computer games and television. And youngsters spend an average of twenty-four hours a week in front of the tube.

But is exercise all that important? More especially, can it help a hyperactive child settle down, concentrate and behave better? Or can it make a depressed child develop better self-esteem and enable him to get along better with his family and his peers at school? My answer is "yes" and there's support for such a point of view.

In discussing the benefits of exercise, Audrey McMahon, a member of the ACLD Scientific Studies Committee commented:

> Exercise promotes good health in several ways:
> 1. It helps in the absorption and utilization of nutrients.
> 2. It promotes oxygenation of the blood.
> 3. It increases circulation to the brain.
> 4. It promotes sweating and helps the body get rid of toxins.
> 5. It stimulates the production of good hormones.
> But achieving a good sweaty, panting workout with a hyperactive child who doesn't have much self discipline isn't easy.

I spent years dreaming up wiles! And it takes one-to-one time and energy.[12]

Here's more: In an article on the benefits of exercise, Bonnie Liebman commented, "If you could sell a drug that could help people lose weight, slow the aging process, prevent a heart attack and increase self-esteem, you'd make a fortune, but the miracle cure already exists and it's not in the shape of a pill. It's exercise and it can work those wonders and more."[13]

In a discussion of the psychological benefits of exercise, Ms. Liebman told of the work of University of Wisconsin psychiatrist John Griest, who showed that running can be as effective as psychotherapy in relieving moderate depression.

Over a ten-week period, running or walking at a comfortable pace for one hour at least three times per week lessened depression as well or better than psychotherapy in the patients Griest studied. Moreover, the benefits of exercise were still present when he rechecked the patients twenty-one months later.[14]

Why does a child feel better after exercise? For one thing, it helps him take his mind off his troubles. And exercising with someone else (as for example, running with his father or a friend) provides him with healthful social contacts.

Equally important, biochemical changes are induced by exercise. Researchers at a number of different institutions cited by Liebman have identified "a class of natural, opiate-like hormones that increase pleasure and diminish pain."[15] The name of this class is beta-endorphin.

Here's still more: In an article in the San Diego Tribune of January 13, 1982, entitled, "Can Running Help Troubled Kids?," Tom Coat told of the work of Mark Shipman, a professor of psychiatry at the University of California at San Diego. Dr. Shipman also served as the medical director of the San Diego Center for Children—a residential and daytime treatment facility for children ages six to thirteen.

According to Coat:

Shipman, a veteran of seventeen marathons began the first of the center studies in 1980. . . . Five years and ten thousand miles of recreation running convinced him that running could cause emotional and behavioral changes. . . . One day while running on the beach, Shipman said he thought about the phenomenon known as "runner's high," a state in which runners have been shown to be calm and able to ward off depression. He wondered if such a high could be used as a natural alternative to drugs for emotionally disturbed children.

Shipman continued, "I can definitely say that running reduced aggression and dependence on medication. . . . In some cases, medication was stopped entirely. . . . That was the most exciting result of the study."[16]

A second behavioral study cited by Coat referred to a doctoral dissertation by Hugh Stevenson, the track and cross country coach at the United States International University in San Diego who said:

We're already seeing effects, especially on hyperactive, aggressive kids. . . . Students who ran and participated in jumping or field exercises for forty minutes a day, at least three times a week, showed less aggression on the days they ran than on the days they did not.[17]

What can you do to get your child to exercise more? Here are suggestions:

1. Begin exercising regularly yourself. Children are parent watchers and parent imitators. I know you're busy—so am I—and you need a twenty-six hour day to do all the things you have to do. Yet, take time for exercise and exercise with your children.

2. Go to your bookstore and look at some of the books or tapes on exercise. There are dozens of them. Pick one you like and start on a regular exercise and fitness plan at home. Here's an inexpensive one I recommend to my patients and their families: *The U.S. Edition of the Official Royal Canadian Air Force Plan for Physical Fitness.* It was first published in 1962 and outlines exercises for people from ages seven through fifty-five.

3. Encourage your child to join organized exercise groups, such as swimming, soccer, track, baseball, basketball, football, tennis or aerobic dance. Help him to choose an activity that will improve his coordination but won't frustrate him too

much. You'll also want to find a teacher or coach who encourages the children with praise and other positive reinforcements.

4. Limit television hours and send your child outside to play.

Section K

CHECKLIST
AND CONCLUSION

49

Checklist for Helping Your Hard-to-Raise Child

C heck off the following items as you complete them. You don't have to try these steps consecutively—the order depends on *your* child's symptoms and *your* available time, money and energy. Good luck!

See chapter(s)

BASIC STEPS:

___ 1. Have a complete physical exam (within the last year), hearing test, eye exam, complete blood count, and urinalysis done on your child.   14

___ 2. "Clean up" your child's diet.   30

___ 3. Give basic nutritional supplements—multiple mineral-vitamin supplement (including B vitamins and vitamin C), calcium, magnesium and zinc.   31–32

___ 4. Emphasize praise, love, touching and "psychological vitamins."   39

___ 5. Consider school readiness and placement.   43

ALLERGIES:

___ 1. Complete the allergy questionnaire (Your Child's Medical History).   13

___ 2. Try Elimination Diet A. Identify foods that your child is allergic to and avoid them.   16

___ 3. Assess sensitivity to dust, molds, pollens or animal danders. Reduce exposures. Consider allergy testing and treatment.   18–19

___ 4. Complete the Chemical Sensitivity Questionnaire. Lighten the chemical load. 20–21

THE YEAST CONNECTION:

___ Complete the Yeast Questionnaire. If your child scores high, 24
___ 1. Follow the *Candida* Control Diet. 28
___ 2. Use nonprescription antifungal agents (garlic, acidophilus and caprylic acid products). 25
___ 3. Consider prescription of nystatin (or Nizoral) by your physician. 25

BIOCHEMICAL CONSIDERATIONS:

___ 1. Give supplemental essential fatty acids. 34–35
___ 2. Try other suggested vitamin and mineral supplements. Consider other appropriate studies, including 31–32
___   a. Laboratory studies for toxic minerals. 32–33
___   b. A blood test for vitamin levels. 31

PERSISTENT HEALTH PROBLEMS:

___ 1. Try Elimination Diet B (the "cave man" diet). 16
      Identify and avoid problem foods.
      Rotate the diet. 17
___ 2. Consult a physician interested and knowledgeable in evaluating the role of diet, allergies, 29–32, 34–38
      5–13, 16–21
      Candida (yeasts) and nutrition in causing 22–28
      or contributing to your child's physical, mental, emotional and learning problems.
      Follow his suggestions if he:
___   a. Orders other biochemical tests including fatty acid and amino acid studies. 34–36
___   b. Tests your child for food sensitivities and prescribes food extracts. 17

50

Conclusion

I finished medical school in 1942. Since that time many changes have taken place in the world around me. Some of these changes can be called fantastic, miraculous or wonderful, while others might be said to be unfortunate, distressing or deplorable. And there are a lot of changes that, like two-edged swords, bring us both benefits and adverse effects. Here are a few examples:

Television entertains and provides marvelous information for people of all ages. A six-year-old child today is apt to know more about world events and life in general than a twelve-year-old—or even an adult—knew a few generations ago. Television entertains shut-ins and educates all of us—if we'll take the time and make the effort.

But the adverse effects of television concern me. Recent studies have shown that the average American child spends more time looking at television than he does in a school room. And each year he looks at thousands of advertisements that encourage him to eat foods that aren't good for him. He also may see so much violence and crime on TV that he's apt to become more aggressive and hostile.

Children also see so much bad manners and bad morals that they begin to accept such behavior as normal. And as pointed out by Tipper Gore in her 1987 book, *Raising PG Children in an X-Rated Society,* television not only encourages violent behavior, it also encourages sexual promiscuity.

Antibiotics help control many dangerous infections and save many lives. Moreover, they have literally "wiped out" many diseases that killed or crippled people during my years in medical school or early years of practice. But antibiotics upset certain fragile body balances and when used excessively or for long periods of time, they promote the overgrowth of the common yeast *Candida albicans.* This yeast in turn puts out a toxin that affects many parts of the body, including the nervous system.

Agribusiness, the supermarket distribution of foods and the decline of the family farm. Unquestionably, most American obtain enough food to maintain their weight. Moreover, one third to one half of Americans—including the poor—consume more calories than they use up. Accordingly, overweight—even obesity—poses a greater threat to most Americans than does underweight.

Many processed foods on supermarket shelves are loaded with sugar, food coloring, processed (hydrogenated) fat, hormones and antibiotics. Growing numbers of observers feel these foods contribute to health problems we're seeing today including obesity, heart disease, hyperactivity and learning problems.

Insecticides and weed killers. These chemicals control pests that would destroy crops; they also kill weeds that would crowd out food-bearing plants. But new pesticide-resistant strains of insects are developing. And toxic products from the both insecticides and weed killers get into our water supply and into our tissues and body fluids, including breast milk.

Petrochemicals and other chemicals. A major American company has for years featured the slogan "Better Living Through Chemistry." Unquestionably, chemistry has contributed to our high standard of living. Today, many necessities, conveniences and luxuries have been made possible because of chemical processes.

For example, petrochemicals are used in polyester clothing, copy-machine paper, fiberboard, electronic equipment and hundreds of other products we use. Although most people seem to tolerate these chemicals, growing numbers complain of "chemical sensitivity."

In addition, many industries produce highly toxic industrial wastes as a by-product of their manufacturing processes. The toxic nature of these substances is recognized by everyone, including those who produce them. Supposedly "safe" methods of disposal are being looked for. Yet, at this time, satisfactory answers haven't been found.

Acid rain, a sulfur-containing by-product of American "smoke-stack" industry is damaging and destroying many American and Canadian forests. Lead from many sources, including lead-containing paints and gasoline, is found in the blood, teeth and brains of all of us.

Happily, during the past ten years, millions of Americans, including those working at the grass-roots level and those in government and our leading universities, are looking at and grappling with many of these problems. And changes are being made. For example, lead is systematically being removed from most gasolines. As a result, recent studies have shown that lead levels in some groups of children are declining.

Health care. Many marvelous advances have been made in health care since I entered medical school almost fifty years ago. Diphtheria, scarlet fever, polio, measles and diarrhea with dehydration killed or crippled many children in the forties and fifties. Now these diseases are rarely seen.

Cataract surgery, total hip replacements and other marvelous advances in surgery relieve suffering and add to the quality of life.

But in spite of these advances, there are problems—grievous problems—as pointed out by Joseph A. Califano in his recent book, *Who Lives, Who Dies, Who Pays.* It seems that we're spending too much money treating things that could easily be prevented. Moreover, too many of us, including those who need health care and those who deliver it, have assumed that if someone else was paying for it, we could consume as many health services as our hearts desired.

It is now obvious to everyone, including leaders in business and industry, that changes must be made. We simply cannot afford to keep on going this way. Moreover, as pointed out by John Naisbitt, more and more people today are taking responsibility for their own health.[1] Nutrition is being seriously entertained as a preventive measure against cancer, heart disease and many other chronic health disorders. Many people are eating less sugar and fat.

Although change is inevitable, it is taking place with "break-neck" speed. Change makes many people uncomfortable and it threatens others, both psychologically and economically. For example: A new hospital is built and filled with expensive equipment and personnel, including a team trained to do heart by-pass surgery for blocked arteries. Yet observers are asking, "Is such surgery really necessary? Does it improve the quality of life? Does it help more than (or as much as) diet and exercise?"

In such a situation it's easy to see how and why physicians who carry out such procedures in hospitals resist change.

Another example is headaches. Millions of people are troubled by severe headaches and undergo sophisticated tests including brain-wave studies and "scans" to search for and rule out blood clots, abcesses, and other rare causes of headache. When such tests are "negative" (as is usually the case), drugs are usually prescribed to help relieve the symptoms.

Yet a few astute physicians beginning in the early 1900s found that the cause of many, and perhaps most, headaches could be identified using a simple, one-week elimination diet. If the headaches disappeared—as was generally the case—

foods were then added back and the troublemakers could be identified. But because these observant physicians were unable to "scientifically prove" their observations, they were usually ignored or put down.

A similar situation exists with muscle and joint pain—even arthritis. In spite of observations by many people that show that such symptoms are often diet related, most physicians, including arthritis specialists, have ignored the diet-arthritis connection—especially since this connection is reported by ordinary folks.

Why is this so? In a recent article published in the *Journal of the American Medical Association,* "The Tomato Effect— Rejection of Highly Efficacious Therapies," James S. Goodwin, M.D., and Jean M. Goodwin, M.D., of the University of New Mexico, told how effective methods of treatments are often rejected because doctors don't understand why or how they work. Many of the concepts and recommendations described in this book still haven't been accepted by many physicians, including those in the medical establishment who often say, "Your observations haven't been proved scientifically. They're based on anecdotal data."

I can understand such criticism because I've seen all sorts of "wild" and unproven ideas come down the pike during the forty-plus years since I finished medical school. Many ideas that initially seemed to possess merit later proved to be passing fads or even hoaxes.

On the other hand, when I review history, I find countless examples of brilliant medical "breakthroughs" that were initially put down, ridiculed or rejected by the establishment.

For example, the British doctor James Lind, in the 1740s, found that by giving the British sailors limes, the dread and often fatal disease scurvy would be prevented. Yet because Lind couldn't explain how and why limes helped, his recommendations were rejected. Thousands of British sailors died of scurvy in the next fifty years because limes and other fresh fruits and vegetables weren't made available on all British ships. One hundred and eighty-three years elapsed between Lind's initial observations and the discovery of vitamin C by the Hungarian biochemist Albert Szent-Györgi.

Another story: Ignaz Semmelweis, a twenty-five-year-old physician, discovered a simple way of preventing a dreaded fatal disease, "childbed fever." Women in labor who were delivering their babies in hospitals were dying in epidemic proportions. The cause: doctors were carrying out pelvic examinations on their patients in labor after performing autopsies on women who had died of "childbed fever." The solution: Semmelweiss posted a sign on the door of his obstetrical ward: "Carefully wash your hands before every pelvic examination." And the patients on his ward remained well while women on other wards continued to die.

What happened to Semmelweis? He was ridiculed and fired from his hospital appointments because he chose to rock the boat. It wasn't until about twenty-five years later, in the 1870s, with the work of Lister and Pasteur, that the medical community (and the world) began to realize the validity of Semmelweis's observations.

And so it is today. Laura and I have gathered information for this book from many sources (including the medical and lay literature). Although some of our material comes from reports in the scientific literature, much of it is based on my personal experiences with thousands of patients during the past thirty years.

Moreover, I learned from the clinical observations and reports of dozens of other physicians who have made similar observations and shared them with me.

I've also listened to and heard from tens of thousands of parents and teachers in the United States, Canada and England who also know beyond a shadow of a doubt that what a child eats (or doesn't eat) plays a major role in causing hyperactivity and related behavior and learning problems.

I freely admit that I possess no "panacea"—no quick fix—and no magic answer for your hard-to-raise child. Yet I believe with every fiber within me that *he can and will be helped if you'll follow the leads Laura and I have discussed with you.*

Several years ago, at a yeast conference in Dallas, my good friend, Phyllis Saifer, M.D., of Berkeley, California, said, "When it comes to helping patients with yeast-related illness *I have more questions than answers."*

This same statement sometimes applies to helping children with nervous system symptoms and emotional and learning problems. But, as Confucius pointed out, "A journey of a thousand miles starts with one step." I hope reading this book will be the first step on the high road to health and happiness for your child—and your family.

APPENDIX A
The Feingold Diet
and Controversy

If you've spent much time trying to help your hard-to-raise child, chances are you've heard about the work of the late Benjamin Feingold, M.D., of California, and the "Feingold diet." This pioneer physician helped make people everywhere aware that what a child eats can affect his behavior.

Moreover, through his leadership and the unselfish work of thousands of parents who became members and leaders of the Feingold Association of the United States (FAUS) (P.O. Box 10085, Alexandria, VA 22310), countless hyperactive children and their families have been helped.

Here are comments by Patricia Frederick, a long-time Feingold leader, published in a recent issue of the The *Feingold Association of the Washington Area Newsletter:*

> Why did I put my heart out to the Feingold Association? It is very simple. The Feingold diet saved my daughter, my marriage and my life. . . . Here's my story. . . .
>
> Dawn, our second child . . . barely ever slept. At six months she was crawling and at nine months she was running at full force. She suffered from many ear infections, had various unexplainable skin rashes, and was congested most of the time. . . .
>
> Dawn was a constant-motion child who cried so very often. She didn't cry, she screamed! . . . As she grew, her activity level grew.
>
> We spent all of her first 2½ years trying to find out just what was the problem. . . . We had her to an ear, nose and throat specialist, an allergist, the lab for total body X rays, blood tests, urine tests and also attended many highly recommended parent effectiveness training courses. Nothing worked.
>
> Her sleep patterns tormented us because she didn't sleep!

Her activity level was so unpredictable that you didn't go anywhere.

Our allergist had been doing some reading and highly recommended that we get Dr. Feingold's book, "Why Your Child Is Hyperactive." He told us over the phone about diet management. . . . We had done everything else, it certainly couldn't hurt. Three days later a new Dawn was born into our home. This child *walked* into the kitchen and *asked* for some cereal. The same child had never walked, and talking was usually in a yell. . . . She was even smiling. And she had slept through the entire night.[1]

In my opinion, Dr. Feingold's observations on the relationship of diet to hyperactivity might be compared to the pioneer explorations of Christopher Columbus in 1492. Both men were often ignored or ridiculed. Yet because they persisted, in each case a "new world" was opened up.

Here's another parallel: When Columbus discovered America, the Vikings had preceded him. Yet their voyages made little or no impression on the world. Similarly, beginning over sixty years ago a few allergy pioneers (including W. R. Shannon and Albert Rowe) observed that what a person ate could profoundly affect the nervous system.[2,3,4]

In the next several decades other physicians, including Theron Randolph, Hal Davison, Steve Lockey, Frederic Speer and Susan Dees, reported other food-related nervous system manifestations. These included headache, hyperactivity, irritability, confusion, depression and convulsive disorders.[5,6,7,8,9,10] Yet just as the continent of North America was overlooked until Columbus came along, the diet-hyperactivity "continent" was overlooked by most of the medical community and the public until Feingold came along.

Here's a third parallel between the discoveries of Columbus and Feingold: Naturally, Columbus could only lead the way and it took thousands of explorers and map makers who came after him to prepare a full topographical survey of the North American continent. Similarly, it will take thousands of parents, physicians, psychologists, biochemists, immunologists, nutritionists, toxicologists and other researchers to explore and map out all of the still unknown parts of the "continent" of hyperactivity.

Because the relationship of diet to hyperactivity continues
to be controversial and because the Feingold diet has been so
prominently featured in this controversy, I think you'll be interested in learning more about the Feingold diet and how it
got started.

A handful of allergists, including Theron Randolph,[11]
Frederic Speer[12] and Stephen Lockey[13] in the 1950s, noted
that coal-tar derivatives, including food colors and dyes, at
times were responsible for a variety of adverse (allergic) reactions. These included hives, asthma, gastrointestinal allergy
and irritation of the vulva.

Feingold, a San Francisco allergist and immunologist with
the Kaiser Permanente Medical Center, became interested
in these adverse reactions to food colors and flavors in the
1960s. In his book *Why Your Child Is Hyperactive* he tells his
story:

> In the summer of 1965 a woman entered my office. . . . She was
> suffering from acute hives. . . . She looked, and obviously felt,
> miserable.
>
> I read the medical history of this patient, examined her and
> tested her for allergy. Since the tests were negative, I con-
> cluded that artificial food colors and flavors might be involved.
> Food additives had been a causative factor in previous cases of
> hives that I had seen. I immediately placed her on a diet to
> which she quickly responded. The skin condition vanished
> within seventy-two hours.
>
> Then, some ten days following the diet prescription, I re-
> ceived an unusual call from the center's chief of psychiatry. He
> asked, "What did you do with that patient?" and I replied that
> we had simply "placed her on the elimination diet."
>
> The psychiatrist then revealed that this woman had been
> in psychotherapy for about two years. She'd been hostile and
> aggressive, unable to get along with her husband or family or

coworkers. In less than two weeks, these conditions had also cleared.[14]

Following the response of this patient, Dr. Feingold and his staff began to look for other patients whose behavioral disturbances were induced by artificial colors and flavors and by foods containing salicylates, the major ingredient in ordinary aspirin tablets.

During the next several years of using his elimination diet on allergic patients, most often children, Feingold began to hear increasing numbers of reports that behavioral patterns in many of these children had changed. Moreover, a few parents reported that "disruption at home and in school had almost stopped; that learning ability had improved."[15]

In June 1973 Dr. Feingold described his experiences in treating children with hyperactivity and other behavioral disturbances at a meeting of the allergy section of the American Medical Association in New York City. His presentation caught the attention of reporters, including science writers, and led to extensive coverage by the national media.

Soon afterward Clyde Hawley, M.D., and Robert W. Buckley, M.D., of California, confirmed Feingold's observations. Moreover, these physicians carried out a simple study that clearly demonstrated that tiny amounts of food dyes purchased at the supermarket caused violent behavioral reactions in some of their patients.[16]

Two groups of dietary ingredients were eliminated by Feingold. Group I includes all foods that contain synthetic colors and flavors as well as the preservatives BHT and BHA. Group II foods comprise a number of fruits, vegetables and miscellaneous items containing "salicylates."*

According to Dr. Feingold, salicylates are also related to aspirin, willowbark and oil of wintergreen.

After Feingold's book was published, a national "Feingold Association" was formed, with chapters across the country. And according to Dr. Buckley:

---

*The salicylate-containing foods include almonds, apples (also cider and cider vinegar), apricots, all berries, cherries, cloves, coffee, cucumbers and pickles, currants, grapes and raisins (also wine and wine vinegar), green peppers (also chilies), nectarines, oranges, peaches, plums, prunes, tangerines, tomatoes and all teas.

They placed consumer pressure on the government for stricter regulation of the sort of chemicals placed in junk food. The massive food industry acted to defend its image and its right to indiscriminately use azo and aniline chemicals.

They organized a nutrition foundation which received contributions from the Coca Cola Company, Oscar Meyer Co., Procter & Gamble, Campbell Soup, Nestle Co., Dow Chemical and the Strange Company, which makes artificial colors and flavors.

They held press conferences to claim that indecisive and occasionally inept research did not demonstrate a scientific proof to account for the benefit which Feingold reported. They concluded it was safe to continue using the additives.[17]

I could write hundreds of pages to tell you more about the controversy that has surrounded the Feingold diet and other aspects of the diet-behavior controversy during the last decade. Yet I don't feel it is relevant or necessary to load you up with all this material as a lot of it is "water under the bridge." Nevertheless, it's appropriate to summarize briefly some of the things that have taken place.

The Feingold controversy in many ways resembles the "food allergy controversy." Here are some of these similarities:

1. Reports of food dyes causing behavioral changes were made by practicing physicians and their patients. Such individuals lacked the funds, personnel and facilities needed to support their clinical observations with scientific studies.

2. The scientists who did not see these reactions (and who

did not visit with the parents or teachers who observed them) tended to be skeptical.

3. Many of these skeptics reacted with hostility—and arrogance—and challenged those who reported them to "scientifically prove" their "anecdotal observations" by using scientific studies.

4. Talking about a diet-behavior relationship was uncomfortable, inconvenient and threatening to many people, and to companies and corporations manufacturing and marketing foods loaded with colors, flavors and additives. If they accepted the Feingold findings and recommendations, such companies would find them inconvenient and costly. Those feeling threatened also included physicians, psychiatrists and other professionals who customarily blamed hyperactivity and related disturbed behavior on other causes. Moreover, such professionals usually used other methods of treatment, including psychotherapy and medication.

5. The egos of scientific "experts" understandably are threatened when new observations in their fields come from "ordinary folks." Accordingly, they tend to reject them as "unproven," "anecdotal" or "unscientific."*

6. Carrying out controlled experiments to study diet and behavior relationships are expensive, and time consuming, and present many difficult challenges even under the most favorable circumstances.

7. Unfortunately, in my opinion, a number of the early studies (that were supposedly "scientific") were organized and carried out by investigators who weren't objective. Moreover, their studies were funded by those who had a financial interest

---

*A friend of mine interested in this subject commented:

> I'll tell you why "experts" in the fields of allergy, neurology, psychiatry, psychology, nutrition, education and pediatrics have rejected the diet-behavior relationship for so many years.
>
> By definition "an expert is an authority who knows all there is to know about his field." And if he admits he doesn't know that what a child eats can make him hyperactive and cause other behavioral changes . . . then by definition he's no longer an expert. And no person wants to give up his expert status!

> Another friend put it more simply. He said, "What a person isn't up on he's down on."

in proving that what a child ate had little or nothing to do with his behavior.

In many ways, those of us who have found that dietary ingredients cause hyperactive behavior remind me of the fable of the blind men who examined an elephant. The man who felt the trunk described the animal in one way, while another, perched on the animal's head (or at his tail or underside), told a different story. Similarly, different observers examining the "hyperactivity elephant" have developed divergent hypotheses to explain the causes of hyperactivity.

For example, because Dr. Feingold was interested in artificial food dyes and flavorings, he emphasized the role of these substances in causing hyperactivity. Moreover, recent double-blind controlled cross-over studies by Egger, Soothill and associates showed that food colors were a major cause of hyperactivity in the patients they studied.[18]

But Feingold, like Columbus, didn't know that the "hyperactivity continent" was bigger than he realized. And countless physicians and parents have found that adverse reactions to many common foods also cause hyperactivity.

If you're familiar with the Feingold diet, or if you've found that it has helped your child (or even if it hasn't), you're apt to ask, "Why is it that you, Dr. Feingold and many others have found that what a child eats can make him hyperactive, yet some researchers who carried out 'scientific studies' have been unable to confirm this relationship?"

In responding to this frequently asked question, in my 1980 article in the *Journal of Learning Disabilities* entitled, "Can What a Child Eats Make Him Dull, Stupid, or Hyperactive?" I said:

> 1. Most of the studies . . . investigated only the role of food colors and dyes and paid no attention to sugar, milk, chocolate, wheat, corn and other foods that commonly cause allergic reactions in children. Accordingly, many of the children studied by researchers remained hyperactive because they continued to eat foods (and breathe chemicals and inhalants) to which they were allergic.
> 2. [There was] lack of understanding of the fundamental principles involved in masked, hidden or delayed-onset food

allergy by those conducting the studies. . . . When an individual who is sensitive to a food avoids it for 4 to 14 days . . . and then returns the food to his diet, sharp and exaggerated symptoms will usually develop.

Moreover, such symptoms usually develop within a few minutes to a few hours after eating the food. In contrast, if the food is avoided for 3 or more weeks, the individual usually loses some of his sensitivity. So when challenges are carried out after a child has been on an elimination diet for 3 to 6 weeks, no reaction may occur even though the child was or is sensitive to one of the eliminated foods.

3. Studies by Swanson and Kinsbourne suggest that the quantities of food color administered by some of the "negative" studies were only ⅓ to ⅕ as much as the typical American child consumes in a day. And these investigators noted that a majority of the hyperactive children they studied showed measurable nervous system reactions when given larger amounts of food colors and dyes (following a 4-day period of avoidance).[19]

THE QUESTION OF SALICYLATE-CONTAINING FOODS

Here's another aspect of the Feingold diet that has caused confusion . . . the question of salicylates. In the 182 families who participated in my five-year study, food colors, especially red, were reported to be the second most common cause of hyperactivity (sugar ranked first). Although I learned about the relationship of food colors to hyperactivity from Dr. Feingold, I've been unable to confirm his observations about the harmful effects of the salicylates.

Because ordinary aspirin is loaded with "salicylates," in working with my hyperactive patients I usually ask parents, "Does aspirin upset your child in any way? Does it make him swell or wheeze? Does it bother his nervous system?"

In most of my patients (unless they're bothered by nasal polyps or asthma, or give a history of problems with aspirin), I ask parents to give the child (age five or older) an adult-size aspirin tablet three times a day and to note any effects on the child's behavior.

Although I see an occasional child whose parents report, "Aspirin makes my child overactive," in perhaps nineteen out of twenty of my patients, parents report, "No effect." So when a concentrated salicylate, such as aspirin, doesn't disturb a child, it seems to me that parents needn't eliminate the many nutritional fruits and vegetables that contain salicylates.*

After all, salicylate-containing foods like apples, oranges, coffee and tomatoes are common allergy-provoking foods. But so are milk, wheat, eggs, corn and chocolate, which don't contain salicylates.

However, recent studies support the hypothesis that salicylates may contribute to hyperactivity. Joseph J. McGovern, Jr., M.D., of Oakland, California, and Robert Gardner, Ph.D., professor of animal science at Brigham Young University, studied thirteen hyperactive children under scientifically controlled conditions.[21] Their study was designed to explore the relationship between naturally occurring "phenolic food compounds" (PFC's) and hyperactivity.

The PFC's are low molecular weight chemicals in foods that contain the phenol ring in their structure. Among these compounds are the salicylates.

In carrying out their studies these investigators used sublingual drops of various substances, including eight common foods, animal danders, molds and house dust and also preparations of salicylates and other phenolic fractions found in foods.

Of the children studied, each child reacted adversely to an average of seven test substances. Eighty percent of the children reacted to challenge with salicylates.

Furthermore, Australian researchers studied eighty-six

*Gary Oberg, M.D., of Crystal Lake, Illinois, commented:

Maybe the salicylates in the foods of some of Dr. Feingold's patients had little or nothing to do with the reactions he observed. Instead, the children may have been reacting in an allergic manner to other components of these foods that by coincidence also contained salicylates.[20]

children who had improved on an elimination diet. "Nearly three-quarters reacted to double-blind challenge with salicylates but not placebo." Yet these researchers found the Feingold diet "unsuitable for the management of food-related behaviour disturbances . . . [because] laboratory analyses have shown that many foods allowed on the Feingold diet are rich in salicylates."[22]

Do salicylate-containing foods play an important role in causing hyperactivity? At this point I don't really know. Yet, if your child's puzzle remains incomplete, you may need to search for a salicylate piece.

APPENDIX B
Other Sources
of Information

U.S. AND CANADIAN SOURCES OF HELP AND INFORMATION

1. *Association for Children with Learning Disabilities (ACLD)*. This nonprofit organization, with over two hundred state and local affiliates, was incorporated in 1964 "for the purposes of advancing the education and general well-being of children with learning disabilities." It sponsors national, state and local meetings, and feature speakers with varying backgrounds. This organization also distributes books, articles and service directories on learning disabilities and related disorders. For information, send a stamped, self-addressed envelope to ACLD, 4156 Library Road, Pittsburgh, PA 15234, or in Canada to ACLD, 1901 Yonge Street, Suite 504, Toronto, Ontario M4S 2Z3.

2. *Update*. This quarterly periodical is published by the Gesell Institute of Human Development. Recent issues of this periodical have discussed nutritional, environmental, psychological and other factors that play a part in causing illness. For further information, send a stamped, self-addressed envelope to *Update*, 310 Prospect Street, New Haven, CT 06511.

3. *Human Ecology Action League (HEAL)*. This national, nonprofit organization (with chapters in many cities) publishes a quarterly magazine, "The Human Ecologist." This periodical contains news on recent developments in environmental medicine, including sources of books, food, clothing and other supplies. For information about the newsletter or a support group in your area, send a stamped, self-addressed envelope to "HEAL," 2421 W. Pratt, Suite 1112, Chicago, IL 60645.

4. *Feingold Association of the United States (FAUS)*. For

many years this nonprofit organization has worked to help hyperactive children and their families. There are many local chapters throughout the country. For further information, send a stamped, self-addressed envelope to FAUS, P.O. Box 6550, Alexandria, VA 22306.

5. *The Price-Pottenger Nutrition Foundation.* This nonprofit, educational foundation publishes a quarterly bulletin devoted to nutritional topics. For further information, send a stamped, self-addressed envelope to PPNF, P.O. Box 2614, La Mesa, CA 92041.

6. *Canadian Schizophrenia Foundation,* 2229 Broad Street, Regina, Saskatchewan S4P 1Y7, Canada. This is the Canadian "sister organization" of the Huxley Institute. Its goals and purposes are identical. Certain classes of membership in either of these organizations include subscriptions to the quarterly *Journal of Orthomolecular Medicine* and a quarterly newsletter.

7. *The Journal of Orthomolecular Medicine,* publication office 2229 Broad Street, Regina, Saskatchewan S4P 1Y7, Canada. This journal provides information on a wide variety of topics including *Candida albicans,* vitamins, trace minerals and other subjects relevant to lay persons as well as to professionals.

8. *The People's Medical Society,* 33 East Minor Street, Emmaus, PA 18049. This organization is the project of the Soil and Health Society, a nonprofit, tax-exempt organization. It was organized to create a national citizen's group to promote preventive-health practices and to contain medical costs. Services include a regular newsletter. Membership fee is $20 per year.

9. *The Environmental Health Association of Dallas, Inc. (EHAD).* EHAD provides information and support to individuals with chronic health disorders, and publishes a newsletter, *Twentieth Century Living.* For further information, send a stamped, self-addressed envelope to EHAD, P.O. Box 224121, Dallas, TX 75264.

10. *The Center for Science in the Public Interest (CSPI).* This center provides many excellent materials on nutrition. Their monthly sixteen-page publication, *Nutrition Action,* is well written, interesting and authoritative. For further infor-

mation, send a stamped, self-addressed envelope to CSPI, 1775 S Street, N.W., Washington, D.C. 20009.

11. *Western New York (WNY) Allergy and Ecology Association*, 437 Linwood Avenue, Buffalo, NY 14209. Available through this organization is a newsletter that reviews relevant literature and contains general information for individuals with food and chemical sensitivity and yeast-connected health disorders. The price for ten issues per year is $10. To obtain a single issue send a stamped, self-addressed envelope and $1.00.

12. *Nutrition for Optimal Health Association (NOHA)*. Available from this nonprofit organization are educational materials including tapes, books and a newsletter. For further information, send a stamped, self-addressed envelope to NOHA, P.O. Box 380, Winnetka, IL 60093.

13. *Allergy Information Association (AIA) of Canada*, Room 7, 25 Poynter Drive, Weston, Ontario M9R 1KB, Canada. This organization founded in 1964 publishes an excellent quarterly newsletter, *Allergy Shot*, that provides information on allergies and a wide variety of related health topics.

14. *Access to Nutritional Data*, P.O. Box 52, Ashby, MA 01431. Information about nutrition is exploding and almost impossible to keep up with. This organization publishes monthly file cards summarizing the nutritional literature. Subscription rates are $80 for six months, $150 for twelve months.

15. *Insta-Tape, Inc.*, 810 South Myrtle Avenue, P.O. Box 1729, Monrovia, CA 91016. This company provides educational tapes for professionals and nonprofessionals, dealing with a variety of topics relating to allergy, clinical ecology and nutrition.

16. *Sara Sloan Nutra*, P.O. Box 13825, Atlanta, GA 30324. Available from this source are a nutrition newsletter and a variety of helpful books and pamphlets directed especially toward improving the nutritional status of children.

17. *Metabolic Update*. A monthly audio-tape service designed to alert the listener to fast-breaking advances in nutrition, by Jeffrey Bland, Ph.D., of the Linus Pauling Institute. $200 per year, $20 per copy. For information write to *Metabolic Update*, 15615 Bellevue-Redmond Road, Suite E, Bellevue, WA 98008.

18. *Brain/Mind Bulletin.* News from the *Leading Edge.* This newsletter edited by the author of *The Aquarian Conspiracy,* Marilyn Ferguson, brings together information on psychology, human potential and brain function. Moreover, it probes into the territory of social innovation and local and world issues of various types. Available from Interface Press, Box 42211, 4717 North Figueroa Street, Los Angeles, CA 90042, for $35 per year.

19. *Human Ecology Foundation of Canada,* 465 Highway 8, Dundas, Ontario L9H 4V9, Canada. This foundation publishes a quarterly newsletter. It was organized to provide information for those interested in obtaining safe sources of food, clothing and housing. Annual membership fee is $20.

20. *Executive Health.* This six- to eight-page, highly authoritative publication discusses vitamins, minerals, fatty acids, exercise, and many other subjects. Published monthly by Executive Health Publications, P.O. Box 589 Rancho Santa Fe, CA 92067. Subscriptions are $30 per year in the United States, Canada and Mexico.

21. *Huxley Institute for Biosocial Research (HIBR),* 900 North Federal Highway, Suite 330, Boca Raton, FL 33432. This nonprofit national organization carries on a number of educational activities, including training seminars for physicians and yearly symposia for the public. Its goals include providing both professionals and nonprofessionals with the latest findings in nutrition and more especially in orthomolecular medicine and psychiatry.

22. *Schizophrenia Association of Greater Washington (SAGW),* Wheaton Place Office Building, North, #404, Wheaton, MD 20902. This organization was founded primarily to help individuals with schizophrenia, depression and other mental illnesses. However, it now also serves as a resource organization for both professionals and nonprofessionals interested in nutrition, preventive medicine and new approaches to health care.

23. *The International Journal of Biosocial Research,* P.O. Box 1174, Tacoma, WA 98401. This quarterly publication "is a peer-review interdisciplinary journal devoted to research on the environmental, genetic, biochemical and nutritional factors affecting human behavior and social groupings."

24. *En-Trophy Institute,* Box 984, Station "A," Hamilton, Ontario L8N 3R1, Canada. This organization publishes the *En-Trophy Review,* a "unique" holistic approach to your food and health.

25. *The People's Doctor.* This is an informative, stimulating and provocative newsletter, by "medical heretic" Robert Mendelsohn, M.D. Although trained as a pediatrician, Mendelsohn has given up traditional pediatrics and has become an articulate and controversial advocate of alternative methods of health care. For more information, write to *The People's Doctor,* P.O. Box 982, Evanston, IL 60204.

26. *American Academy of Environmental Medicine,* P.O. Box 16106, Denver, CO 80216. This organization will send names of physicians interested in food and chemical sensitivities and environmental medicine to anyone who sends a stamped, self-addressed envelope. They will also furnish names of these physicians to anyone who calls them.

27. *Prevention, Best Ways, Let's Live* and *Your Good Health.* I've read many informative and reliable articles on nutrition and preventive medicine in these publications. Moreover, five to ten years after publication in these magazines, much of the same information was published in distinguished medical journals. Look for these and other fine health magazines at your local newsstand.

28. *Academic Therapy.* Academic Therapy Publications publishes this "practical" journal five times each year for teachers in the field of learning disabilities and other specialists working with kids who learn differently. In addition, this firm publishes 125 high-interest and low-level novels for young people, ages nine to eighteen, who are reading two or three years below level. For further information, contact: Academic Therapy Publications, 20 Commercial Boulevard, Novato, CA 94947-6191. Request a free catalog.

29. *The Preventive Medicine Doctor.* This pamphlet by M. J. Packovich, M.D., published by Tecbook Publications, P.O. Box 5002, Topeka, KS 66605, price $1.39, lists the names and addresses of 140 publications and 121 associations, including both orthodox and alternative health-care approaches. Many of these offer newsletters, booklets and magazines for low cost or without charge.

30. *Kup's Komments.* A holistic journal for the public and health practitioners by Roy Kupsinel, M.D., P.O. Box 550, Oviedo, FL 32765.

31. *Once Daily.* "A new digest of dental health for people who want sound teeth and healthy bodies," by Jerome Mittleman, D.D.S., 263 West End Avenue, #2-A, New York, NY 10023.

32. *Allergy Alert.* A monthly newsletter by Sally Rockwell, discussing food, chemical and other allergies and yeast-connected health disorders. For further information send a stamped, self-addressed envelope to *Allergy Alert,* P.O. Box 15181, Seattle, WA 98115. Also available from this source is *Rotation Game,* "a self-help survival kit for those with food allergies," and a handbook of recipes entitled *Coping with Candida.*

BRITISH AND AUSTRALIAN SOURCES OF HELP AND INFORMATION

1. *Hyperactive Children's Support Group,* 59 Meadowside, Angmering, Littlehampton, West Sussex BN16 4BW, England.

2. *Action Against Allergy,* 43 The Downs, London SW20 8HG, England. This association is working to help people with chronic illness related to foods, chemicals and yeasts. Chairperson: Mrs. Amelia Nathan Hill.

3. *The McCarrison Society,* Miss Pauline Atkin, Secretary, 23 Stanley Court, Worcester Road, Sutton, Surrey SM2 65D, England.

4. *Sanity,* 77 Moss Land, Pinner, Middlesex HA5 3AO, England.

5. *Schizophrenia Association of Great Britain,* Tyr Twr, Ooanfair Hall, Caernarvon OL55 1TT, Wales.

6. *The Journal of Alternative Medicine,* 30 Station Approach, West Byfleet, Surrey KT14 GNF, England.

7. *Clinical Ecology Society,* The Medical Center, Michael J. Radcliffe, M.D., President, Hythe, Southampton SO4 52B, England.

8. *Austro-Asian Society for Environmental Medicine,* c/o

Clive F. H. Pyman, M.D., 20 Collins Street, Coats Building, Suite 4, Melbourne, Victoria, Australia.

9. *The Allergy Self-Help Centre,* Unit 4, 42 Osborne Place, Stirling 6021, Western Australia.

10. *Hyperactive Help,* P.O. Box 337, Subiaco 6008, Western Australia.

11. *Allergy Association of Australia,* Adelaide Branch, 37 Second Avenue, Sefton Park 5083, South Australia.

12. *Allergy Association of Australia,* New South Wales Branch, 61 Cambewaira Avenue, Castle Hill, Sydney 2154, Australia.

13. *Allergy Association of Australia,* Melbourne Branch, P.O. Box 298, Ringwood, Victoria 3134, Australia.

Reading List

Note: * Denotes books of special interest to physicians;
      ** denotes my favorite books.

ALLERGY, IMMUNOLOGY, CLINICAL ECOLOGY AND ENVIRONMENTAL MEDICINE

*Bell, I. R. *Clinical Ecology: A New Medical Approach to Environmental Illness.* Bolinas, CA: Common Knowledge Press, 1982. This little book is packed full of useful information. Highly recommended.

Connolly, P., and associates of the Price-Pottenger Nutrition Foundation. *The Candida Albicans Yeast-Free Cookbook.* New Canaan, CT: Keats Publishing, 1985. Many helpful yeast-free recipes.

Faelten, S., and editors of *Prevention* magazine. *Allergy Self-Help Book.* Emmaus, PA: Rodale Press, 1983. Comprehensive, authoritative, well written. Covers traditional allergies as well as food and chemical allergies. Explains provocative testing and neutralization therapy. Excellent. I recommend it.

**Forman, R. *How to Control Your Allergies.* New York: Larchmont Book Co., 1979. A superb little book. One of my favorites. Clearly and succinctly tells about some of the allergy controversies you'll run into. Easy to read. Highly recommended.

**Gerrard, J. W., ed. *Food Allergy: New Perspectives.* Springfield, IL, Charles C. Thomas, 1980. This book is written by a university professor of pediatrics. *Must reading for physicians interested in a more comprehensive look at food allergy* and the newer (but controversial) methods of studying and treating it using provocative testing and neutralizing doses of food extracts. Although written for professionals, nonprofessionals whose children suffer from food allergies will find it interesting.

Golos, N., and F. Golbitz. *Coping with Your Allergies.* New York: Simon & Schuster, 1979. An excellent reference source. Full of practical tips for individuals and families with food and chemical sensitivities. Practical. Highly recommended.

———. *If This Is Tuesday It Must Be Chicken.* New Canaan, CT: Keats Publishing, 1983. People with food allergies should rotate their diets. This book will tell you how. Useful.

———, J. O'Shea and F. Waickman. *Environmental Medicine: How to Diagnose and Manage Allergies.* New Canaan, CT., Keats Publishing, 1986. This is a textbook for allergy patients, their doctors and all concerned lay people.

Jones, M. *The Allergy Cookbook.* Emmaus, PA: Rodale Press, 1984. A carefully researched, authoritative book that will help you make tasty meals while avoiding food allergens. Excellent.

Levin, A., and D. L. Dadd. *Consumer Guide for the Chemically Sensitive.* 1982. Available from Alan S. Levin, M.D., 450 Sutter, Suite 1138, San Francisco, CA 94105. If you suffer from chemical sensitivities, get this book. Well done, thorough, comprehensive.

———, and M. Zellerback. *Type 1/Type 2 Allergy Relief Program.* New York: Berkley Publishing, 1984. Another excellent book that tells you about traditional allergies and food and chemical sensitivities and explains the difference. Recommended.

Mackarness, R. *Eating Dangerously.* New York: Harcourt Brace Jovanovich, 1976. This book on food allergies sold a quarter of a million copies in England under the title *Not All in the Mind.* Interesting. Tells you how to do sublingual testing for foods.

———. *Living Safely in a Polluted World.* New York: Stein & Day, 1983. Another interesting book.

Mandell, M., and L. Scanlon. *Dr. Mandell's Five-Day Allergy Relief System.* New York: Pocket Books, 1979. This bestselling book contains many patient stories. It describes sublingual testing and the fascinating experiences of the author. Interesting. Well done.

Nichols, V. *Cookbook and Guide to Eating—Diversified Diet for Allergies,* available from 3350 Fair Oaks Drive, Xenia, OH 45385. Chock full of information that will help you rotate your child's diet.

*Philpott, W. H., and B. K. Kalita. *Brain Allergies.* New Canaan, CT: Keats Publishing, 1986. This book is full of interesting material on allergies and other dietary factors that affect brain function.

**Randolph, T., and R. Moss. *An Alternative Approach to Allergies.* New York: Bantam Books, 1982. An excellent, readable, up-to-date, comprehensive discussion of the Randolph approach to food and chemical sensitivities.

**Rapp, D. J. *Allergies and Your Family.* New York: Sterling, 1981. This interesting, easy-to-read book was written by one of America's best-known allergists. Authoritative, highly recommended.

Rippere, V. *The Allergy Problem: Why People Suffer and What Should Be Done.* Wellingborough, Northamptonshire, England: Thorsons Publishing, 1983. This British book is interesting and well done.

Soyka, F., and A. Edmonds. *The Ion Effect.* New York: Bantam Books, 1978. Excellent. Talks about how electrical charges in the air affect how you feel. Interesting.

**Speer, F. *Allergy of the Nervous System.* Springfield, IL: Charles C. Thomas, 1970. Allergy affects the nervous system as often as it does the nose, lungs or skin. This book is an excellent reference source for physicians. Introduction by the late Walter Alvarez of the Mayo Clinic. A favorite of mine.

**Stevens, L. J. *The Complete Book of Allergy Control.* New York: Pocket Books, 1986. Excellent, comprehensive, well researched.

**Truss, C. O. *The Missing Diagnosis.* Birmingham: Truss, 1983. Available in many bookstores and can also be ordered from P.O. Box 26508, Birmingham, AL 35226. This book, written for physicians and the public, describes the brilliant pioneer observations on the relationship of *Candida albicans* (yeasts) to a whole host of human illnesses. Highly recommended. If you or other family members suffer from yeast-connected health problems, read this book and lend it to your physician.

NUTRITION AND PREVENTIVE MEDICINE

Banick, A. E., and C. Wade. *Your Water and Your Health.* New Canaan, CT: Keats Publishing, 1981. A useful source of information about your drinking water and what you can do about it.

Bland, J. *Hair Tissue Mineral Analysis.* New York, Thorsons Publishing, 1984. A comprehensive, succinct discussion of this important, yet controversial, subject.

————. *Nutraerobics.* New York: Harper & Row, 1983. Authoritative, interesting. Written by the director of the Linus Pauling Institute, a highly qualified authority in the field of nutrition.

*————. *Yearbook of Nutritional Medicine, 1984–1985.* New Canaan, CT: Keats Publishing, 1985. Superb book. Contains much authoritative information on fatty acids, amino acids, carbohydrate metabolism, zinc, megavitamins and other related subjects.

————. *Your Health Under Siege: Using Nutrition to Fight Back.* Brattleboro, VT: Stephen Greene, 1982.

Brody, J. *Jane Brody's Nutrition Book.* New York: W. W. Norton, 1981. An authoritative book on nutrition by the popular *New York Times* columnist.

———. *Jane Brody's New York Times Guide to Personal Health.* New York: Avon, 1983. Interesting, authoritative.

**Burros, M. F. *Keep It Simple: Thirty-Minute Meals from Scratch.* New York: Pocket Books, 1982. Practical, well written, interesting. One of my favorites.

**Cheraskin, E., W. M. Ringsdorf, Jr., and A. Brescher. *Psychodietetics.* New York: Bantam Books, 1976. Excellent. Interesting, easy to read. A long-time bestseller. Carefully researched. You'll like this book.

———, and E. L. Sisley. *The Vitamin C Connection.* New York: Bantam Books, 1984. Over one third of Americans take extra vitamin C. This book will tell you lots more about it

**Cousins, N. *Anatomy of an Illness.* New York: Bantam Books, 1981. One of my favorites. Fascinating. You'll like it. Tells how big doses of vitamin C, laughter and a positive mental attitude helped the author conquer an incurable illness.

DiCyan, E. *A Beginner's Introduction to Trace Minerals.* New Canaan, CT: Keats Publishing, 1984. Sound information on a subject you need to know about.

**Dufty, W. *Sugar Blues.* New York: Warner Books, 1976. Another one of my favorites. Chock full of fascinating information.

Gaby, A. *The Doctor's Guide to Vitamin B_6.* Emmaus, PA: Rodale Press, 1985. A well-written, comprehensively researched book with up-to-date information on an important nutrient.

Garrison, R., and E. Somer. *The Nutrition Desk Reference.* New Canaan, CT: Keats Publishing, 1985. A solid storehouse of invaluable information for the professional or the educated layman.

**Goldbeck, N., and D. Goldbeck. *The Supermarket Handbook: Access to Whole Foods.* New York: New American Library, 1976. A longtime favorite. Practical and useful.

Goodwin, M., and G. Pollen. *Creative Food Experiences for Children.* Washington, DC: CSPI, 1980. Available from CSPI Publications, 1755 S Street, N.W., Washington, D.C. 20009. I like this book and the many other publications from the Center for Science in the Public Interest (CSPI).

**Hall, R. H. *Food for Nought.* New York: Harper & Row, 1977. Comprehensive, carefully researched book. One of my favorites. (Out of print. Check with your public library.)

Hoffer, A., and M. Walker. *Orthomolecular Nutrition.* New Canaan, CT: Keats Publishing, 1978. Linus Pauling used the term orthomolecular to convey the idea that many chronic mental disorders could be corrected by "straightening" the concentration of molecules in the brain. This book, written by orthomolecular psychiatrist Abram Hoffer, will tell you more about this important subject.

*Horrobin, D. *Clinical Uses of Essential Fatty Acids.* Montreal: Eden Press, 1983. An informative book for professionals interested in learning more about fatty acids.

Hunter, B. T. *Additives Book.* New Canaan, CT: Keats Publishing, 1980. I've heard Beatrice Trum Hunter talk many times and I've read and reread her books. They're carefully researched and authoritative. I recommend all of them, especially this one and *The Great Nutrition Robbery.*

———. *The Great Nutrition Robbery.* New York: Charles Scribner's Sons, 1978. Authoritative, well written. One of my favorites.

———. *The Sugar Trap and How to Avoid It.* Boston: Houghton Mifflin, 1982. I've found that sugar plays a major role in causing hyperactivity. I especially recommend this authoritative, well-written book. (Out of print. Check with your library.)

Jacobson, M. F. *Eater's Digest: The Consumer's Fact Book of Food Additives.* Garden City, NY: Doubleday, Anchor Books, 1976. Available from CSPI Publications, 1755 S Street, N.W., Washington, DC 20009. Good reference source.

Lansky, V. *The Taming of the C.A.N.D.Y. Monster.* Wayzata, MN: Meadowbrook Press, 1978. An interesting book that could help you feed your youngster. However, some of the recipes contain sugar.

Lesser, M. *Nutrition and Vitamin Therapy.* New York: Bantam Books, 1981. Interesting. Recommended.

*Levine, S. and P. Kidd. *Antioxidant Adaptation: Its Role in Free Radical Pathology.* San Leandro, CA: Biocurrents Division, 1985. Available from Allergy Research Group, 400 Preda Street, San Leandro, CA 94577. A new book for professionals.

Mindell, E. *Vitamin Bible.* New York: Warner Books, 1980. Good reference source on the various vitamins.

Montagu, A. *Touching: The Human Significance of the Skin.* New York: Harper & Row, 1972. Hard-to-raise children need to be touched. Get this book. It'll tell you why.

**Ott, J. N. *Health and Light.* New York: Pocket Books, 1983. Improper lighting at school or at home can contribute to hyperactivity. This book will tell why. An important reference source. By all means, read it.

Our Bodies, Ourselves. New York: Simon & Schuster, 1985. Lots of information about self-care and what you can do to keep your family healthy.

Passwater, R. A. *EPA—Marine Lipids.* New Canaan, CT: Keats Publishing, 1982. A good reference source. A short, inexpensive booklet.

———. *Evening Primrose Oil.* New Canaan, CT: Keats Publishing, 1981. Another good reference.

———. *Beginner's Introduction to Vitamins.* New Canaan, CT: Keats Publishing, 1983. Inexpensive. Authoritative.

*———, and E. M. Cranton. *Trace Elements, Hair Analysis and Nutrition.* New Canaan, CT: Keats Publishing, 1983. An authoritative book chock full of information.

Pfeiffer, C. C. *Mental and Elemental Nutrients.* New Canaan, CT: Keats Publishing, 1976. A good reference source for vitamins and minerals.

———. *Zinc and Other Micro-nutrients.* New Canaan, CT: Keats Publishing, 1978. An excellent reference source for the trace minerals. One of my favorites.

Price, W. A. *Nutrition and Physical Degeneration.* Berkeley, CA: Parker House, 1981. Available from Price-Pottenger Foundation, P.O. Box 2614, La Mesa, CA 92014. I recommend this important book. Serious students of nutrition should read how modern diets contribute to degenerative disease.

Rudin, D. O., and C. Felix. *The Omega-3 Phenomenon: The Nutritional Breakthrough of the Eighties.* New York: Rawson-Macmillan, 1987. Rudin is an outstanding authority on fatty acids.

Schauss, A. *Nutrition and Behavior.* New Canaan, CT: Keats Publishing, 1985. This Keats booklet contains much helpful information. Recommended.

**Schroeder, H. A. *The Poisons Around Us.* New Canaan, CT: Keats Publishing, 1978. This book, by a Dartmouth scientist, is one of my favorites. Much information about cadmium and other toxic minerals. A "five-star" book. Highly recommended.

———. *Trace Elements and Man.* Old Greenwich, CT, Devon-Adair, 1973. Another superlative book by one of my favorite authors.

Sheinkin, D., M. Schacter, and R. Hutton. *Food, Mind and Mood.* New York: Warner Books, 1980. An interesting book. Discusses many different methods of detecting food sensitivity.

Sloan, S. *The Brown Bag Cookbook.* Charlotte, VT: Williamson Publishing, 1984.

———. *Nutritional Parenting.* New Canaan, CT: Keats Publishing, 1982. For over twenty years Sara Sloan helped Atlanta and Fulton County children eat good food in their school lunches. This pamphlet and other publications by Sara Sloan will help you in the important task of getting more nutritious foods served to your child at school. To get more information from Ms. Sloan, write to Sara Sloan, Nutra, P.O. Box 13825, Atlanta, GA 30324.

**Smith, L. H. *Feed Your Kids Right.* New York: Dell, 1980. An interesting, provocative book by the colorful pediatrician and controversial and popular author Lendon Smith. You'll love all his books.

————. *Foods for Healthy Kids.* New York: Berkley Publishing, 1984. You'll like this interesting book.

**Williams, R. J. *Physician's Handbook of Nutritional Science.* Springfield, IL: Charles C. Thomas, 1978. An important basic reference source. One of my favorites.

*————, and D. K. Kalita. *A Physician's Handbook on Orthomolecular Medicine.* New Canaan, CT: Keats Publishing, 1979. Interesting, authoritative.

Wright, J. V. *Dr. Wright's Guide to Healing with Nutrition.* Emmaus, PA: Rodale Press, 1984. A fascinating book by a former medical columnist for *Prevention* magazine.

Wunderlich, R. C., Jr. *Sugar and Your Health.* Saint Petersburg, FL: Good Health Publications, Johnny Reads, Inc., 1982. Pediatrician Ray Wunderlich has long worked to help children and their parents by changing their diets. I highly recommend his books and booklets.

————, and D. Kalita. *Nourishing Your Child.* New Canaan, CT: Keats Publishing, 1984. An excellent resource book. I recommend it. Directed especially toward the parents of the hyperactive child.

HYPERACTIVITY AND CHILD BEHAVIOR

Brown, R., and M. Connelly. *How to Have a Party for Your Hyperactive Child and Survive, How to Organize Your Child and Save Your Sanity, How to Travel with Your Active Children, If There's Nothing Wrong with My Child Then What's Wrong with Him?* Available from Cottage Park Publications, P.O. Box 458, Vienna, VA 22180, 1980. These inexpensive booklets contain a number of useful suggestions. I recommend them.

Cott, A. *Dr. Cott's Help for Your Learning-Disabled Child.* New York: Times Books, 1985. This renowned orthomolecular physician describes his biochemical approach to treating hyperactivity and learning problems.

**Dodson, F. *How to Discipline with Love.* New York: New American Library, 1978. One of my favorites. I recommend it highly.

**————. *How to Parent.* New York: New American Library, 1973. One of my favorites. I especially like the chapter "Can You Teach a Dolphin to Type?"

Feingold, B. F. *Why Your Child Is Hyperactive.* New York: Random House, 1975. A classic by the pioneer who made everyone aware that food colors and dyes could cause hyperactivity.

**Flesch, R. *Why Johnny Still Can't Read.* New York: Harper & Row, 1981. A classic. Highly recommended, especially if your child experiences trouble in reading.

**Ginott, H. *Between Parent and Child.* New York: Avon, 1969. One of my favorites. Superb. Full of many practical suggestions. I especially like the chapter on communicating with your child using the "say it back" technique.

Hinds, J. M. *The Invisible Epidemic: Learning Disabilities, Their Many Interrelated Causes, Prevention, Recognition and Intervention.* Available from All Star Printing, 1025 20th Street South, Birmingham, AL 35205.

**Ilg, F., L. Ames and S. Baker. *Child Behavior.* New York: Harper & Row, 1981. A superb, authoritative book. Section 4 is especially appropriate for parents of the hard-to-raise child. Highly recommended.

**Johnson, S. *The One Minute Mother* and *The One Minute Father.* New York: William Morrow, 1983. These books will help you help your children develop self-esteem. Highly recommended.

Kane, P. *Food Makes the Difference.* New York: Simon & Schuster, 1985. An excellent, well-researched, comprehensive book about diet and behavior.

Mitchell, J. *Help for the Hyperactive Child.* White Hall, VA: Betterway Publications, 1984. A sensitive, informative guide by a mother "who's been there." You'll identify with her feelings of hope and despair.

**Rapp, D. J. *Allergies and the Hyperactive Child.* New York: Cornerstone, 1980. Doris Rapp, M.D., through her clinical and research studies and her books, has played a significant role in making everyone aware of the role of allergies in causing hyperactivity. This book should be on your reference shelf.

**————. *The Impossible Child.* Tacoma, WA: Life Sciences Press, 1986. Another superb book by Dr. Rapp. Written for parents and teachers. A must book for both. Available from Practical Allergy Research Foundation, P.O. Box 60, Buffalo, NY 14223.

Reed, B., S. Knickelbine and M. Knickelbine. *Food, Teens and Behavior.* Manitowoc, WI: Natural Press, 1983. Another excellent book on diet and behavior.

Schauss, A. *Diet, Crime and Delinquency.* Berkeley, CA: Parker House, 1981. An interesting book.

Stevens, S. *The Learning-Disabled Child: Ways That Parents Can Help.* Winston-Salem, NC: John F. Blair, 1980. A helpful, informative guide for parents of children with learning problems.

Notes

Preface

1. A. H. Rowe, Sr., *Allergies and Your Child* (New York: Holt, Rinehart & Winston, 1972), pp. 259–274.

2. A. H. Rowe, Sr., "Allergic Toxemia and Migraine Due to Food Allergy," *California Western Medicine* (Vol. 33, 1930), p. 785.

3. H. J. Rinkel, T. G. Randolph and M. Zeller, *Food Allergy* (Springfield, IL: Charles C. Thomas, 1951).

4. T. G. Randolph, "Allergy as a Causative Factor of Fatigue, Irritability, and Behavior Problems in Children," *Journal of Pediatrics* (Vol. 31, 1947), p. 560.

5. J. Glaser, *Allergy in Childhood* (Springfield, IL: Charles C. Thomas, 1956), pp. 299–309.

6. J. Glaser, in W. G. Crook, ed., *Your Allergic Child* (New York: Medcom Press, 1973), p. 50.

7. F. Speer, "The Allergic Tension-Fatigue Syndrome," *Pediatric Clinics of North America* (Vol. 1, 1954), p. 1029.

8. W. G. Crook and others, "Systemic Manifestations Due to Allergy. Report of Fifty Patients and a Review of the Literature on the Subject," *Pediatrics* (Vol. 27, 1961), pp. 790–799.

9. J. W. Gerrard and M. Esperance, "Nocturnal Enuresis: Studies in Bladder Function in Normals and Enuretics," *Canadian Medical Association Journal* (Vol. 101, 1969), p. 269.

10. J. W. Gerrard, *Understanding Allergies* (Springfield, IL: Charles C. Thomas, 1973), pp. 9–17.

11. W. C. Deamer and others, "Allergic Tension-Fatigue Syndrome," Scientific Exhibit, American Academy of Pediatrics, San Francisco, October 1970.

12. W. C. Deamer, "Pediatric Allergy: Some Impressions Gained over a 27-Year Period," *Pediatrics* (Vol. 48, 1971), p. 930.

13. W. C. Deamer, "Recurrent Abdominal Pain: Recurrent Controversy," (Letters) *Pediatrics* (Vol. 46, 1973), p. 307.

14. J. P. Kemp, "Recurrent Abdominal Pain," (Letters) *Pediatrics* (Vol. 46, 1970), p. 972.

15. J. P. McGovern and others, "Allergic Headache," in F. Speer, ed., *Allergy of the Nervous System* (Springfield, IL: Charles C. Thomas, 1970), pp. 47–68.

16. J. C. Breneman, "Allergic Cystitis: The Cause of Nocturnal Enuresis," *General Practice* (Vol. 20, 1959), p. 84.

17. B. D. Schmitt, "School Phobia . . . The Great Imitator: The Pediatrician's Viewpoint," *Pediatrics* (Vol. 48, 1971), p. 433.

18. R. T. Stone and G. J. Barbero, "Recurrent Abdominal Pain in Childhood," *Pediatrics* (Vol. 45, 1970), p. 732.

19. W. G. Crook, *Your Allergic Child* (New York: Medcom Press, 1973).

20. W. G. Crook, *Can Your Child Read? Is He Hyperactive?* (Jackson, TN: Professional Books, 1975).

21. W. G. Crook, *Tracking Down Hidden Food Allergy* (Jackson, TN: Professional Books, 1978).

22. W. G. Crook, "Can What a Child Eats Make Him Dull, Stupid or Hyperactive?" *Journal of Learning Disabilities* (Vol. 13, 1980), pp. 53–58.

23. C. O. Truss, *The Missing Diagnosis* (Birmingham, AL: Truss, 1983), pp. 71–75.

24. W. G. Crook, *The Yeast Connection* (New York: Vintage Books, 1986).

25. L. J. Stevens, G. E. Stevens and R. Stoner, *How to Feed Your Hyperactive Child* (New York: Doubleday, 1977).

26. L. J. Stevens and R. Stoner, *How to Improve Your Child's Behavior Through Diet* (New York: Doubleday, 1979).

27. L. J. Stevens, *The Complete Book of Allergy Control* (New York: Pocket Books, 1986).

Chapter 1
The Hard-to-Raise Child Resembles a Jigsaw Puzzle

1. Personal communication with G. Oberg.

Chapter 3
The Pitfalls of Labeling Your Hard-to-Raise Child

1. C. O. Truss, *The Missing Diagnosis* (Birmingham, AL: Truss, 1983), p. 79.

2. S. M. Baker, "A Biochemical Approach to the Problem of Dyslexia," *Journal of Learning Disabilities* (Vol. 18, No. 10, Dec. 1985), p. 581.

3. S. M. Baker, "The Language of Illness," *Update* (Vol. 4, No. 3, Winter 1986), pp. 3–6.

4. S. M. Baker, "Whole Person Medicine," Health by Choice Conference, Atlanta, 1986. Tapes available from Insta-Tape, Inc., P.O. Box 1729, Monrovia, CA 91016.

5. Baker, "A Biochemical Approach to the Problem of Dyslexia," p. 581.

6. Ibid., p. 582.

Chapter 4
Defining Terms You'll Run Into

1. *Diagnostic and Statistical Manual of Mental Disorders*, Third Edition, (DSM-III) (Washington, DC: American Psychiatric Association, 1980).

Chapter 5
Is the Incidence of Hard-to-Raise Children Increasing?

1. P. Schrag and D. Divoky, *The Myth of the Hyperactive Child* (New York: Pantheon Books, 1975).

Chapter 6
The Nutritional Disaster of the Twentieth Century

1. E. Cheraskin, W. M. Ringsdorf, Jr., and A. Brecher, *Psychodietetics* (New York: Bantam Books, 1974).

2. E. Cheraskin, W. M. Ringsdorf, Jr., and J. W. Clark, *Diet and Disease* (Emmaus, PA: Rodale Press, 1968).

3. R. J. Williams, *Nutrition Against Disease* (New York: Bantam Books, 1971), p. 38.

4. R. H. Hall, "Beware of Those Fabricated Foods," *Executive Health* (Vol. XII, No. 7, April 1976), pp. 1–2.

5. H. A. Schroeder, *The Poisons Around Us: Toxic Metals in Food, Air and Water* (Bloomington, IN: Indiana University Press, 1974), pp. 121–122.

6. J. Wurtman, quoted in J. Brody, *Jane Brody's Nutrition Book* (New York: W. W. Norton, 1981), p. 386.

7. Personal communication with P. Charren.

8. J. Gussow, "It Makes Even Milk a Dessert," *Clinical Pediatrics* (Vol. 12, No. 2, Feb. 1973), p. 70.

Chapter 7
Our Polluted Planet and Chemical Sensitivity

1. F. Lyman, "Dredging for Dollars," *Environmental Action* (Feb. 1981).
2. T. G. Randolph and R. W. Moss, *An Alternative Approach to Allergies* (New York: Harper & Row, 1980), p. 50.
3. S. D. Lockey, Sr., "Allergic Reactions Due to F, D and C Dyes Used in Coloring and Identifying Agents in Various Medications," Bulletin. Lancaster General Hospital, Lancaster, PA, 1948.
4. B. F. Feingold, *Why Your Child Is Hyperactive,* (New York: Random House, 1975).
5. "Poisoning the Well," *Environmental Action* (Oct. 1984), p. 4.
6. F. S. Sterrett, *Long Island Pediatrician* (Summer 1982).
7. Randolph and Moss, *An Alternative Approach to Allergies,* p. 84.
8. W. Rea, "Cardiovascular Disease Triggered by Foods and Chemicals," in J. W. Gerrard, ed., *Food Allergy: New Perspective,* (Springfield, IL: Charles C. Thomas, 1980), pp. 99–143.

Chapter 8
The Role of Antibiotics

1. K. Iwata and Y. Yamamoto, "Glycoprotein Toxins Produced by *Candida albicans.*" Reprinted from the proceedings of the Fourth International Conference on the Mycoses, June 1977. PAHO, Scientific Publications #356.
2. S. S. Witkin, "Defective Immune Responses in Patients with Recurrent Candidiasis," *Infections in Medicine* (Vol. 2, No. 3, May/June 1985).
3. C. O. Truss, *The Missing Diagnosis* (Birmingham, AL: Truss, 1983), pp. 39–42, 71–75 and 93–95.
4. W. G. Crook, *The Yeast Connection* (New York: Vintage Books, 1986), pp. 189–196 and 375–378.

Chapter 9
If You'd Had a Magic Wand or an Aladdin's Lamp—

1. G. Brewer and T. Brewer, *What Every Pregnant Woman Should Know: The Truth About Diet and Drugs in Pregnancy* (New York: Penguin Books, 1979–1981), pp. 42–69.
2. L. B. Ames, *Is Your Child In the Wrong Grade?* (New York: Harper & Row, 1970), p. 8.

Chapter 10
Types of Allergy and the Allergy Controversy

1. A. H. Rowe, Sr., *Food Allergy: Its Manifestations, Diagnosis and Treatment* (Philadelphia: Lea & Febiger, 1931), p. 785.

2. H. Rinkel, T. G. Randolph and M. Zeller, *Food Allergy* (Springfield, IL: Charles C. Thomas, 1951).

3. T. G. Randolph, "Allergy as a Causative Factor of Fatigue, Irritability and Behavior Problems of Children," *Journal of Pediatrics* (Vol. 31, 1947), p. 560.

4. F. Speer, "The Allergic Tension-Fatigue Syndrome," *Pediatric Clinics of North America* (Vol. 1, 1954), p. 1029.

5. C. May, "Food Allergy," *Pediatric Clinics of North America* (Vol. 22, No. 1, Feb. 1975), p. 217.

6. W. G. Crook, "Food Allergy—The Great Masquerader," *Pediatric Clinics of North America* (Vol. 22, No. 1, Feb. 1975), pp. 227–238.

7. J. Gerrard, *Understanding Allergies* (Springfield, IL: Charles C. Thomas, 1973), p. 39.

8. K. Ishizaka and T. Ishizaka, "Identification of Gamma E Antibodies as a Carrier of Reagenic Activity," *Journal of Immunology* (Vol. 99, 1967), p. 1187.

9. F. Speer, personal communication.

10. W. C. Deamer, as quoted by W. G. Crook in *You and Allergy* (Jackson, TN: Professional Books, 1980), p. 4.

11. W. T. Kniker, "Deciding the Future for the Practice of Allergy and Immunology," *Annals of Allergy* (Vol. 55, No. 2, Aug. 1985), p. 107.

12. W. G. Crook, "What is Scientific Proof?" *Pediatrics* (Vol. 65, 1980), p. 638.

Chapter 11
Allergy Can Make Your Child Hyperactive, Tired or Nervous

1. B. R. Hoobler, "Some Early Symptoms Suggesting Protein Sensitization in Infancy," *American Journal of Diseases of Children* (Vol. 12, 1916), p. 129.

2. W. R. Shannon, "Neuropathic Manifestations in Infants and Children as a Result of Anaphylactic Reactions to Foods Contained in Their Dietary," *American Journal of Diseases of Children* (Vol. 24, 1922), p. 89.

3. I. S. Kahn, "Pollen Toxemia," *Journal of the American Medical Association* (Vol. 88, 1927), p. 241.

4. A. H. Rowe, Sr., *Food Allergy: Its Manifestations, Diagnosis and Treatment* (Philadelphia: Lea & Febiger, 1931), p. 785.

5. T. G. Randolph, "Allergy as a Causative Factor of Fatigue, Irritability and Behavior Problems of Children," *Journal of Pediatrics* (Vol. 31, 1947), p. 560.

6. F. Speer, "The Allergic Tension-Fatigue Syndrome," *Pediatric Clinics of North America* (Vol. 1, 1954), p. 1029.

7. F. Speer, "The Allergic Tension-Fatigue Syndrome in Children," *International Archives of Allergy* (Vol. 12, 1958), p. 207.

8. Ibid.

9. W. G. Crook and others, "Systemic Manifestations Due to Allergy. Report of Fifty Patients and a Review of the Literature on the Subject," *Pediatrics* (Vol. 27, 1961), pp. 790–799.

10. W. G. Crook, "Can What a Child Eats Make Him Dull, Stupid or Hyperactive?" *Journal of Learning Disabilities* (Vol. 13, No. 5, 1980), pp. 53–58.

11. D. J. Rapp, "Does Diet Affect Hyperactivity?" *Journal of Learning Disabilities* (Vol. 11, No. 6, June/July 1978), pp. 56–62.

12. D. J. Rapp, *Allergies and the Hyperactive Child* (New York: Sovereign Books, 1979).

13. D. J. Rapp, *The Impossible Child* (Buffalo, NY: Practical Allergy Research Foundation, 1986).

14. J. O'Shea and S. F. Porter, "Double-Blind Study of Children with Hyperkinetic Syndrome Treated with Multi-Allergen Extract Sublingually," *Journal of Learning Disabilities* (Vol. 14, No. 4, April 1981).

15. J. Egger and others, "Controlled Trial of Oligoantigenic Treatment in the Hyperkinetic Syndrome," *Lancet* (Vol. 1 (8428), March 9, 1985), pp. 540–545.

16. F. Hare, *The Food Factor in Disease* (London: Longmans, Green, 1905).

17. J. Glaser, "Migraine in Pediatric Practice," *American Journal of Diseases of Children* (Vol. 88, 1954), p. 92.

18. J. Munro and others, "Food Allergy in Migraine," *Lancet* (Vol. 8184), July 5, 1980), pp. 1–4.

19. J. Egger and others, "Is Migraine Food Allergy?" *Lancet* (Vol. 1 (8355), Oct. 15, 1983), pp. 865–869.

Chapter 12
Allergy Can Make Your Child Sick

1. J. D. Bullock and others, "Recurrent Abdominal Pain," (Letters) *Pediatrics* (Vol. 46, 1970), p. 969.

2. W. G. Crook, "Recurrent Abdominal Pain," (Letters) *Pediatrics* (Vol. 46, 1970), p. 971.

3. R. T. Stone and G. J. Barbero, "Recurrent Abdominal Pain in Childhood," *Pediatrics* (Vol. 45, 1970), p. 732.

4. A. H. Rowe, Sr., "Allergic Toxemia and Migraine Due to Food Allergy," California Western Medicine (Vol. 33, 1930), p. 785.

5. J. D. Bullock and others, "Recurrent Abdominal Pain," (Letters) *Pediatrics* (Vol. 46, 1970), p. 971.

6. J. C. Breneman, "Allergic Cystitis: The Cause of Nocturnal Enuresis," General Practice (Vol. 20, 1959), p. 84.

7. J. W. Gerrard and M. Esperance, "Nocturnal Enuresis: Studies in Bladder Function in Normals and Enuretics," *Canadian Medical Association Journal* (Vol. 101, 1969), p. 269.

8. A. Harrison, (Letters) *Pediatrics* (Vol. 48, 1971), p. 166.

9. J. Gerrard and others, (Letters) *Pediatrics* (Vol. 48, 1971), p. 994.

10. T. Matsumura, T. Kuroume and I. Fukushima, "Significance of Food Allergy in the Etiology of Orthostatic Albuminuria," *Journal of Asthma Research* (Vol. 3, 1966), p. 325.

11. J. P. McGovern, T. J. Haywood and A. A. Fernandez, "Allergy and Serious Otitis Media," *Journal of the American Medical Association* (Vol. 200, 1967), p. 124.

12. C. O. Truss, *The Missing Diagnosis* (Birmingham, AL: Truss, 1983), p. 75.

Chapter 14
Getting Started

1. G. Stollerman, "The Gold Standard," *Hospital Practice* (January 30, 1985), p. 9.

2. S. Dees and H. Lowenbach, "The Electroencephalograms of Allergic Children," *Annals of Allergy* (Vol. 6, 1948), p. 99.

3. F. J. Kittler and D. G. Baldwin, "The Role of Allergic Factors in the Child with Minimal Brain Dysfunction," *Annals of Allergy* (Vol. 28, 1970), p. 203.

4. J. Egger and others, "Controlled Trial of Oligoantigenic Treatment in the Hyperkinetic Syndrome," *The Lancet* (Vol. 1 (8428), March 9, 1985), pp. 540–545.

5. F. Speer, *Allergy of the Nervous System* (Springfield, IL: Charles C. Thomas, 1970).

Chapter 16
Elimination Diets

1. Daniel 1:1–20, *Good News Bible: The Bible in Today's English Version* (New York: American Bible Society, 1976), pp. 954–955.

Chapter 17
Helping Your Food-Sensitive Child

1. H. J. Rinkel and others, "The Diagnosis of Food Allergy," *Archives of Otolaryngology* (Vol. 79, 1964), p. 71.

2. J. B. Miller, "The Management of Food Allergy." In J. W. Gerrard, ed., *Food Allergy: New Perspectives* (Springfield, IL: Charles C. Thomas, 1980), pp. 274–282.

3. D. H. Sandberg, "Renal Disease Related to Hypersensitivity to Foods." In J. W. Gerrard, ed., *Food Allergy: New Perspectives* (Springfield, IL: Charles C. Thomas, 1980), pp. 157–164.

4. D. J. Rapp, "Hyperactivity and the Tension-Fatigue Syndrome." In J. W. Gerrard, ed., *Food Allergy: New Perspectives* (Springfield, IL: Charles C. Thomas, 1980), pp. 201–204.

5. J. M. Hilsen, "Dietary Control of the Hyperactive Child," *Long Island Pediatrician* (Summer 1982), pp. 25–32.

6. J. B. Miller, "A Double-Blind Study of Food Extract Injection Therapy: A Preliminary Report," *Annals of Allergy* (Vol. 38, 1977), pp. 185–191.

7. D. J. Rapp, "Double-Blind Confirmation and Treatment of Milk Sensitivity," *Medical Journal of Australia* (Vol. 4, 1978), pp. 571–572.

8. D. J. Rapp, "Weeping Eyes in Wheat Allergy," *Transactions, American Society of Otolaryngologic and Ophthalmologic Allergy* (Vol. 18, 1978), pp. 149–150.

9. D. J. Rapp, "Food Allergy Treatment for Hyperkinesis," *Journal of Learning Disabilities* (Vol. 12, 1979), pp. 42–50.

10. J. O'Shea and S. F. Porter, "Double-Blind Study of Children with Hyperkinetic Syndrome Treated with Multi-Allergen Extract Sublingually," *Journal of Learning Disabilities* (Vol. 14, No. 4, April 1981).

11. D. King, "Can Allergic Exposure Provoke Psychological Symptoms? A Double-Blind Test," *Biological Psychiatry* (Vol. 16, 1982), pp. 3–17.

12. The American College of Allergists' Proposed Position Statement on Clinical Ecology, 1985. (ACA, 800 E. Northwest Hwy., Mt. Prospect, IL 60056).

Chapter 18
Is *Your* Child Allergic to Airborne Particles He Breathes?

1. I. S. Kahn, "Pollen Toxemia," *Journal of the American Medical Association* (Vol. 88, 1927), p. 241.

2. L. Sternberg, "Seasonal Somnolence: A Possible Pollen Allergy," *Journal of Allergy* (Vol. 14, 1942), p. 89.

Chapter 19
How to Help Your Inhalant-Sensitive Child

1. Allergy Information Association, *Home Care Products,* p. 2.

Chapter 20
Do Chemical Exposures "Turn *Your* Child On"?

1. W. Rea, "Cardiovascular Disease Triggered by Foods and Chemicals." In J. W. Gerrard, ed., *Food Allergy: New Perspectives* (Springfield, IL: Charles C. Thomas, 1980), pp. 99–143.
2. A. S. Levin and others, "Immune Complex Mediated Vascular Inflammation in Patients with Food and Chemical Allergies," *Annals of Allergy* (Vol 47, 1981), p. 138.
3. J. J. McGovern, J. A. Lazaroni, M. F. Hicks and others, "Food and Chemical Sensitivity, Clinical and Immunological Correlates," *Archives of Otolaryngology* (Vol. 109, May 1983), pp. 292–297.

Chapter 21
How You Can Avoid Chemicals

1. K. A. Blume, *Air Pollution in the Schools,* The Human Ecology Research Foundation, 505 N. Lake Shore Drive, Chicago, IL 60611, 1968.

Chapter 22
The Yeast Connection: A Medical Breakthrough

1. C. O. Truss, "Tissue Injury Induced by *Candida Albicans:* Mental and Neurologic Manifestations," *The Journal of Orthomolecular Psychiatry* (Vol. 7, 1978), pp. 17–37.
2. C. O. Truss, *The Missing Diagnosis* (Birmingham, AL: Truss, 1983), p. 71.
3. Ibid., p. 72.
4. Personal communication with A. Lieberman.
5. G. P. Bodey and V. Fainstein, *Candidiasis* (New York: Raven Press, 1985).
6. K. Iwata, in *Recent Advances in Medical and Veterinary Mycology.* (Tokyo: University of Tokyo Press, 1977).
7. K. Iwata and K. Uchida, "Cellular Immunity in Experimental Fungus Infections in Mice," *Medical Mycology,* Flims, January 1977.
8. K. Iwata and Y. Yamamoto, "Glycoprotein Toxins Produced by *Candida Albicans,"* Reprinted from the proceedings of the Fourth

International Conference on the Mycoses, June 1977. PAHO, Scientific Publications #356.

9. Ibid.

10. K. Iwata, in *Recent Advances in Medical and Veterinary Mycology* (Tokyo: University of Tokyo Press, 1977).

11. S. S. Witkin, "Defective Immune Responses in Patients with Recurrent Candidiasis," *Infections in Medicine* (Vol. 2, No. 3, May/June 1985), p. 130.

12. C. O. Truss, "Metabolic Abnormalities in Patients with Chronic Candidiasis," *Journal of Orthomolecular Psychiatry* (Vol. 13, No. 2, 1984), pp. 66–93.

13. L. Galland, "Nutrition and Candidiasis," *Journal of Orthomolecular Psychiatry* (Vol. 14, No. 1, 1985), pp. 50–60.

Chapter 26
Overcoming Yeast-Connected Illness . . . Questions and Answers

1. W. G. Crook, *The Yeast Connection* (New York: Vintage Books, 1986), pp. 286–287.

2. FDA Drug Bulletin (Aug. 1984).

3. Personal communication with A. Lieberman.

4. A. Liebeskind, "*Candida albicans* as an Allergenic Factor," *Annals of Allergy* (Vol. 20, 1962), pp. 394–396.

5. C. O. Truss, "Tissue Injury Induced by *Candida albicans,*" *Journal of Orthomolecular Psychiatry* (Vol. 7, No. 1, 1978), pp. 17–37.

Chapter 27
Using Antibiotics Wisely

1. L. Pauling, "Vitamin C and Infectious Disease," *Executive Health* (Vol. 19, No. 4, 1983), pp. 1–3.

2. G. Eby, D. Davis and W. Halcomb, "Reduction in Duration of Common Colds by Zinc Gluconate Lozenges in a Double-Blind Study," *Antimicrobial Agents and Chemotherapy* (Vol. 25, No. 1, 1984), pp. 20–24.

Chapter 29
If Sugar Is a No-No, What Can You Use?

1. Council on Scientific Affairs, American Medical Association, "Aspartame: Review of Safety Issues," *Journal of the American Medical Association* (Vol. 254, No. 3, July 19, 1985), p. 402.

2. R. Wurtman, "Neurochemical Changes Following High-Dose As-

partame with Dietary Carbohydrates," *New England Journal of Medicine* (Vol. 309, Aug. 18, 1983), pp. 429–430.

3. A. Kulczycki, "Aspartame Induced Urticaria," *Annals of Internal Medicine* (Vol. 104, No. 2, Feb. 1986), pp. 207–208.

4. R. N. Hoover and P. H. Strasser, "Artificial Sweeteners and Human Bladder Cancer," *Lancet* (Vol. 1, 1980), pp. 837–840.

5. Council on Scientific Affairs, American Medical Association, "Saccharin: Review of Safety Issues," *Journal of the American Medical Association* (Vol. 254, No. 18, Nov. 8, 1985), p. 2624.

Chapter 30
What Is a Good Diet?

1. E. Blume, "Overdosing on Protein," *Nutrition Action Health Letter* (Vol. 14, March 1987), pp. 1, 4–6.

2. J. Brody, *Jane Brody's Nutrition Book* (New York: W. W. Norton, 1981), pp. 358–359.

3. S. Sloan, *The Brown Bag Cookbook* (Charlotte, VT: Williamson Publishing, 1984).

4. S. Sloan, *The Care and Feeding of Healthy Kids* (New York: Accent Books, 1985).

Chapter 31
A Guide to Vitamin Supplementation

1. L. Pauling, *How to Live Longer and Feel Better* (New York: W. H. Freeman, 1986), p. 48.

2. A. Gaby, *The Doctor's Guide to Vitamin B_6* (Emmaus, PA: Rodale Press, 1984), pp. 12–13.

3. Personal communication with S. Pilar.

4. R. Williams and D. Davis, "Differential Nutrition—A New Orientation from which to Approach the Problems of Human Nutrition," *Perspectives in Biology and Medicine* (Vol. 29, Winter 1986), pp. 199–202.

5. A. Brenner, "The Effects of Megadoses of Selected B Complex Vitamins on Children with Hyperkinesis: Controlled Studies with Long-Term Follow-Up," *Journal of Learning Disabilities* (Vol. 15, No. 5, May 1982), pp. 258–264.

6. M. Coleman, "Serotonin Concentrates in Whole Blood of Hyperactive Children," *Journal of Pediatrics* (Vol. 78, 1971), pp. 985–990.

7. M. Coleman and others, "A Preliminary Study of the Effect of Pyridoxine Hydrochloride in a Subgroup of Hyperkinetic Children:

A Double-Blind Crossover Comparison with Methylphenidate," *Biological Psychiatry* (Vol. 145, 1979), pp. 741–751.

8. B. Rimland, E. Callaway and P. Dreyfus, "The Effects of High Doses of Vitamin B₆ on Autistic Children: A Double-Blind Crossover Study," *American Journal of Psychiatry* (Vol. 135, 1978), pp. 472–475.

9. L. Pauling and D. R. Hawkins eds., "High Dosage Levels of Certain Vitamins in the Treatment of Children with Severe Mental Disorders," *Orthomolecular Psychiatry* (New York: W. H. Freeman, 1973).

10. B. Rimland and G. E. Larson, "Nutritional Ecological Approaches to the Reduction of Criminality, Delinquency and Violence," *Journal of Applied Nutrition* (Vol. 33, 1981), pp. 116–137.

11. B. Rimland, "Megavitamin Therapy for Autism and Related Disorders," (Publication 39A) Institute for Child Behavior Research, 4157 Adams Avenue, San Diego, CA 92116.

12. D. Lonsdale and R. Shamberger, "Red Cell Transketolase as an Indicator of Nutritional Deficiency," *American Journal of Clinical Medicine* (Vol. 33, No. 2, 1980), pp. 205–211.

13. J. W. Cromer, Jr., and H. I. Fritz, "A Trial of Combined Megavitamins in Treating Childhood Hyperkinesis," *Ohio Journal of Science* (Suppl.), 75:43, 1978.

14. C. B. Everson, T. O. Tiernan, and H. I. Fritz, "Efficacy of First Void Urine Sample for Characterization of Selected Neurotransmitters, Metabolites and Amino Acids in the Urine of Hyperactive Children Treated with Supplemental High Dose Water Soluble Vitamins," *Ohio Journal of Science,* 84093, 1984.

15. R. Harrell and others, "Can Nutritional Supplements Help Mentally Retarded Children? An Exploratory Study," *Proceedings of the National Academy of Sciences USA* (Vol. 78, Jan. 1981), pp. 574–578.

16. F. Ilg, L. Ames and S. Baker, *Child Behavior* (New York: Harper & Row, 1981), p. 328.

17. D. Davis, "Using Vitamin A Safely," *Osteopathic Medicine* (Vol. 3, No. 10, Oct. 1978), p. 31.

18. L. Pauling, "Evolution and the Need for Ascorbic Acid," *Proceedings of the National Academy of Sciences, U. S. A.* (Vol. 67, 1970), pp. 1643–1648.

19. L. Pauling, "Orthomolecular Environment of the Mind; Orthomolecular Theory," *American Journal of Psychiatry* (Vol. 131, 1974), pp. 1251–1257.

20. L. Pauling, "Case for Vitamin C in Maintaining Health and Preventing Disease," *Modern Medicine* (July 1976), pp. 68–72.

21. L. Pauling, *How to Live Longer and Feel Better* (New York: W. H. Freeman 1986).

22. Personal communication with J. Bland.

23. R. Good, as quoted in a promotional brochure, United Sciences of America, Dallas, TX, April 1986, and in an address to the American Academy of Environmental Medicine, Clearwater, FL, October 27, 1986.

Chapter 32
A Guide to Mineral Supplementation

1. L. Galland, "Nutrition and Candidiasis," *Journal of Orthomolecular Psychiatry* (Vol. 14, No. 1, 1985), pp. 50–60.

2. K. M. Hambidge and J. Baum, "Low Levels of Zinc in Hair of Children with Poor Growth and Appetites," *Pediatric Research* (Vol. 6, 1972), p. 868.

3. K. M. Hambidge and others, "Concentration of Chromium in the Hair of Normal Children and Children with Diabetes Mellitus," *Diabetes* (Vol. 17, No. 8, Aug. 1968), pp. 517–519,

4. Personal communication with J. Bland.

5. E. Cranton, "Update on Hair Analysis in Clinical Medicine," *Journal of Holistic Medicine* (Vol. 7(2), Fall/Winter 1985), pp. 171–173.

6. J. Bland, *Hair Tissue Mineral Analysis* (New York: Thorsons Publishing, 1984), p. 7.

7. H. Schroeder, *Trace Elements and Man* (Old Greenwich, CT: Devon-Adair, 1973).

8. H. Schroeder, *The Poisons Around Us* (Bloomington, IN: Indiana University Press, 1974).

Chapter 33
Toxic Minerals

1. N. Nusser, "Affluent Kids Also Harmed by Toxic Lead," *The Wall Street Journal* (July 24, 1981).

2. M. Waldholz, "Lead Poisoning Takes a Big, Continuing Toll as Cures Prove Elusive," *The Wall Street Journal* (May 27, 1982).

3. H. L. Needleman and others, "Deficits in Psychological and Classroom Performances of Children with Elevated Dentine Lead Levels," *New England Journal of Medicine* (Vol. 300, 1979), pp. 689–695.

4. M. Marlowe and others, "Hair Content as a Predictor of Learning Disabilities," *Journal of Learning Disabilities* (Vol. 17, No. 7, 1984), pp. 418–421.

5. A. Sohler, M. Kruesi and C. Pfeiffer, "Blood Lead Levels in Psychiatric Outpatients Reduced by Zinc and Vitamin C," *Journal of Orthomolecular Psychiatry* (Vol. 6, No. 3, 1977), p. 275.

6. Personal communication with S. Baker.

7. "What Every Parent Should Know about Lead???" is available from Tennessee Technological University, Cookeville, TN 38501. (Brochure)

8. H. Schroeder, *Trace Elements and Man* (Old Greenwich, CT: Devon-Adair, 1973), pp. 97–114.

9. Personal communication with Ellen Grant.

10. Personal communication with C. Pfeiffer.

11. R. Papioannou and C. Pfeiffer, "Pure Water for Drinking. A Review of Essential and Toxic Metals in Health and Disease," *Journal of Orthomolecular Medicine* (Vol. 1, No. 3, 1986), p. 187.

12. G. Fasciana, "Are Dental Fillings Hurting You? The Hazard of Having Mercury in Your Mouth." Keats Publishing Co., 27 Pine St., P. O. Box 876, New Canaan, CT 06840.

13. B. W. Eggleston, B. W., "Effect of Dental Amalgam and Nickel Alloys on T Lymphocytes: Preliminary Report. *Journal of Prosthetic Dentistry*, pp. 617–619, May 1984.

14. W. G. Crook, THE YEAST CONNECTION, third edition, pp. 387–390.

15. For more information contact Toxic Element Research Foundation (TERF) P.O. Box 2589, Colorado Springs, CO 80901.

16. R. Papioannou and C. Pfeiffer, "Pure Water for Drinking," p. 190.

17. Ibid., p. 190.

Chapter 34
The Importance of Essential Fatty Acids

1. D. O. Rudin, "The Major Psychoses and Neuroses as Omega-3 Essential Fatty Acid Deficiency Syndrome: Substrate Pellagra," *Biological Psychiatry* (Vol. 16, No. 9, 1981), pp. 837–850.

2. D. O. Rudin, "The Dominant Diseases of Modernized Societies as Omega-3 Essential Fatty Acid Deficiency Syndrome: Substrate Beriberi," *Medical Hypotheses* (Vol. 8, 1982), pp. 17–47.

3. D. O. Rudin and C. Felix, *The Omega-3 Phenomenon: The Nutritional Breakthrough of the 80's* (New York: Rawson-Macmillan, 1987).

4. D. Horrobin, *Clinical Uses of Essential Fatty Acids* (Montreal: Eden Press, 1983).

5. D. Horrobin, *Prostaglandins* (Montreal: Eden Press, 1978).

6. C. O. Truss, "Metabolic Abnormalities in Patients with Chronic Candidiasis," *Journal of Orthomolecular Psychiatry* (Vol. 13, No. 2, 1984), pp. 66–93.

7. S. M. Baker and L. Galland, "Whole Person Medicine," Health by Choice Conference, Atlanta, April 1986. Tapes are available from Insta-Tape, Inc., P.O. Box 1729, Monrovia, CA 91016.
8. D. Horrobin, *Prostaglandins,* p. 1.
9. D. O. Rudin, "The Dominant Diseases of Modernized Societies," p. 22.
10. Ibid., pp. 24–25.
11. Personal communication with A. Schauss.
12. L. Galland, "Fatty Acids and the Cell Code," *Update* (Vol. 3, No. 3, Spring 1984), p. 6.
13. Personal communication with D. Horrobin.
14. I. Colquhoun and S. Bunday, "A Lack of Essential Fatty Acids as a Possible Cause of Hyperactivity in Children," *Medical Hypotheses* (Vol. 7, 1981), p. 677.
15. S. M. Baker, "Fat Is Not Just to Hold Your Pants Up," *Update* (Vol. 3, No. 2, Winter 1984), p. 1.

Chapter 36
Amino Acids

1. Personal communication with S. Baker.
2. J. Pangborn, "Aspects of Amino Acid Metabolism in Health and Clinical Practice," NOHA Program, Oct. 6, 1982.
3. M. Salaman, "Amino Acid Testing," *Let's Live* (August 1984), p. 82.
4. J. Pangborn, "Aspects of Amino Acid Metabolism in Health and Clinical Practice," NOHA Program, Oct. 6, 1982.
5. R. Wurtman, "Nutrients That Modify Brain Function," *Scientific American* (April 1982), p. 50.
6. S. Baker, *Child Behavior* (New York: Harper & Row, 1981), pp. 316–317.

Chapter 37
Hypoglycemia

1. E. Cheraskin, W. M. Ringsdorf, Jr., and A. Brecher, *Psychodietetics* (New York: Bantam Books, 1974), pp. 71–72.
2. J. Anderson, *Fiber and Food* (Lexington, KY: HCF Diabetes Foundation, P.O. Box 22124, 1985).
3. D. Rapp, *Allergies and the Hyperactive Child* (New York: Sovereign Books, 1979), pp. 58–59.
4. Personal communication with T. Randolph.
5. W. Philpott and D. Kalita, *Brain Allergies* (New Canaan, CT: Keats Publishing, 1980), p. 118.

Chapter 38
Phosphates and Behavioral Disturbances

1. M. Walker, "Phosphates and Hyperactivity: Is There a Connection?," *Academic Therapy* (Vol. 17, March 1982), pp. 439–446.
2. L. Galland, "The Chemistry of Healing: Magnesium and the Battle for Light," *Update* (Vol. 4, No. 2, Spring 1985), p. 4.

Chapter 39
What Are Psychological Vitamins?

1. S. Johnson, *One Minute Mother* (New York: William Morrow, 1983), p. 47.
2. J. Gaylin, "The Importance of Being Praised," *Family Weekly* (March 21, 1982), p. 19.
3. J. Bowlby, *Attachment and Loss* (New York: Basic Books, Inc., 1969).
4. L. H. Kaplan, *Oneness and Separateness: From Infant to Individual* (New York: Simon and Schuster, 1978).
5. M. H. Klaus and J. H. Kennel, *Bonding, the Beginning of Parent-Infant Attachment* (New York: New American Library, 1983).
6. A. Montagu, *Touching: The Human Significance of the Skin* (New York: Columbia University Press, 1971), pp. 15–16.
7. A. T. Henderson, "A Hypothesis on the Etiology of Hyperactivity with a Pilot Study Report of Related Drug Therapy," *Pediatrics* (Vol. 52, No. 4, Oct. 1973), p. 625.

Chapter 40
Changing Your Child's Behavior

1. W. C. Crook, "Dr. Crook Discusses Children—And How You Can Make Them Mind" (Jackson, TN: Professional Books, 1987).

Chapter 41
Communicating with Your Child

1. H. Ginott, *Between Parent and Child* (New York: Avon Books, 1965), pp. 24–25.
2. Ibid., pp. 25–26.
3. F. Dodson, *How to Discipline with Love* (New York: Signet, 1977), p. 61.
4. Ibid., pp. 56–57.

Chapter 42
Understanding *Your* Feelings

1. Lendon Smith, *Feed Your Kids Right* (New York: Dell, 1979).

Chapter 43
Helping Your Child Succeed in School

1. L. B. Ames, *Is Your Child in the Wrong Grade in School?* (New York: Harper & Row, 1967), p. 8.
2. F. L. Ilg, L. B. Ames and S. M. Baker, *Child Behavior* (New York: Harper & Row, 1981), pp. 239–240.
3. E. Denhoff, "Detecting Potential Learning Problems at Preschool Medical Examinations," *Texas Medicine* (Vol. 65, 1969), pp. 56–59.
4. R. Flesch, *Why Johnny Still Can't Read* (New York: Harper & Row, 1981), pp. 3–4.

Chapter 45
Should Your Child Take Drugs to Control His Behavior?

1. C. Bradley, "The Behavior of Children Receiving Benzedrine," *American Journal of Psychiatry* (Vol. 94, 1937), pp. 577–585.
2. D. Rapp, *Allergies and the Hyperactive Child* (New York: Sovereign Books, 1979), p. 38.

Chapter 46
Mental Retardation, Autism and Tourette's Syndrome

1. B. Rimland, E. Callaway and P. Dreyfus, "The Effects of High Doses of Vitamin B_6 on Autistic Children: A Double-Blind Crossover Study," *American Journal of Psychiatry* (Vol. 135, 1978), pp. 472–475.
2. G. LeLord and others, "Effects of Pyridoxine and Magnesium on Autistic Symptoms: Initial Observations," *Journal of Autism and Developmental Disorders* (Vol. 11, No. 2, 1981), pp. 219–230.
3. J. Martineau and others, "Effects of Vitamin B_6 on Averaged Evoked Potentials in Infantile Autism," *Biological Psychiatry* (Vol. 16, No. 7, 1981), pp. 625–639.
4. Personal communication with M. Mandell.
5. Personal communication with T. Randolph.

Chapter 47
Miscellaneous Measures That May Help Your Child

1. J. Wright, *Dr. Wright's Book of Nutritional Therapy* (Emmaus, PA: Rodale Press, 1979), p. 352.
2. A. P. Krueger, "Air Ions as Biological Agents—Fact or Fancy? (Part I)," *Immunology and Allergy Practice* (Vol. 4, No. 4, 1982), p. 140.
3. Ibid., pp. 129–140.
4. A. P. Krueger, "Air Ions as Biological Agents—Fact or Fancy? (Part II)," *Immunology and Allergy Practice* (Vol. 4, No. 5, 1982), pp. 173–183.
5. F. Soyka, *The Ion Effect* (New York: E. P. Dutton, 1977).
6. L. Ponte, "How Artificial Light Affects Your Health," *The Reader's Digest* (Feb. 1981), p. 134.
7. J. N. Ott, *Light, Radiation and You* (Old Greenwich, CT: Devon-Adair, 1982), pp. 130–133.
8. Personal communication with J. O'Brian.
9. J. Brody, "Surprising Health Impact Discovered for Light," *The New York Times* (Nov. 13, 1984).
10. A. Pike, "Light and Life: How Light Benefits the Body," *Let's Live* (Vol. 52, No. 8, 1984).
11. "Getting an F for Flabby—U.S. Youths Come Up Short on Endurance, Strength and Flexibility," *Time* (Jan. 26, 1987), pp. 64–65.
12. Personal communication with A. McMahon.
13. B. Liebman, "Exer-Guide: A Look at the Benefits of Exercise," *Nutrition Action* (Vol. 8, No. 11, Nov. 1981), p. 9.
14. Ibid., pp. 10–11.
15. Ibid., p. 11.
16. T. Coat, "Can Running Help Troubled Kids?" *San Diego Tribune* (Jan. 13, 1982).
17. Ibid.

Chapter 49
Conclusion

1. J. Naisbitt, *Megatrends* (New York: Warner Books, 1982).

Appendix A
The Feingold Diet and Controversy

1. P. Frederick, "Feingold Success Story," *The Feingold Association of the Washington Area Newsletter* (Issue #100, July/Aug. 1985), pp. 4–5.

2. W. R. Shannon, "Neuropathic Manifestations in Infants and Children as a Result of Anaphylactic Reactions to Foods Contained in Their Dietary," *American Journal of Diseases of Children* (Vol. 24, 1922), p. 89.

3. A. H. Rowe, Sr., "Allergic Toxemia and Migraine Due to Food Allergy," *California Western Medicine* (Vol. 33, 1930), p. 785.

4. A. H. Rowe, Sr., *Food Allergy: Its Manifestations, Diagnosis and Treatment* (Philadelphia: Lea and Febiger, 1931).

5. T. G. Randolph, "Allergy as a Causative Factor of Fatigue, Irritability, and Behavior Problems in Children," *Journal of Pediatrics* (Vol. 31, 1947), p. 560.

6. T. G. Randolph, H. J. Rinkel and M. Zeller, *Food Allergy* (Springfield, IL: Charles C. Thomas, 1951).

7. H. Davison, "Allergy of the Nervous System," *Quarterly Review of Allergy* (Vol. 6, 1952), p. 157.

8. S. D. Lockey, Sr., "Reactions to Hidden Agents in Foods and Drugs Can Be Serious," *Annals of Allergy* (Vol. 35, 1975), pp. 239–242.

9. F. Speer, "The Allergic Tension-Fatigue Syndrome," *Pediatric Clinics of North America* (Vol. 1, 1954), p. 1029.

10. S. Dees, "Neurological Allergy in Children," *Pediatric Clinics of North America* (Vol. 1, 1954), p. 1017.

11. T. Randolph, *Human Ecology and Susceptibility to the Chemical Environment* (Springfield, IL: Charles C. Thomas, 1962), pp. 20–24.

12. F. Speer and R. Dockhorn, *Allergy and Immunology in Children* (Springfield, IL: Charles C. Thomas, 1973), pp. 290–291.

13. S. D. Lockey, Sr., "Allergic Reactions Due to F, D and C Yellow #5 Tartrazine, and Aniline Dye Used as a Coloring and Identifying Agent in Various Steroids." *Annals of Allergy* (Vol. 17, 1959), pp. 719–721.

14. B. F. Feingold, *Why Your Child Is Hyperactive* (New York: Random House, 1974), pp. 1–2.

15. Ibid., p. 11.

16. C. Hawley and R. Buckley, "Food Dyes and Hyperkinetic Children," *Academic Therapy* (Vol. 10:1, 1974), pp. 27–32.

17. R. Buckley, "The Food Dye Controversy," *Somatics* (Vol. 3[1], Autumn 1980), p. 23.

18. J. Egger and others, "Controlled Trial of Oligoantigenic Treatment in the Hyperkinetic Syndrome," *Lancet* (Vol. 1 (8428), March 9, 1985), p. 543.

19. W. G. Crook, "Can What a Child Eats Make Him Dull, Stupid or Hyperactive?," *Journal of Learning Disabilities* (Vol. 13, 1980), pp. 53–58.

20. Personal communication with G. Oberg.

21. J. J. McGovern and R. Gardner, "Natural Food-Borne Aromatic-Induced Behavioral Disturbances in Children with Hyperkinesis," *National Journal of Bio-social Research* (Vol. 4, No. 1, 1983), pp. 40–42.

22. A. Swain and others, "Salicylates, Oligoantigenic Diets, and Behavior," *Lancet* (July 6, 1985), p. 41.

Index

ABOUT THE AUTHORS

WILLIAM G. CROOK. M.D., received his medical education and training at the University of Virginia, the Pennsylvania Hospital, Vanderbilt, and Johns Hopkins. He is a Fellow of the American Academy of Pediatrics, the American College of Allergists, and a member of Alpha Omega Alpha as well as many other medical organizations.

He is the author of numerous scientific articles and five previous books, including *The Yeast Connection,* a national best seller. He has served as a Visiting Professor at Ohio State University, and the Universities of California (San Francisco) and Saskatchewan. He lives with his wife in Jackson, Tennessee. He has three daughters and four grandchildren.

LAURA J. STEVENS is the author of four previous books, including *How to Feed Your Hyperactive Child* and *The Complete Book of Allergy Control.* She lives in West Lafayette, Indiana, with her husband and two teen-aged sons.